EM
IN

2nd

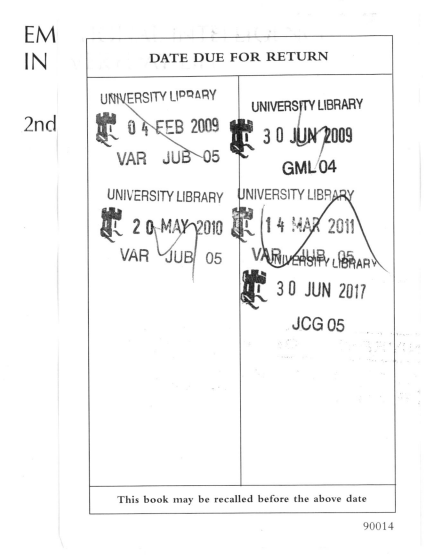

# EMOTIONAL INTELLIGENCE IN EVERYDAY LIFE

2nd Edition

*edited by*

**Joseph Ciarrochi**
*University of Wollongong*

**Joseph P. Forgas**
*University of New South Wales*

**John D. Mayer**
*University of New Hampshire*

**Ψ Psychology Press**
Taylor & Francis Group

NEW YORK AND HOVE

1005036141

Published in 2006
by Psychology Press
270 Madison Avenue
New York, NY 10016
www.psypress.com

Published in Great Britain
by Psychology Press
27 Church Road
Hove, East Sussex BN3 2FA
www.psypress.co.uk

*Psychology Press is an imprint of the Taylor & Francis Group*

10   9   8   7   6   5   4   3   2   1

Typeset in Meridien by Macmillan India, Bangalore, India.
Printed and bound in the USA by Sheridan Books, Inc., Ann Arbor, MI, on acid-free paper.
Paperback cover design by Anú Design.

**Library of Congress Cataloging-in-Publication Data**
Emotional intelligence in everyday life / edited by Joseph Ciarrochi, Joseph Forgas, and
John D. Mayer — 2nd ed.
     p. cm.
   Includes bibliographical references and index.
   ISBN 1-84169-434-7 (hardcover : alk. paper) — ISBN 1-84169-435-5 (pbk. : alk. paper)
   1. Emotional intelligence. I. Ciarrochi, Joseph. II. Forgas, Joseph P. III. Mayer,
John D., 1953–

BF576 .E465 2005
152.4 — dc22                                                                    2005016131

ISBN10: 1-84169-434-7 (hbk)
ISBN10: 1-84169-435-5 (pbk)

ISBN13: 9-78-1-84169-434-7 (hbk)
ISBN13: 9-78-1-84169-435-5 (pbk)

# CONTENTS

## PART II
## APPLICATIONS OF EMOTIONAL INTELLIGENCE
## RESEARCH TO EVERYDAY LIFE

## PART III
## INTEGRATION AND CONCLUSIONS

# ABOUT THE EDITORS

**Joseph Ciarrochi** received his Ph.D. degree from the University of Pittsburgh, a postdoctoral fellowship in emotion research from the University of New South Wales, and currently has a position as lecturer in psychology at the University of Wollongong. He has been conducting cutting-edge research in how emotions influence thinking and behavior and how emotional intelligence can best be measured and used. His findings have been published in the top journals in psychology and have been presented at numerous international conferences. In addition to conducting research, Dr. Ciarrochi has been developing training programs that are designed to increase people's social and emotional intelligence.

**Joseph P. Forgas** is a Scientia Professor of Psychology at the University of New South Wales, Sydney. He received his DPhil degree from the University of Oxford and subsequently was awarded a DSc degree from the same university. He has written or edited 14 books and is the author of more than 120 scholarly articles and chapters. He is a fellow at the Academy of Social Sciences, Australia; the American Psychological Society; and the Society of Personality and Social Psychology. His current research focuses on the role of affect in social thinking and interpersonal behavior. This work has received international recognition, including the Research Prize from the Alexander von Humboldt foundation (Germany) and a Special Investigator Award from the Australian Research Council.

**John (Jack) D. Mayer** pioneered research in emotional intelligence. Since the late 1970s, he has studied the interaction of emotion and thought. Between 1990 and 1993, Dr. Mayer coauthored the first peer-reviewed scientific articles on emotional intelligence, with his colleague Dr. Peter Salovey of Yale University. Since then Dr. Mayer has further examined how to measure and use emotional intelligence. At the same time, he has developed a conceptual model for the more general study of human personality. He has published more than 70 scientific articles, book chapters, and tests. Dr. Mayer is currently a professor of psychology at the University of New Hampshire, he has served on the editorial boards of *Psychological Bulletin* and the *Journal of Personality* and has been a National Institute of Mental Health Postdoctoral Scholar at Stanford University. Dr. Mayer received his Ph.D. and M.A. degrees in psychology at Case Western Reserve University and his B.A. degree from the University of Michigan. Dr. Mayer's current work on emotional intelligence has been featured widely in the media. He has spoken on the topic in academic, business, and government forums, both nationally and internationally.

# LIST OF CONTRIBUTORS

**Brian Bienn**
EI Skills Group, USA

**John T. Blackledge**
University of Wollongong, Australia

**Marc A. Brackett**
Yale University, USA

**Maureen Buckley**
Sonoma State University, USA

**David R. Caruso**
Yale University and EI Skills Group, USA

**Joseph Ciarrochi**
University of Wollongong, Australia

**Maurice J. Elias**
Rutgers University, USA

**Julie Fitness**
Macquarie University, Sydney, Australia

**Judith Flury**
University of Texas at Arlington, USA

**Joseph P. Forgas**
University of New South Wales, Sydney, Australia

**Glenn Geher**
State University of New York at New Paltz, USA

**Lisa Hunter**
Columbia University, USA

**William Ickes**
University of Texas at Arlington, USA

**Susan A. Kornacki**
EI Skills Group, USA

**Jeffrey S. Kress**
The Jewish Theological Seminary, USA

**Gerald Matthews**
University of Cinncinnati, USA

**John D. Mayer**
University of New Hampshire, USA

**Richard D. Roberts**
Educational Testing Service (ETS), USA

**Carolyn Saarni**
Sonoma State University, USA

**Peter Salovey**
Yale University, USA

**Carrie L. Wyland**
University of New South Wales, Sydney, Australia

**Moshe Zeidner**
University of Haifa, Israel

# LIST OF FIGURES

# LIST OF TABLES

# INTRODUCTION

John D. Mayer
Joseph Ciarrochi

Few areas of psychology have generated so much popular interest as emotional intelligence (EI). Over the past decade, EI has been a topic of best-selling books, magazines, and newspaper articles. It has also been the topic of considerable scientific research. There are several explanations for the explosion of interest in EI. One explanation is that emotional intelligence somehow fits the zeitgeist—the intellectual spirit—of the times. A persistent theme of contemporary life is that we can solve technical problems far better than human problems. The promise of emotional intelligence is that it might help us solve at least one aspect of human problems, namely, conflicts between the heart and the head. A second, everyday explanation for the interest is that the EI concept implies (to some observers) that people without much academic ability might still be highly successful in life if they are high in EI. Another reason for its popularity may be that the concept provides critics of traditional intelligence tests with ammunition to attack those tests (after all, one might not need traditional intelligence to succeed). And finally, journalists and writers have written lively, popular accounts of EI and its potential role in everyday life. Such accounts have challenged the view that human nature involves a continuous conflict between the head and the heart. Moreover, they have led people to believe that EI may make us healthy, rich, successful, loved, and happy. Such bold and important claims need to be evaluated scientifically. This is what the first edition of the book sets out to do.

It has now been five years since the first edition was written, and the field has changed dramatically. Indeed, so much new and interesting work has been conducted that we felt it time to thoroughly revise the first edition. This second edition updates the connection between the reader and cutting edge research from leaders in the field.

## ☐ A Dialogue about Human Nature

Beginning in the twentieth century, psychologists began to insert themselves into the debate on human nature. They helped inform political scientists about why people vote in certain ways; informed aeronautical engineers about how to design the cockpit of airplanes; and informed computer scientists on the ways that people think. Most relevant here, they also began to inform psychotherapists and others about how people felt, and what those feelings meant.

Such pronouncements about why people do the things they do, and the nature of human nature, long predates psychology, of course. As our species evolved tens of thousands of years ago, Homo sapiens must have found themselves increasingly self-aware of a largely mysterious and unpredictable world. This self-awareness went hand-in-hand with the development of language and culture to communicate information about life and existence. From the earliest times, philosophers, religious prophets, mystics, and poets have provided greatly sought (and sometimes forcibly imposed) directions on how life should be lived. From Ancient Greece came political philosophy and the invention of democracy. From China came a code of family life evolved in the form of Confucianism. From the Middle East came monotheism and the commandments of Moses.

The forms of government, the religions, and the moralities in use today are descendants of earlier systems of thought. In general, those systems that survived and flourished did so in part, because they worked. That is, thoughts evolve as well as organisms, and only those systems of thinking survived that were useful enough to assist with daily living. When the expertise is completely wrong, it is deemphasized and eventually ignored. The conversation between the experts and audience flourishes when experts are helpful, and vanishes when they are not. We can see the process today: communism's view of humanity as "economic man" was simply too restrictive, too simplistic to properly channel human energy. Its followers finally brought about its demise. On a smaller scale, the members of isolated suicide cults die off because their own self-destruction makes it finally impossible to further spread their message. Likewise, the belief that emotions are irrational may be destined for extinction. Emotional intelligence has attracted the attention of the public because it suggests that emotions may make us more, not less, rational.

## ☐ The Dialogue about Feeling

As part of the larger debates on governance, religion, and morality, experts also developed theories of how people should feel. The ancient Greek Stoics argued that thinking was reliable, but that feelings were too subjective, idiosyncratic, and unreliable to be used in constructive ways by society. Although stoicism failed as a movement, its central tenets influenced the Judaism of the time to a slight degree and, to a greater degree, the then-emerging tenets of Christianity. The stoic ideas were therefore conveyed through the branches of some religions. Centuries later, the rational, scholarly, and empirical emphasis of the European Enlightenment appeared to further discredit emotionality. There were some rebellions against this trend, including the European Romantic movement, in which artists, writers, and philosophers argued for the importance of feeling and of following one's heart. Jumping forward in time: the political rebellions of the 1960s also placed a high value on the emotions. For example, in the United States, then Secretary of Defense Robert McNamara referred to himself as a "human computer" who would not let emotion interfere with his thoughts about the War in Vietnam. In contrast, demonstrators against the war followed their feelings of sympathy toward innocent people who were dying, feelings of anger at a government that was responsible for those deaths, and, perhaps, feelings of fear at having to serve in an unpopular war. They believed that the cold, computer-like arguments of people like Robert McNamara were being used to disparage those feelings. Whatever the merits of the arguments, the debate was often characterized as one of reason against feeling. There was little recognition that thought and feeling could be integrated.

# ☐ The Advent of Emotional Intelligence

Emotional intelligence is the latest development in understanding the relation between reason and emotion. Unlike earlier ideas, its unique contribution is to see thought and emotion as adaptively, *intelligently*, intertwined. Whereas Blaise Pascal wrote, famously, that "The heart has its reasons of which reason knows not" [1, p. 113], the concept of emotional intelligence suggests that intelligence may understand emotion, and that emotion may facilitate intelligence.

As with past developments in the view of human nature, there is interplay between the experts in the field, and between those experts and others who are interested in using the knowledge for more practical purposes. Today, emotional intelligence spans two worlds: the world of popular psychology, with its best-selling volumes on the differences between women and men, self-motivation, personality types, healing of the soul, and jazzy newspaper science on the one hand, and the world of careful, painstaking research science on the other. This intersection creates a rather uneasy tension at times, and often misleading cross-talk.

The scientist says, "Here is what I have been working on recently . . ." The journalist replies, "This is really important," and then jazzes up the story in a way that seems close to nutty: "Emotional intelligence is twice as important as IQ!" (This often-made, often-repeated claim cannot be substantiated, as is pointed out in a number of chapters of this volume.)

Readers think the idea is important, and follow the journalistic reports closely. Seeing this, the scientist thinks, "people are interested in what I do (even if they don't quite get it). I'll give them more," and then proceeds to write a carefully analytic piece that might be, however, off the topic, or so advanced as to be unfathomable to nonpsychologists. (A lot of emotional intelligence writing really isn't about emotional intelligence, as several authors note in their chapters.)

At the same time, this intersection between the scientific and popular world can lead to genuine collaboration between the scientist and the public, but only if the scientist cares enough to write clearly, and the interested reader is motivated to think critically.

## ☐ The Rationale for this Book

In the past few years, people have expressed a strong desire for information about emotional intelligence, as is evidenced by the proliferation of popular books, and magazine and newspaper pieces. Scientists have also become fascinated by the topic; there has been a marked increase in serious research within the area. We were motivated to develop this revised volume in response to the curiosity about the concept, and the availability of new information about it in the scientific literature.

In this volume, we have invited internationally renowned scientists and scientific practitioners to present their views and scientific findings related to emotional intelligence. We have asked them to write in an accessible, accurate, and informative fashion, so that people from a wide variety of disciplines and walks of life can easily understand the book. We have asked them to keep their footnotes and citations to a minimum (although you will still find the most important references you need to important works in the area). The result is a collection of essays that are frequently worthwhile and informative, often provocative, and sometimes (we think) wonderful.

Why are experts all of sudden saying there is emotional intelligence? What is the concept, and what does it mean? What does it say about aspects of our everyday life, including our health, economic decisions, relationships, and ability to have a successful a career? This book explains what is known about each of those questions.

## ☐ The Book's Contents

People approaching the area of emotional intelligence do so with different interests, needs, and agendas. The different chapters of this book will no doubt appeal in different ways to different readers. To spare the reader the effort of striking out at random, we will quickly introduce the authors and chapters of this volume. This should help readers find what is closest to what they are looking for.

## Part I: Fundamental Issues

The first part of the book is a general introduction to the field of emotional intelligence and its study. It introduces some of the concepts, measures, and research underlying the general study of emotional intelligence.

What is the field of emotional intelligence? In Chapter 1, "A New Field Guide to Emotional Intelligence," John D. Mayer updates the guide to the field that opened the original edition of this book. In this new version, he again sorts out the interweaving of popular and scientific psychology to provide a field guide of what's what in defining emotional intelligence, measuring it, and what the significance of the area might ultimately be. Mayer, along Peter Salovey (another contributor to this volume), published the articles often credited with beginning the field. He brings his insider's view to bear on the field and clarifies a number of developments, both historical and contemporary, regarding what is happening in the field. If you are new to the area, or unfamiliar with the different meanings of emotional intelligence, or the history of the area, this chapter is a good place to start.

One of the most important issues in the field is how EI is best measured. In Chapter 2, Marc A. Brackett and Glenn Geher examine a variety of psychological tests that have been developed to measure emotional intelligence, all quite different from one another. Here, they pool their collective knowledge and talents to provide a state-of-the art look at what measures of emotional intelligence tell us today. Their chapter critically evaluates the EI tests and describes the strengths and weaknesses of each.

In Chapter 3, Maureen Buckley and Carolyn Saarni address crucial questions concerning how EI develops. They discuss what aspects of a child's learning history promote EI, and what aspects undermine EI. They also present the indicators of EI at each age period, from infancy to adulthood.

The field of emotional intelligence was strongly influenced by several related fields. One of these was the psychological study of "cognition and affect," or, how emotions and thoughts interact. Joseph Forgas has been a central contributor to that field, and his *Handbook of Cognition and Emotion* summarized much of that field. In Chapter 4, Joseph P. Forgas and Carrie L. Wyland describe what a person needs to know about emotions in order to achieve high emotional intelligence. For example, they describe how emotions progress over time and how we tend to overestimate how long negative emotions last. Drawing on their knowledge of cognition and affect, they also describe an important, unexpected finding: the more we try to reason about something, the more our irrelevant moods will bias our thoughts. Their chapter describes a number of other ways that emotions influence our thinking and behavior, and presents a model of these influences.

Substantial research has been conducted on how people cope with stress. In Chapter 5, Moshe Zeidner, Gerald Matthews, and Richard D. Roberts specifically examine the link between coping and emotional intelligence. They argue that no coping strategy is universally effective. The effectiveness of a strategy depends on aspects of the person and the situation. This chapter is critical in connecting modern emotional intelligence research with the decades of coping research that came before it.

## Part II: Applications of Emotional Intelligence Research to Everyday Life

The second part of the book examines how emotional intelligence applies to clinical psychopathology, to education, to interpersonal relationships, to work, to health and finances, and to psychological well-being.

All of us enjoy the pleasures and suffer the pains of interpersonal relations. Julie Fitness has devoted her career to studying the role of emotions in long-term relationships and marriage. In Chapter 6, she discusses ways in which EI may be essential to maintaining a strong, healthy relationship. Fitness also argues that emotional intelligence alone is not sufficient to guarantee marital happiness. Spouses must also want to be married, be committed to the idea of being married, and have values that are consistent with a supportive, caring relationship.

Interpersonal relations begin with a "getting to know you" period. Judith Flury and William Ickes have been conducting cutting edge research on people's ability to read the thoughts and emotions of others. In Chapter 7, they discuss the processes that are involved in accurate emotion perception, and ways in which such perception can be improved. They also describe research that suggests that being emotionally intelligent sometimes means deliberately not trying to know how the other person feels. In other words, sometimes delusions may be as necessary to our happiness as realities.

Educators have expressed a tremendous interest in emotional intelligence. Maurice Elias is an eminent scholar in education and a major force in bringing emotional intelligence into educational contexts. In Chapter 8, he and his colleagues, Jeffrey Kress and Lisa Hunter, discuss the critical need for Social and Emotional Learning (SEL) programs in schools. They then review the wide range of SEL programs that have been adopted in schools and how some of these programs have brought about a number of positive changes in student's lives (better academics, less aggression and drug usage). Elias, Kress, and Hunter's chapter is essential reading to educators and parents and anyone who is interested in how EI can be taught.

There has been a great deal of popular interest in how emotional intelligence can be applied to the business world. David Caruso is not only a trained intelligence researcher, and codeveloper of some central measures of emotional intelligence, but also has served as an executive coach in the business world. He and his colleagues, Brian Bienn and Susan Kornacki, describe the ways in which emotional intelligence is essential to success in the work place, making liberal use of examples. In Chapter 9, "Emotional Intelligence in the Workplace," they describe how emotional intelligence is relevant to selecting and developing a career, and how EI can help people deal effectively with co-workers. The chapter further discusses how EI assessment can be integrated with other forms of assessment to provide people with feedback about their strengths and weaknesses. The chapter concludes with a blueprint for an EI training program within the workplace.

Joseph Ciarrochi has been publishing in the area of emotions and emotional intelligence for over a decade now. His research has increasingly shifted to understanding why people often act with low emotional intelligence and how this state of affairs can be improved. In Chapter 10, Joseph Ciarrochi and his colleague John T. Blackledge present a theory about the cause of human suffering and emotional ineffectiveness. They then use this theory to provide structure to the last four decades of research on individual differences in effective emotional functioning.

Peter Salovey codeveloped the theory of emotional intelligence with John D. Mayer in the early 1990s and has continued work in the field since that time. In Chapter 11, "Applied Emotional Intelligence: Regulating emotions to become healthy, wealthy, and wise," he examines how emotional intelligence may contribute both to our health and our wealth. He shows that the inability to manage emotions effectively can lead to health problems such as heart disease. He also shows how poor management of negative emotions can lead to disastrous financial decisions. His chapter is rich with illustrations of how using better emotional and cognitive strategies may lead us to more fulfilling lives.

## Part III: Integration and Conclusions

In Chapter 12, Joseph Ciarrochi summarizes the key similarities and differences between the different approaches to EI presented in the book. He introduces a distinction between emotional intelligence and emotionally intelligent behavior. This distinction is intended to resolve some of the unnecessary conflicts between different approaches.

One recurrent theme of the book is that the terminology of the field is not always as carefully employed as would be desirable. In Chapter 13, "Clarifying Concepts Related to Emotional Intelligence: A Proposed Glossary," Mayer and Ciarrochi revisit some of the language of the field and make some recommendations about how to clear up its terminology. Using language carefully, they argue, can facilitate work in the field. Our hope is that things will be much better in this regard by the third edition of this volume.

Together, these chapters represent a diversity of approaches, disciplinary outlooks, and perspectives on the concept of emotional intelligence. The field of emotional intelligence is rapidly growing and expanding. We are confident that each of the approaches represented in this volume will inform the reader about what EI is and how it may be important to all aspects of everyday life.

# ☐ Reference

1.  Pascal, B. (1966). *Pensees*. Baltimore: Penguin Books. (Original work published 1643).

I

# FUNDAMENTAL
# ISSUES

CHAPTER 1

John D. Mayer

# A New Field Guide to Emotional Intelligence

## ☐ Introduction

This chapter addresses seven questions about the field of emotional intelligence beginning with: (1) "How did the field begin (and how was it popularized)?" Although the field began in a scientific context, it was then popularized and the scientific and popular concepts diverged. Consequently, one must ask (2) "Which emotional intelligence are we talking about?" The conceptions of EI vary dramatically, leading to, (3) "Is EI a new ability or a repackaged approach to personality psychology?" When it comes time to measure EI, another question is, (4) "What type of data best reflect emotionally intelligent thinking?" It is also useful to ask, (5) "What do we know about how approaches to studying EI interrelate?" The influence of popular claims is addressed in (6) "How important is EI?" and more serious reflections on the field are considered with the question (7) "Why is EI important?"

## ☐ A New Field Guide to Emotional Intelligence

The field of emotional intelligence began within psychology, but is now a subject studied by those in education, human resources, and psychiatry, among others. It is anchored by popular magazines and articles, on the one hand, and rigorous academic work, on the other. Consequently, definitions, claims, measures, and approaches are as diverse as they can possibly be—and the person first encountering the field is likely to wonder how to make sense of it all. To provide a field guide, this chapter will briefly discuss seven questions. First, "How did the field begin (and how was it popularized)?" This question is central to understanding the diversity of constituencies and definitions employed in the field. In fact, the field is so diverse and has so many competing interests, that the second question, "Which emotional intelligence are we talking about?" is truly critical. A closely allied question asks, "Is EI a new ability or a repackaged approach to personality psychology?" When it is time to study EI, critical questions include, "What type of data best reflect emotionally intelligent thinking?" and "What do we know about how approaches to studying EI interrelate?" The last two questions concern the significance of the area. Many astonishing claims have been made for emotional intelligence. One question, "How important is EI?" addresses such claims and asks whether they could possibly be true. The final question "Why is EI important?" is in many ways a rejoinder to the popular claims. That is, if those claims are untrue, does emotional intelligence still matter?

The discussion of the above questions will be focused on upholding reasonable conceptual standards that make a science worth studying. So, throughout the chapter a concerted effort will be made to discuss the field in a critical, careful fashion. In particular, I will advocate for such matters as: (a) a history of the field based on a reasonable understanding of the areas that led up to it, (b) terminology that is consistent with existing research in psychology, (c) measures that are valid, and (d) realism concerning predictive claims. People interpret such things as terminology, validity, and realism differently, of course, and that is where the more serious and interesting controversies arise.

## ☐ How Did the Field Begin (and How Was It Popularized)?

Philosophical considerations of the relations between thought and emotion in Western culture go back over 2000 years [1–2]. Here, however, I concentrate on activities in psychology from 1900 onward, using a five-fold division of years: (1) from 1900 to 1969, during which the psychological study of intelligence and emotions were relatively separate; (2) from 1970 to 1989, when psychologists focused on how emotions and thought influenced one another; (3) from 1990 to 1994, which marked the emergence of emotional intelligence as a topic of study; (4) from 1995 to 1996, when the concept was popularized, and (5) the present era of clarifying research. Table 1.1 provides an overview of these five periods of time and a few key books and articles related to each.

**TABLE 1.1. The emergence of the emotional intelligence concept: An overview**

| | |
|---|---|
| **1900–1969:**<br>*Intelligence and*<br>*Emotions as Separate,*<br>*Narrow Fields* | *Intelligence research.* The realm of psychological testing for intelligence was developed during this period and a sophisticated technology of intelligence tests arose (see [3] for a review).<br>*Emotions research.* In the separate field of emotion, debate centered on the chicken-and-egg problem of which happens first: physiological reaction, or emotion. In other areas of work, Darwin had argued for the heritability and evolution of emotional responses, but during this time, emotion was often viewed as culturally determined, largely a product of pathology, and idiosyncratic (see [4] for a review of Darwin's work).<br>*The search for social intelligence.* As intelligence testing emerged, the focus was on verbal and propositional intelligence. A number of psychologists sought to identify a social intelligence as well; however, efforts in this direction were discouraging and conceptions of intelligence remained cognitive. |
| **1970–1989:**<br>*Precursors to*<br>*Emotional Intelligence* | *Cognition and affect.* The precursors to emotional intelligence were put into place in this two-decade period. The field of *cognition and affect* emerged to examine how emotions interacted with thoughts. Researchers suggested that depressed people might be more realistic and accurate than others and that mood swings might enhance creativity [5]. The field of *nonverbal communication* developed scales devoted to perception of nonverbal information—some of it emotional—in faces and posture [6]. Those in the field of *artificial intelligence* examined how computers might understand and reason about the emotional aspects of stories [7].<br>*Multiple intelligences.* Gardner [8] described an "intrapersonal intelligence," which involved, among other things, the capacity to perceive and symbolize emotions.<br>*Social intelligence.* For example, empirical work on social intelligence found that it divided into social skills, empathy skills, prosocial attitudes, social anxiety, and emotionality (sensitivity) [9]. Brain research began to separate out connections between emotion and cognition (e.g., [10]). Occasional use of the term, "emotional intelligence" was made [11], [12, pp. 103, 107]. |

(*Continued*)

**TABLE 1.1. The emergence of the emotional intelligence concept: An overview**

| | |
|---|---|
| **1990–1993:** <br> *The Emergence of* <br> *Emotional Intelligence* | The four-year period beginning the 1990s saw the first sustained development of the first concept of emotional intelligence. The article, "Emotional Intelligence" provided a first review of areas potentially relevant to an emotional intelligence. At the same time, a demonstration study, including the first ability measure of emotional intelligence under that name, was published. An editorial in the journal *Intelligence* argued for the existence of an emotional intelligence as an actual intelligence (see [13–15]). During this time, further foundations of emotional intelligence were developed, particularly in the brain sciences (e.g., [16]). |
| **1995–1997:** <br> *The Popularization* <br> *and Broadening* <br> *of Emotional* <br> *Intelligence* | Goleman, a science journalist, published the popular book, *Emotional Intelligence*, loosely modeled on the academic writings in the area (see above). The book became a world-wide best seller and was widely copied. *TIME Magazine* used the term "EQ" on its cover. A number of personality scales were published under the name of emotional intelligence (e.g., [17–19]). |
| **1998–present:** <br> *Research on and* <br> *Institutionalization of* <br> *Emotional Intelligence* | A number of refinements to the concept of emotional intelligence took place, along with the introduction of new measures of the concept, and a growing number of peer-reviewed research articles on the topic. These have now become too numerous to enumerate. |

The period from 1900 to 1969 was an era of research into separate areas of intelligence and emotion. During this time, the area of intelligence emerged, and intelligence tests were first developed, explored, and understood. In emotions research, early investigators were focused on a chicken-and-egg problem: would a person who encountered a stressful situation such as meeting a bear in the woods first respond physiologically (e.g., with an increased heart rate) and then feel emotion, or was the emotional feeling primary, followed by physiological changes. A second problem focused on whether emotions held universal meaning, or whether they were culturally determined and idiosyncratic. Darwin had argued that emotions evolved across animal species; this was met with skepticism by social psychologists who believed that emotions were manifested differently in different cultures (see [4] for a review).

The second era, 1970–1989, was a time when several precursors of emotional intelligence were put into place. Whereas intelligence and emotion previously had been considered separate fields, they were now integrated in the new field of "cognition and affect" (i.e., thought and emotion). Within this area, researchers sought lawful rules of what emotions meant and when they arose. In this pursuit, earlier philosophical writings concerning the logic of emotions were rediscovered and examined, notably those of the Enlightenment philosopher Spinoza. Researchers reasserted Darwin's idea that emotions had evolved across species, and that, from an evolutionary perspective, emotions were universal expressions of internal feelings and formed a universal language of relationships. The influence of emotion on thought was examined in extreme cases, such as in depressed individuals, as well as those suffering from bipolar disorder (manic depression).

Researchers in artificial intelligence became interested in whether expert systems could be developed in the form of computer programs that could understand the feelings of characters in stories. To do this required drawing on the same basic laws of emotions and their meanings studied in cognition and affect. There was a small but definite interchange among researchers in artificial intelligence, and those studying cognition and affect (see [20] for a review).

Although the term "emotional intelligence" was used sporadically during this time, it was never defined or described in any definite way—probably because the foundations of the concept were still being developed. Such definitions as arose were precursor definitions, in the sense that they either referred explicitly to emotional intelligence but were unclear; or were clear but failed to refer to emotional intelligence. For example, an unpublished dissertation by Dr. Wayne Payne distinguished an emotional intelligence from more purely cognitive forms of intelligence as follows:

> . . . The facts, meanings, truths, relationships, etc., [of emotional intelligence] are those that exist in the realm of emotion. Thus, feelings are facts. . . . The meanings are *felt* meanings; the truths are emotional truths; the relationships are interpersonal relationships. And the problems we solve are emotional problems, that is, problems in the way we feel [11, p. 165].

This is partway to an emotional intelligence. For example, "the problems we solve are . . . problems in the way we feel," makes sense. Still, at this point much in this definition seems more rhetorical than clear. For example, the concept of *"felt* meanings" or the statement that "feelings are facts," are not explained in the text, and make sense, at best, only looking back from a better developed field.

Another sort of precursor definition was clear, but did not refer to an emotional intelligence. For example, Howard Gardner wrote of intrapersonal intelligence, that the "capacity at work here is *access to one's own feeling life*—one's range of affects or emotions" [21, p. 239]. For Gardner, however, this access to feeling life did not constitute emotional intelligence, but rather was part of a more general self- and social knowing which were intertwined with one another [21, p. 240ff]. Gardner continues to view any separate emotional intelligence as an inappropriate application of the intelligence concept [22]. A number of other areas developed precursors to emotional intelligence. For example, in the literature on child development, a concept of emotional giftedness (also termed "emotional overexcitability") was proposed which, in some ways, also anticipated the concept of emotional intelligence [23, p. 116].

More than an incidental or intuitive use of a term, however, is necessary to mark the origin of a concept and the beginning of its study. A clearer scientific vision of what the concept might mean and a more comprehensive and secure footing for its study in a scientific context are needed. The period from 1990 to 1993 marked the emergence of the concept of emotional intelligence in this sense.

In 1990, my colleague Peter Salovey and I drew together much of the above research and developed a formal theory of emotional intelligence and a coordinated measurement demonstration [13], [15]. We explicitly proposed that a diverse and apparently unrelated group of studies—in aesthetics, brain research, intelligence measurement, artificial intelligence, and clinical psychology, among others—were all addressing the same phenomenon: a heretofore overlooked intelligence. Second, we addressed the potentially contradictory nature of the phrase "emotional intelligence," and provided the first formal definition of the concept and explanation of skills involved. Also in 1990, the first ability scale explicitly intended to measure emotional intelligence was introduced. A follow-up editorial in 1993, in the journal *Intelligence*, called for the serious study of emotional intelligence; EI was characterized as potentially meeting the rigorous definition of an intelligence [14]. For these reasons, the third era, 1990–1993, is generally regarded as the starting point for the study of emotional intelligence (e.g., [19], [24–25]).

The fourth era (1994–1997) marked a rather unusual turn of events as the field became popularized and broadened. It was during this time that the term *emotional intelligence* was popularized in a best-selling book by a science journalist, Daniel Goleman [19]. He and others seized upon it as a banner for a great deal of research and public policy. In the book and the popular accounts that accompanied it, emotional intelligence was said to be, possibly, the best predictor of success in life, to be accessible by virtually anyone, and to be like "character." The book's combination of lively writing, extraordinary claims for the concept, and loose description of the concept created an explosion of activity in a new, and increasingly fuzzily defined area. Moreover, many people and companies hoped to join in the excitement. Tests were sold as measures of emotional intelligence that were not originally defined that way, associations of educators and business people were created to teach and consult on emotional intelligence, and many other popular books attempted to ride the coattails of the success of the 1995 popularization.

During the period beginning in 1997 and extending to the present, a working out of the now multiple concepts of emotional intelligence gradually has been taking place. New measures of emotional intelligence have been developed, and serious research is taking place within the field, of which this volume is one important example. The field is complicated by the fact that it possesses both scientific and popular aspects. These often conflicting constituencies have led to definitions of emotional intelligence that are nearly unrelated to one another. It is for that reason that the next section addresses the question of which emotional intelligence one is talking about.

## ☐ Which Emotional Intelligence Are We Talking About?

### Definitions

There are now so many conceptions of emotional intelligence—and they are so different from one another—that any approach to the field must begin by distinguishing among them. Definitions of EI have ranged from the focused, in which EI is conceived of as a traditional intelligence involving the emotions, to the diffuse and sprawling, in which EI is conceived of as a broader collection of often-studied attributes such as persistence, optimism, and sociability. In other words, one cannot engage in a discussion of the topic without first asking, "*Which* emotional intelligence are we talking about?"

Perhaps the only thing that definitions of EI share in common is that they all describe one or more aspects of personality. By "personality" is meant the collective functioning of the larger psychological subsystems of the individual, including his or her motives, emotions, cognitions, and the self [26]. The long-term qualities of the system—such as how happy, honest, or intelligent the personality is—are called traits. From this perspective, traits—be they ability traits such as intelligences, or social traits such as extraversion—all refer to one or another aspect of personality. The key question regarding whether something ought to be named emotional intelligence is whether what is described is particularly relevant to the terms "emotion" and "intelligence."

Here, I will examine three approaches to EI that arguably have generated the most interest and/or research attention thus far. The three are: (1) the EI ability model my colleague Salovey and I developed, and the measures of it we developed with Caruso, (2) Goleman's definition of EI and the Emotional Competency Inventory (ECI) he developed with Boyatzis, and (3) the Bar-On definition and the Bar-On EQ-i. There are, of course, other scales, but these three have thus far dominated empirical research, and due to their diversity, provide a good overview of possibilities within the field [17], [19], [27–28].

## The EI Ability Model and the MSCEIT

The definition of EI employed in the ability model views it as a general, traditional, intelligence made up of specific, interrelated abilities. In this model, emotions are viewed as evolved signal systems and each emotion conveys a specific meaning. For example, fear conveys the possibility that one is under attack and will need to escape; happiness conveys the hope of joining with others. This idea of reasoning with and about emotional information is reflected in the following definition:

> Emotional intelligence refers to an ability to recognize the meanings of emotion and their relationships, and to reason and problem-solve on the basis of them. Emotional intelligence is involved in the capacity to perceive emotions, assimilate emotion-related feelings, understand the information of those emotions, and manage them [29, p. 267].

The Mayer-Salovey-Caruso Emotional Intelligence Test (MSCEIT), which is geared to this definition, measures four areas of EI skills: the abilities to (a) perceive emotion, (b) use emotion to facilitate thought, (c) understand emotional meanings, and (d) manage emotions in oneself and others.

## Goleman's Theory and the Emotional Competence Inventory

Goleman [19], [30] often characterizes EI as a list of personal and social characteristics. He offers little in the way of a formal definition, but does offer longer descriptions of the qualities involved. I have created a briefer description from some of his writings that closely follows his original description. It states that:

> Emotional intelligence is a broad description of an individual's functioning or character that includes abilities such as being able: (i) to motivate oneself, (ii) to persist in the face of frustrations, (iii) to control impulses, (vi) to delay

gratifications, (vii) to regulate moods, (viii) to keep distress from swamping the ability to think, (ix) to empathize, and (x) to hope [19, p. 34]. At other times, EI may be reflected in, or equated to, the capacities (i) to experience enthusiasm, (ii) to feel confident, (iii) to be socially adroit, and (iv) overall, to have good character [19, pp. 79, 115, 285].

Goleman's concept of EI has been measured with the Emotional Competence Inventory. The overall subscales of this instrument have been approximately the same from 1998, although the exact set of sub-scales has varied slightly from report to report. One version stated that the attributes of EI included such qualities as: (1) emotional self aware-ness, (2) accurate self-assessment, (3) self-confidence, (4) emotional self-control, (5) trustworthiness, (6) conscientiousness, (7) adaptability, and continues through a dozen more attributes to, (19) conflict management, (20) building bonds, and (21) teamwork and collaboration [31].

### Bar-On's Theory and the Bar-On EQ-i

Bar-On defines EI as: *"An array of noncognitive capabilities, competencies, and skills that influence one's ability to succeed in coping with environmental demands and pressures"* [17, p. 14, italics in original]. In other words, it is any ability or skill that is not specifically cognitive. His Bar-On EQ-i, measures a num-ber of areas of areas, including (1) emotional self-awareness, (2) assertive-ness, (3) self-regard, (4) self-actualization, (5) independence, (6) empathy, (7) interpersonal relationship, (8) social responsibility, (9) problem solving, (10) reality testing, (11) flexibility, (12) stress tolerance, (13) impulse con-trol, (14) happiness, and (15) optimism [17].

### Evaluative Questions

Several questions may help clarify the differences among the models just presented. For example, "Does a given model sensibly group together ele-ments that go together?" More specifically, "Does it make sense to group together abilities, such as accurately perceiving emotion, and accurately understanding emotions—as is done in the ability model and the MSCEIT?" Or, "Does it make sense to group together impulse control and optimism—as is done in Bar-On's approach?" A second question is "Do the group of attributes in a model have enough to do specifically with 'emotion' and 'intelligence' to justify the label 'emotional intelligence'?" Depending upon how one answers these questions and others, one will likely take a specific perspective on the field.

# ☐ Is EI a New Ability or a Repackaged Approach to Personality?

## EI: Part of the Personality System

Is EI a renamed approach to measuring broad aspects of personality, or is it new? It depends in part on which approach to EI one is speaking about. The key questions involved here are "Does EI describe something that can reasonably be called a single thing—related to emotion and intelligence—that has not specifically been studied before?,"or "Does EI duplicate already-existing conceptions of personality and/or intelligence?" To assess these questions, it helps to start with an overall map of the human personality system.

## Conceptions of EI and Four Areas of Personality

### *Personality's Areas*

The personality system is composed of a number of interrelated areas. One contemporary approach divides it into four general areas and their blends. This division is called the systems set and breaks down personality into areas of (1) energy development, (2) knowledge guidance, (3) conscious self-regulation, and (4) social implementation [32–34]. The four parts will be introduced first, and then used to compare and contrast different approaches to EI.

The first area, *energy development*, involves channeling mental motives, guiding them with emotions, and directing an individual's actions toward sensible goals. To do this, emotions amplify, diminish, and redirect motives. The overall function of the area is to ensure that the individual's mental energy is maintained at appropriate levels and directed toward socially attainable goals. The interleaving of motives with emotions gives rise to the shorthand name to this area, the *energy lattice*.

The second area, *knowledge guidance*, develops, maintains, and applies knowledge so as to inform a person's plans and decisions. The overall aims of the area are to ensure that a person's plans and actions are developed in the context of the best knowledge possible. The area consists of a person's mental models of the self, including one's self-concept. It also consists of mental models of world, including such models as what trees, dirt, stones, and water are like, the names of animals, what other people are like, and more formal knowledge including of language and numbers. In addition, the area includes intelligences that act on the knowledge. This idea of knowledge and the intelligences that work with such information gives rise to the shorthand name for the area, the *knowledge works*.

The third area, *conscious self-regulation*, intervenes when issues arise in mental functioning that require special attention, reassessment, and sometimes, revision. The overall goal of conscious self-regulation is to ensure the smooth and productive function of the psychological system, as well as its improvement over the short and long term. More basically, the area consists of conscious awareness, the capacity for self-reflection, self-regulation, and will. The area's responsibility for oversight leads to its shorthand name, the *conscious executive*.

The fourth area, *social implementation*, carries out social activities by adjusting them according to the social situation involved. The goal of this area is to ensure the individual's expression of personality in the social arena is effective and skilled. More basically, the area contains mental models of social actions and scripts, and social skills useful to carrying them out; it also includes lower level, more naturalistic styles of behavior such as the outgoing sociability of extroversion or the avoidant sensibilities of the introvert. The responsibility of these functions for assisting the individual in maintaining a social self-presentation leads to a shorthand name for the area of the *social actor*.

## EI and the Personality System

With this generic model as a guide, the parts of personality measured by the various scales of EI—and a comparison general scale of personality—can be examined. The comparison scale of personality is the California Psychological Inventory (CPI, [35]). The CPI is composed of a number of individual scales based on folk conceptions of mental health, including scales of Self-Acceptance, Empathy, Responsibility, Socialization, Good Impression, Well-Being, Tolerance, Intellectual Efficiency, Flexibility, and Self-Control.

I took the subscales of the MSCEIT, EQ-i, ECI, and CPI and assigned them to the area above they most reflected, or to one of several blended areas. The results are shown in Table 1.2. Table 1.2 leads off with the "energy development" area—concerning motives and emotions. Subscales from several measures describe that area. Both the ECI's need for achievement scale, and the Bar-On EQ-i's happiness and stress tolerance scales are relevant to these areas. The MSCEIT is not shown under this area because it does not assess aspects of this sort of energy development.

In knowledge guidance—concerning knowledge and intelligence—the EQ-i's problem solving and reality testing scales appeared relevant, as did the ECI's organizational awareness, and service orientation (see Table 1.2).

**TABLE 1.2.  Four main areas of personality, their principal blends, and the attributes relevant to each area measured by major tests of EI\* and a comparison scale of personality\*\***

| Test | Areas of personality and test subscales assessing aspects of them |
|------|-------------------------------------------------------------------|
| **I. Energy development** | |
| EQ-i | 12. Stress tolerance |
|  | 14. Happiness |
| ECI | 9. Achievement orientation |
| CPI | 15. Achievement via conformance |
|  | 16. Achievement via independence |
| *Emotion–knowledge blend* | |
| MSCEIT | 1. Perceiving emotions |
|  | 2. Emotional facilitation of thought |
|  | 3. Understanding emotions |
|  | 4. Emotional management |
| EQ-i | 6. Empathy |
|  | 15. Optimism |
| ECI | 8. Optimism |
|  | 11. Empathy |
| CPI | 7. Empathy |
|  | 13. Well-being |
| **II. Knowledge guidance** | |
| EQ-i | 8. Social responsibility |
|  | 9. Problem solving |
|  | 10. Reality testing |
| ECI | 12. Organizational awareness |
|  | 13. Service orientation |
| CPI | 14. Tolerance |
|  | 17. Intellectual efficiency |
|  | 18. Psychological mindedness |
| *The self blend* | |
| EQ-i | 1. Emotional self-awareness |
|  | 3. Self-regard |
|  | 4. Self-actualization |
| ECI | 1. Emotional self-awareness |
|  | 2. Accurate self-assessment |
|  | 4. Emotional self-control |
|  | 3. Self-confidence |
| CPI | 5. Self-acceptance |
| **III. Conscious self-regulation** | |
| EQ-i | 13. Impulse control |
| ECI | 10. Initiative |
| CPI | 10. Self-control |

*(Continued)*

**TABLE 1.2. Four main areas of personality, their principal blends, and the attributes relevant to each area measured by major tests of EI\* and a comparison scale of personality\*\***

| Test | Areas of personality and test subscales assessing aspects of them |
|---|---|
| *The enactor blend* | |
| EQ-i | 5. Independence |
| | 11. Flexibility |
| ECI | 7. Adaptability |
| CPI | 1. Dominance |
| | 3. Sociability |
| | 6. Independence |
| | 19. Flexibility |
| **IV. Social implementation** | |
| EQ-i | 2. Assertiveness |
| | 7. Interpersonal relationship |
| ECI | 5. Trustworthiness |
| | 14. Developing others |
| | 15. Inspirational leadership |
| | 16. Influence |
| | 17. Communication |
| | 18. Change catalyst |
| | 19. Conflict management |
| | 20. Building bonds |
| | 21. Teamwork and collaboration |
| CPI | 2. Capacity for status |
| | 4. Social presence |
| | 9. Socialization |
| | 11. Good impression |
| | 12. Communality |
| *Whole personality characteristics* | |
| ECI | 6. Conscientiousness |
| CPI | 8. Responsibility |
| | 20. Femininity/masculinity |

\*The major tests of EI are the Mayer-Salovey-Caruso Emotional Intelligence Test (MSCEIT), the Bar-On Emotional Quotient Inventory (EQ-i), and the Emotional Competencies Inventory (ECI).
\*\*The personality inventory is the California Psychological Inventory (CPI).

Within personality, there exists a smaller blended area that integrates energy development and knowledge guidance, the "Emotional—Knowledge Blend." This area involves knowledge of emotions and emotional contributions to intellect. The MSCEIT test's four scales were classified as describing that area: (1) accurate perception of emotion,

(2) emotional facilitation of thought, (3) understanding emotions, and (4) emotional management (although the last scale might equally have been placed in the "Self Blend" area; see Table 1.2). Both the ECI and Bar-On EQ-i also measure attributes within this area. The EQ-i measures empathy and optimism. The ECI measures emotional self-awareness, optimism, and empathy (see Table 1.2).

Concerning conscious self-regulation, both the ECI and Bar-On EQ-i contain scales of impulse control and initiative. There is a closely related blend between conscious regulation and knowledge that includes the EQ-i's and ECI's scales related to emotional self-awareness, and accurate self-awareness more generally. Measures of self-regard and self-actualization are included there as well.

Finally, subscales also pertain to the area of social action. The Bar-On EQ-i assesses assertiveness and interpersonal relationships in this area. The ECI assesses trustworthiness, developing others, inspirational leadership, influence, communication, conflict management, and other features of this realm.

## Evaluative Questions

As before, one or two questions can help focus the description above. Most germane is the question, "Does EI describe something that can reasonably be called a coherent ability related to both emotion and intelligence?"—because if it doesn't then EI becomes a collection of individual variables, and one might better talk about a type or constellation of personality qualities. Perhaps, for example, the MSCEIT covers a new, not-before-studied aspect of personality regarding how one joins thought and emotion. Another question is, "If two tests that share the name EI draw on different parts of personality, broadly speaking, are they named correctly and will they interrelate?"

Of course, the answer to these questions also can be addressed empirically, for example, by seeing if the scales correlate with one another or with preexisting scales of personality or not. This issue will be considered in greater detail in an ensuing section—but first there is one remaining question about measurement that needs to be addressed.

## ☐ What Type of Data Best Reflect Emotionally Intelligent Thinking?

Suppose that we have selected a conception of EI from one of the three approaches above. A further concern involves identifying what kind of data best reflects mental abilities. The three approaches above all suggest that EI is an ability or collection of skills. Multiple kinds of data about a person can be examined—self-judgment data, criterion-report data, and observer-report data (among many others)—and each is good for a specific purpose. Which is best for the purpose here? [36–37].

The gold standard in measuring mental skills, intelligences, and achievement more generally, is a criterion-report test (also known as ability testing and/or performance testing). In criterion report testing, the individual is asked to produce the solution to a problem and then that solution is compared to a criterion of correctness. An example of a criterion-report item on an emotional intelligence test might involve presenting a picture of a happy face, as judged by experts, and then asking the individual what emotions are expressed by the face. The individual might respond, "happy," and obtain a correct score, or "sad" and obtain an incorrect score. This approach is considered appropriate for measuring abilities, because there is some objective verification that what the person believes is correct really is correct. The MSCEIT represents such a criterion-report test.

An alternative form of testing intelligence employs self-judgment data. Self-judgment testing typically involves having the individual make a judgment or endorsement as to what he or she is like. It draws on an individual's self-concept. Examples of self-judgment items in the EI area might be, "I am very accurate in reading the emotions in others' faces." Self-judgment data is very valuable in assessing things like a person's present mood (for which the individual is, arguably, the ultimate authority). It is rarely used to measure mental abilities, however, as people are relatively poor judges of their own mental capacities. For example, in the traditional intelligence field, criterion-report IQ does not correlate well with self-judged intelligence, with correlations rarely exceeding near-chance levels (e.g., between $r = .00$ and $.30$ [38]). The Bar-On EQ-i is a self-report scale, as are some forms of the ECI.

A third approach to measuring emotional intelligence is to use observer-report data. This makes particular sense if one considers emotional intelligence to refer to effective behavior. In observer ratings, an observer—someone who knows the person—decides whether a person is emotionally intelligent or not. Within organizational settings it is sometimes the custom to measure "360 degrees of feedback," from all around the individual. So, a manager in a company would receive feedback from subordinates, colleagues, and supervisors on a number of competencies believed related to emotional intelligence. Although observer ratings are often of use for certain easily spotted social qualities such as extraversion, they are less accurate for an assessment of intelligent behavior, for which correlations are little higher than those for self-report [39–40]. To a great extent, intellectual processing is hidden within cognitive processes; it is also likely that intelligent behavior frequently goes "over the heads" of those who witness it [41]. Some have argued that those who meet certain social goals (i.e., making people happy) are higher in EI and those goals are easy to specify; still, higher EI people may also set more nuanced goals (e.g., making *some people* happy). As already mentioned, some forms of the ECI are self-judgment; others, however, employ observer judgments [42].

## ☐ What Do We Know About How Approaches to Studying EI Interrelate?

Research in EI has been abundant over the past several years. It would be neither possible nor advisable to review everything that is known about EI at this point, given space limitations (but see Chapter 2 for a detailed review). A quick overview of how these measurement approaches interrelate with one another and with measures of personality is, however, central to understanding the field. To accomplish this, three issues are briefly covered: (a) to what degree are the three approaches to EI the same? (b) How do the measures relate empirically to preexisting scales of intelligence, personality, and/or other areas? And (c) What are some primary findings surrounding each approach.

### The Three Approaches Yield Three Unrelated Measurement Instruments

The review above indicated that three markedly different definitions of emotional intelligence have been employed in the field. One, the ability approach using the MSCEIT test, defines EI as an intelligence concerning emotions, and measures it as an ability. The other two approaches define EI as a broad constellation of personality attributes. Those two approaches employ self- or observer-judgments to measure the entity.

As might be expected from such different definitions and measurement procedures, the approaches are empirically quite distinct. Generally speaking, one would expect measures that assess the same entity to intercorrelate at the $r = .70$ level or above. In the case of these scales, however, their correlations (where known) are low. The correlation between the MSCEIT and EQ-i, for example, is $r = .20$ in one study [43]. No published data exist yet in regard to relations between either the ECI and the other measures. Some conclusions can be drawn that the ECI and EQ-i are likely to share some overlap—at least in their self-judgment forms, given that the two also have overlap with the Big Five scale (see below).

## EI Measured as an Ability Has Good Discriminant Validity Relative to Preexisting Scales

The MSCEIT test is relatively independent of preexisting intelligence scales, correlating in the $r = .00$ to $.30$ range with them. The MSCEIT is similarly independent of preexisting personality scales, correlating in the $r = .00$ to $.35$ range with them. All told, the MSCEIT appears to measure something new [44].

## EI Measured as Broad Constellations of Personality Attributes Has High Overlap with Preexisting Scales of Personality

The Bar-On EQ-i and ECI—as well as other self-judgment scales of EI—all have high overlap with preexisting scales of personality psychology. For example, one commonly used contemporary scale of personality is the Big Five, a collection of five traits including Neuroticism–Stability, Extraversion–Introversion, Openness–Closedness, Friendliness–Hostility, and Conscientiousness–Carelessness. Despite the dissimilar sounding names of the scales, the Bar-On EQ-i has a multiple $R$ with the Big Five of $R = .75$. Similarly, the ECI has been reported to have "strong overlap in most of its dimensions . . ." [with the Big Five] and therefore to contribute, "only a minimal amount of variance above the NEO-PI" [45]. Another self-judgment scale of EI, the Schutte scale, similarly has high overlap with the Big Five, $R = .52$, and $R = .70$ with a scale of well-being [43].

## General Personality Models of EI Are Largely Duplicating Preexisting Measures of Emotional Intelligence

To be sure, the EQ-i and ECI have a number of provocative findings associated with them (e.g., [46–47]). The challenge here is to know what findings are uniquely due to some aspect of EI and what are due more generally to the overlap with positive self-judgment. Generally speaking, the $R = .75$ between a test such as the EQ-i and the Big Five translates as a person's self-description of themselves as outgoing, emotionally stable and positive, friendly, and conscientious. "It would," wrote one group of researchers discussing their findings with the EQ-i, "be useful to examine the incremental predictive power of these variables above the prediction achieved by basic personality dimensions assessed by measures like the NEO-FFI. Unfortunately," the authors continue, "almost none of the studies using the scale have done so [47, p. 170]."

Put another way, we don't yet know whether correlations between such tests and various criteria are really due to EI, or to a positively self-judged personality. Guidelines for psychological testing indicate that tests should minimize what's termed "construct-irrelevant variance"—things the test measures that aren't part of the concept they intend to measure [48]. The high correlation between self-report EI tests and personality measures suggest that either they might be renamed as measures of self-judged personality, or that, as measures of EI, they contain a great deal of construct-irrelevant variance.

## When EI is Measured as an Ability It is Useful for Predicting Important Outcomes

The relative independence of the MSCEIT from other measures makes its interpretation more straightforward. A recent review of findings regarding the MSCEIT and the criteria with which it correlates attempted to convey a summary of the overall pattern of MSCEIT correlations with other variables:

> The high EI individual, relative to others, is less apt to engage in problem behaviors and avoids self-destructive, negative behaviors such as smoking, excessive drinking, drug abuse, or violent episodes with others. The high EI person is more likely to have possessions of sentimental attachment around the home and to have more positive social interactions, particularly if the individual scored highly on emotional management. Such individuals may also be more adept at describing motivational goals, aims, and missions [44, p. 210].

## Evaluating Questions Regarding EI

In considering the findings regarding EI, one must carefully consider the central issue of any test: what is its validity? Validity refers to whether the test measures what it claims to measure. It would involve positive answers to questions such as, "Does the test use a clear and reasonable definition of EI?" "Does the test comprehensively cover what it is supposed to measure?" and "Is the test relatively free of construct-irrelevant variance?" From yet another perspective, one might ask, "Might the test really be better considered an omnibus measure of personality, if it measures assorted personality traits?"

# ☐ How Important is EI?

The theory of emotional intelligence that Salovey and I published in 1990 [15] made only the claim—controversial enough at the time—that such an intelligence might exist. Claims for emotional intelligence escalated markedly with its popularization. Emotional intelligence was said to be "as or more important as IQ" in predicting success in life [19, p. 34].

To claim that emotional intelligence outpredicts intelligence means that it should have correlations with criteria at above the $r = .50$ level. For example, IQ predicts school grades at such a level—a stiff hurdle. Such a claim was bound to catch the attention of psychologists. Those searching for evidence for the claims of the various popularizations were to be disappointed. For example, a Bell Labs study of engineers was said to indicate that emotionally intelligent engineers outperformed others at work. The study in question, however, involved no psychological measurements at all, and emotion was barely mentioned [49].

It was perhaps popular claims such as this that led some psychologists to dismiss the area entirely. For example, one research team in the *Journal of Personality and Social Psychology* [50] concluded that "as presently postulated, little remains of emotional intelligence that is unique and psychometrically sound." And they have since proceeded in their attempts to distinguish myths from science in the field [51].

Rather than retreat from such claims, however, the popular claims escalated—doubled, in fact. Goleman's 1998 follow-up book on his original popularization stated that "emotional competence mattered *twice* as much" as IQ and expertise [30, p. 31]. The figure was based on a survey of job descriptions. For example, a job description might say the applicant "needs to be calm under pressure, a good negotiator, and work well with all kinds of people." Because all of the foregoing are classified as emotional intelligence in Goleman's 25-feature model, it is unsurprising that such descriptions appeared twice as often as comments regarding intelligence and expertise in such descriptions. (There may also be issues of tact that encourage publicly de-emphasizing intelligence.) Job performance is, of course, not best measured by the study of job descriptions. Understanding what actually predicts success requires employing actual measures of personality and predicting actual on-the-job performance. Goleman [30] does describe a further study in his Appendix 2, which may have examined actual leader behavior, but the brief overview and broad definition of EI he employs combine to make it difficult to interpret.

So, there is little or no evidence thus far that emotional intelligence is the best predictor of success in life, let alone twice as important as IQ. This led us to the next question, "Why is emotional intelligence important—if at all?"

# ☐ Why is EI Important?

The study of personality is important to the discipline of psychology. Studies of personality, however, should be carefully labeled as to what they are measuring and assessing. Otherwise, they simply cloud work in the field. The remaining comments refer to the study of emotional intelligence as a mental ability, and measured as a mental ability. The importance of EI extends to (a) understanding ourselves and others, (b) improving individual assessment and prediction, and (c) contributing to social and cultural practices.

## Understanding Ourselves and Others

### Understanding EI Helps Approach Emotions as Signals

The ability theory of EI highlights how emotions serve as a source of important information. For example, the feelings of people in a situation provide important signals about what is going on and how those individuals will interact. Analyzing situations in part according to their emotional information can help people make better decisions.

### Understanding EI Can Enhance Self-Management

People often report that their head and heart are in conflict when making important decisions. Choosing between the head and the heart is a necessity only so long as they are viewed as two separate systems. If, however, thoughts and feelings are seen as integrated—as they are viewed in the ability theory of EI—then emotional intelligence can be used to reason through at least some of the conflicts, understanding a dilemma more completely, and be used to integrate both thoughts about feelings, and feelings about thoughts.

### Emotional Intelligence Enhances Understanding of What It is to be a Human Being

People sometimes label others "hopeless romantics," or as "thinking with their hearts rather than their heads." There is now a way of understanding such thinking. Although some such individuals may merely be oversentimental, or overemphasize feelings, some among them are likely to be undertaking sophisticated information processing.

## Improving Assessment and Prediction

### EI Enhances the Understanding of Intelligence

Psychologists have sought to understand the major mental abilities, including especially the intelligences, how best to define them and what they predict. Emotional intelligence is a fascinating, and yet admittedly unusual instance of a potentially standard intelligence, as such it enriches the discussion about what an intelligence is and how it operates.

## EI Enhances the Fairness of IQ Testing

Psychologists strive to be as fair as possible in measuring mental abilities. When a new mental ability is uncovered and successfully measured, it is possible to improve the fairness of personality assessment by recognizing, for example, intelligences that a person might possess but that have heretofore gone unrecognized.

## Emotional Intelligence Can be Used to Predict Important Outcomes

Although popular versions of the concept have often claimed that EI is a sort of super personality trait, more powerful than IQ, my colleagues and I have never made such claims. EI does, however, often predict between 1% and 15% of the variance of selected outcomes. What makes its predictions of particular importance is the social weight placed on the kinds of outcomes it predicts. These outcomes include higher and better social networks, and reduced fighting and violence, drug use, and other negative behaviors among those high in EI. Even a modest prediction in those areas, given that it is nonoverlapping with other measures, is potentially of practical significance.

## Contributing to Social and Cultural Practices

### EI Provides a Rationale for Taking Emotions Seriously in Educational and Organizational Contexts

The establishment of an emotional intelligence, and the outline of how it operates, provides a rationale for teaching about emotions, their meanings, and how they operate more generally in our educational programs, and for creating specialties in the understanding of emotion. Emotional knowledge can be learned, just as knowledge in any other area can be learned. It is at least possible that increasing such knowledge can help many people live more socially connected lives. This is not a panacea, of course. Like other technologies, emotional knowledge can be used for bad ends as well as good. For example, increased emotional knowledge can provide less well-intentioned individuals with strategies to emotionally manipulate others.

That said, it is my hope that emotional knowledge will have a greater positive than negative impact. Societies that recognize the importance of their citizen's feelings may help create a more humane environment for those who live within them. When this emotional humanity is balanced with the other rights and responsibilities of the individual and society, the world may be the better for it.

# ☐ References

1. Mayer, J. D., Salovey, P., & Caruso, D. R. (2000). Emotional intelligence as zeitgeist, as personality, and as a standard intelligence. In R. Bar-On & J. D. A. Parker (Eds.), *Handbook of emotional intelligence* (pp. 92–117). New York: Jossey-Bass.
2. Solomon, R. C. (2000). The philosophy of emotions. In M. Lewis & J. M. Haviland-Jones (Eds.), *Handbook of emotions* (pp. 3–15). New York: Guilford.
3. Fancher, R. E. (1985). *The intelligence men: Makers of the IQ controversy.* New York: W. W. Norton.
4. Ekman, P. (1973). *Darwin and facial expression: A century of research in review.* New York: Academic Press.
5. Mayer, J. D. (1986). How mood influences cognition. In N. E. Sharkey (Ed.), *Advances in cognitive science* (pp. 290–314). Chichester, UK: Ellis Horwood.
6. Buck, R. (1984). *The communication of emotion.* New York: Guilford Press.
7. Dyer, M. G. (1983). The role of affect in narratives. *Cognitive Science, 7,* 211–242.
8. Gardner, H. (1983). *Frames of mind: The theory of multiple intelligences.* New York: Basic Books.
9. Marlowe, H. A. (1986). Social intelligence: Evidence for multidimensionality and construct independence. *Journal of Educational Psychology, 78,* 52–58.
10. TenHouten, W. D., Hoppe, J. E., Bogen, J. E., & Walter, D. O. (1985). Alexithymia and the split brain: IV. Gottschalk-Gleser content analysis, An overview. *Psychotherapy and Psychosomatics, 44,* 113–121.
11. Payne, W. L. (1986). A study of emotion: Developing emotional intelligence: Self-integration; relating to fear, pain and desire. *Dissertation Abstracts International, 47,* 203A (UMI No. AAC 8605928).
12. Van Ghent, D. (1953). *The English novel: Form and function.* New York: Harper & Row Publishers.
13. Mayer, J. D., DiPaolo, M. T., & Salovey, P. (1990). Perceiving affective content in ambiguous visual stimuli: A component of emotional intelligence. *Journal of Personality Assessment, 54,* 772–781.
14. Mayer, J. D., & Salovey, P. (1993). The intelligence of emotional intelligence. *Intelligence, 17,* 433–442.
15. Salovey, P., & Mayer, J. D. (1990). Emotional intelligence. *Imagination, Cognition, and Personality, 9,* 185–211.
16. Damasio, A. R. (1994). *Descartes' error.* New York: G. P. Putnam's Sons.
17. Bar-On, R. (1997). *Bar-On Emotional Quotient Inventory: Technical manual.* Toronto, Canada: Multi-Health Systems.
18. Cooper, R. K., & Q-Metrics. (1996–1997). *EQ Map: Intepretation guide.* San Francisco: AIT & Essi Systems.
19. Goleman, D. (1995). *Emotional intelligence.* New York: Bantam.

20. Mayer, J. D. (2000). Emotion, intelligence, emotional intelligence. In J. P. Forgas (Ed.), *The handbook of affect and social cognition* (pp. 410–431). Mahwah, NJ: Lawrence Erlbaum & Associates, Inc.

21. Gardner, H. (1993). *Frames of mind: The theory of multiple intelligences* (10th anniv. ed.). New York: Basic Books.

22. Gardner, H. (1999). Who owns intelligence? *Atlantic Monthly, 283,* 67–76.

23. Dabrowski, K., & Piechowski, M. M. (1977). *Theory of levels of emotional development: Vol. 1. Multilevelness and positive disintegration.* Oceanside, NY: Dabor Science Publications.

24. Epstein, S. (1998). *Constructive thinking: The key to emotional intelligence.* New York: Praeger Publishers.

25. Sternberg, R. J. (2001). Measuring the intelligence of an idea: How intelligent is the idea of emotional intelligence? In J. Ciarrochi, J. P. Forgas & J. D. Mayer (Eds.), *Emotional intelligence in everyday life: A scientific inquiry* (pp. 187–194). Philadelphia: Psychology Press.

26. Mayer, J. D. (1998). A systems framework for the field of personality. *Psychological Inquiry, 9,* 118–144.

27. Mayer, J. D., & Salovey, P. (1997). What is emotional intelligence? In P. Salovey & D. Sluyter (Eds.), *Emotional development and emotional intelligence: Educational implications* (pp. 3–31). New York: Basic Books.

28. Mayer, J. D., Salovey, P., Caruso, D. R., & Sitarenios, G. (2003). Measuring emotional intelligence with the MSCEIT V2.0. *Emotion, 3,* 97–105.

29. Mayer, J. D., Caruso, D. R., & Salovey, P. (1999). Emotional intelligence meets traditional standards for an intelligence. *Intelligence, 27,* 267–298.

30. Goleman, D. (1998). *Working with emotional intelligence.* New York: Bantam.

31. Goleman, D. (2000). Leadership that gets results. *Harvard Business Review, 78,* 78–90.

32. Mayer, J. D. (2001). Primary divisions of personality and their scientific contributions: From the trilogy-of-mind to the systems set. *Journal for the Theory of Social Behaviour, 31,* 449–477.

33. Mayer, J. D. (2003). Structural divisions of personality and the classification of traits. *Review of General Psychology, 7,* 381–401.

34. Mayer, J. D. (2004). How does psychotherapy influence personality: A theoretical integration. *Journal of Clinical Psychology, 60,* 1291–1315.

35. Gough, H. G. (1994). *California Psychological Inventory.* Palo Alto, CA: Consulting Psychologists Press.

36. Funder, D. C. (2001). *The personality puzzle.* New York: W. W. Norton & Company.

37. Mayer, J. D. (2004). A classification system for the data of personality psychology and adjoining fields. *Review of General Psychology, 8,* 208–219.

38. Paulhus, D. L., Lysy, D. C., & Yik, M. S. M. (1998). Self-report measures of intelligence: Are they useful as proxy IQ tests? *Journal of Personality Psychology, 66,* 525–554.

39. Borkenau, P., & Liebler, A. (1993). Convergence of stranger ratings of personality and intelligence with self-ratings, partner ratings, and measured intelligence. *Journal of Personality and Social Psychology, 65,* 546–553.

40. Reynolds, D. J., & Gifford, R. (2001). The sounds and sights of intelligence: A lens model channel analysis. *Personality and Social Psychology Bulletin, 27,* 187–200.

41. Wiggins, N., Hoffman, P. J., & Taber, T. (1969). Types of judges and cue utilization in judgments of intelligence. *Journal of Personality and Social Psychology, 12,* 52–59.

42. Boyatzis, R. E., Goleman, D., & Rhee, K. S. (2000). Clustering competence in emotional intelligence: Insights from the Emotional Competence Inventory. In R. Bar-On & J. D. A. Parker (Eds.), *Handbook of emotional intelligence: Theory, development, assessment, and application at home, school, and in the workplace* (pp. 343–362). San Francisco: Jossey-Bass.

43. Brackett, M., & Mayer, J. D. (2003). Convergent, discriminant, and incremental validity of competing measures of emotional intelligence. *Personality and Social Psychology Bulletin, 29,* 1147–1158.

44. Mayer, J. D., Salovey, P., & Caruso, D. R. (2004). Emotional intelligence: Theory, findings, and implications. *Psychological Inquiry, 60,* 197–215.

45. Murensky, C. L. (2000). The relationships between emotional intelligence, personality, critical thinking ability and organizational leadership performance at upper levels of management. *Dissertation Abstracts International: Section B. The Sciences and Engineering, 61*(2-B), 1121 (UMI No. AAI9962991; ISSN/ISBN 0419-4217).

46. Hemmati, T., Mills, J. F., & Kroner, D. G. (2004). The validity of the Bar-On emotional intelligence quotient in an offender population. *Personality and Individual Differences, 37,* 695–706.

47. Parker, J. D. A., Summerfeldt, L. J., Hogan, M. J., & Majeski, S. A. (2002). Emotional intelligence and academic success: Examining the transition from high school to university. *Personality and Individual Differences, 36,* 163–172.

48. Joint Committee on Standards. (1999). *Standards for educational and psychological testing.* Washington, DC: American Educational Research Association.

49. Kelly, R., & Caplan, J. (1993). How Bell Labs creates star performers. *Harvard Business Review, 71,* 128–139.

50. Davies, M., Stankov, L., & Roberts, R. D. (1998). Emotional intelligence: In search of an elusive construct. *Journal of Personality and Social Psychology, 75,* 989–1015.

51. Matthews, G., Zeidner, M., & Roberts, R. D. (2002). *Emotional intelligence: Science and myth.* Cambridge, MA: MIT Press.

2
CHAPTER

Marc A. Brackett
Glenn Geher

# Measuring Emotional Intelligence: Paradigmatic Diversity and Common Ground

In 1990, Peter Salovey and John Mayer published an article [1] that has since served as the academic foundation for research on Emotional Intelligence (EI). In that landmark article, these researchers synthesized the (then) disparate fields of emotion and intelligence into a unifying theory that would pave the way for a great deal of theoretical and empirical work over the past 15 years. They defined EI as "the ability to monitor one's own and others' feelings and emotions, to discriminate among them and to use this information to guide one's thinking and actions" [1, p. 189]. In the same year, they published a second article on EI, which provided an initial empirical demonstration of how EI might be measured, and how individual differences in EI might predict important things about a person's life, including the ability to respond empathically to others [2].

Since Salovey and Mayer's [1] introduction of EI to the academic literature, the definitions of EI across time and across researchers have varied. In a recent thorough review of the EI literature, Matthews, Zeidner, and Roberts [3] delineate the particulars of several different conceptualizations of EI and recommend that EI researchers move toward a more consensual model. For instance, they explain the current predominant "ability" model of EI espoused by Mayer and Salovey [4], which proposes that four fundamental emotion-related abilities comprise EI, including (a) perception/expression of emotion, (b) use of emotion to facilitate thinking, (c) understanding of emotion, and (d) management of emotion in oneself and others. They also describe an alternative model by Bar-On [5], which suggests that the fundamental areas of EI are intrapersonal skills, adaptability, stress management, and general mood. Clearly, these conceptualizations differ.

# ☐ Models of Emotional Intelligence

To provide clarity, two organizational schemes have been developed to categorize different classes of EI theories and measurement tools. Mayer, Salovey, and Caruso [6] discuss the distinctions between "ability" and "mixed" models of EI. Ability models conceptualize EI as a set of mental abilities or skills that pertain to the accurate processing of emotion-relevant information. For instance, Mayer et al. [6] discuss the ability to manage one's own emotions (e.g., having the ability to calm down after being angered) as an element of EI. In fact, their model [6] and new performance test, the Mayer-Salovey-Caruso Emotional Intelligence Test (MSCEIT [7]) is comprised exclusively of such psychological abilities.

In contrast, mixed-models focus on self-perceived abilities, skills, and personality traits. For instance, Bar-On's [5] model of EI includes an emotion-related ability such as "stress tolerance" and basic personality traits such as "optimism." Because both perceived abilities and traits are in the conceptual framework, proponents of this approach have generally employed self-report measures as opposed to performance measures to assess EI. On the Emotion Quotient Inventory (EQ-i [5]), for example, "stress tolerance" is conceptualized as a fundamental ability underlying EI; however, the EQ-i only measures one's perceived ability, and not one's actual ability to tolerate stress.

Petrides and Furnham [8] use a slightly different scheme by referring to "ability EI" versus "trait EI." In their framework, ability EI corresponds to models, such as the one by Mayer et al. [6], that underscore the importance of cognitive abilities in defining EI. Alternatively, trait EI corresponds to models, which emphasize traits that are relevant to individual differences in emotional processes. According to Petrides and Furnham [8], these different models of EI are so conceptually different that they warrant different names. They further argue (and we agree) that such different models should, in fact, not exist under the same semantic umbrella. From their perspective, EI scholars should work toward the development of two fully separate classes of constructs: trait EI and ability EI.

In addition to mixed- or trait-based and ability measures, Brackett et al. [9] developed self-report scales that map directly onto performance tests such as the MSCEIT. These researchers developed the Self-Rated

Emotional Intelligence Scale (SREIS) in order to test the relationship between people's beliefs about their emotion-related abilities (i.e., the perception, use, understanding, and management of emotion) and their actual knowledge about or reasoning capacity with these abilities.

In spite of the heterogeneity among EI measures, several core constructs seem to emerge among the different conceptualizations of EI. Matthews et al. [3] provide a definition of EI that encompasses aspects of several current models of EI. They define EI as "the competence to identify and express emotions, understand emotions, assimilate emotions into thought, and regulate both positive and negative emotions in the self and others" [3, p. 3]. While this definition maps most closely onto Mayer, Salovey, and Caruso's [6] ability model, all models of EI address these basic elements in varying degrees. Accordingly, an emotionally intelligent individual is capable of knowing how others feel, understanding how he or she feels him or herself, using emotions adaptively to make decisions, and regulating emotions effectively in intrapersonal and interpersonal contexts.

Because there are a number of ways of assessing EI, including performance and self-report measures, it is important to consider the distinctions among the different EI tests. In this chapter we review and examine the reliability and validity of some of the most widely used EI measurement tools. We also report on their intercorrelations (when available), whether the EI tests are distinguishable from other mental abilities and well-established personality attributes, and whether they predict important aspects of everyday life, including psychological health and adaptive behavior.

## ☐ Issues Regarding the Measurement of Emotional Intelligence

In their early conceptual writing about EI, Salovey and Mayer [1] knowingly anticipated and considered the empirical study of the construct. They discussed issues regarding the utility of EI, stating "[conclusions regarding this construct] await the findings of well designed experiments and correlational studies" [1, p. 201]. Given the nature of empirical work in psychology, strategies for measuring EI thereby became necessary.

Several issues that underlie EI measurement became apparent as researchers tried to operationally define the construct and its corresponding elements. First, researchers needed to create measures that corresponded accurately to their particular EI conceptualizations. For adherents of ability-based models, that implied the need for "performance measures." A performance measure of EI is an index of EI that assesses individual differences in specific emotion-relevant abilities. The Emotional Accuracy Research Scale (EARS [10], [11]) was one of the first such performance measures of EI. This scale was designed to tap the emotion-identification component of EI by having participants rate the emotions of targets who had written emotionally laden vignettes. In general, higher scores were thought to indicate more ability in identifying emotions of others. The scoring system of this and other performance measures will be described in more detail later.

For adherents of mixed-models of EI, there was also a need to create measures. Generally, researchers working in this tradition have leaned toward self-report indices, a method that is quite common in the measurement of personality traits. For instance, Bar-On [5] developed the EQ-i to tap his largely trait-based model of EI. The EQ-i includes self-report items designed to tap 15 subscales that are thought to comprise five higher order EI domains.

## ☐ Basic Psychometric Issues Pertinent to Emotional Intelligence Measurement

From a measurement perspective, indices of EI should be both reliable and valid. A useful EI measure should exhibit test–retest reliability (i.e., yield similar scores in the same participants across time) and high internal reliability (i.e., the items in the scale should be positively intercorrelated). Such a measure should have content validity (i.e., include items that reasonably tap the multiple conceptual facets of the construct) and convergent validity (i.e., correlate positively with other EI measures). Further, such a measure should demonstrate discriminant validity (i.e., be either uncorrelated or only modestly correlated with conceptually distinct measures such as the Big Five personality traits). Similarly, a good EI index should demonstrate incremental validity (i.e., account for variability in important outcomes after competing predictor variables are statistically controlled for). Also, from a utilitarian standpoint, a good EI measure should have criterion validity (i.e., scores should predict both psychological and behavioral outcomes that are conceptually related to EI). For a broader and more in-depth analysis of psychometric issues applied to EI, see [12].

## ☐ Psychometric Qualities and Validity of Different EI Measures

A good deal of research on the validation of EI measures has been conducted. Here, we provide a summary of the psychometric findings for many of the widely used EI measures. These measures are summarized in

Table 2.1. Consistent with recent the literature on EI (e.g., [6], [8–9], [20]), we organize this section into performance-based and self-report indices of EI.

## Performance Measures of EI

In this section we briefly review some of the best-known EI performance tests that were designed to tap aspects of Mayer et al.'s [6] model of EI. Due to our focus on current measures of EI, we direct the reader elsewhere [3–4], [21] for reviews of related ability tests, including the Levels of Emotional Awareness Scale (LEAS [22]) and the Diagnostic Assessment of Non-Verbal Affect—Adult Facial Expressions (DANVA-AF [23]). Here, we review the EARS (Emotional Accuracy Research Scale [11]) and the MSCEIT (Mayer-Salovey-Caruso Emotional Intelligence Test [7]).

### EARS

The Emotional Accuracy Research Scale (EARS) was designed to measure the emotion-perception component of the ability model by having participants try to identify which emotion (of two options presented across several items) particular targets reported feeling. Emotionally laden stories written by actual targets were used as the basis of participants' judgments. For each participant, two EI scores were computed. The *target-agreement* score corresponded to the degree to which participants' choices matched the actual judgments of the targets themselves. The *consensus-agreement* score corresponded to the degree to which participants' choices were consistent with the group consensus. A weighted-consensus scoring procedure was implemented such that participants' consensus scores increased more for choosing options that were highly popular among the group of judges compared with options that were less popular among the judges.

The initial version of the EARS [11] demonstrated some promise; however, findings regarding the psychometric properties of the EARS also raised some concerns. The internal reliability coefficients (Cronbach's alphas) for the target and consensus subscores were .24 and .53, respectively. These coefficients are, indeed, poor by any standards. In spite of such poor internal reliability, the EARS demonstrated some convergent validity across two studies. In particular, consensus scores were positively related to self-reported empathy ($r = .24$) and the ability to agree with a consensus regarding emotion judgments of targets presented in dynamic video-based presentations (e.g., $r = .36$; see [13]).

**TABLE 2.1. Summary of several indices of emotional intelligence in adults**

| Performance measure | Relevant recent publication | Brief measure description | Facets of EI included |
|---|---|---|---|
| **EARS** Emotional Accuracy Research Scale | [10–11], [13] | An early performance measure of emotion-perception ability; participants read emotionally laden stories and make judgments regarding how the targets of several emotionally laden stories felt; agreement-with-target and agreement-with-consensus scores are computed | Ability to accurately perceive emotions in others (i.e., the emotion-perception branch of the ability model) |
| **MSCEIT** Mayer-Salovey-Caruso Emotional Intelligence Test | [14–15] | The newest index of the ability-model version of EI; can be scored in terms of both agreement with a broad consensus and agreement with judgments from emotion experts; participants make judgments regarding several emotion-relevant stimuli (such as how much fear a particular face demonstrates on a 1–5 scale) | Ability to accurately perceive emotions in oneself and others, use emotions to facilitate thinking, understand emotional meanings, and to effectively manage emotions |
| *Self-report measures* | | | |
| **SSRI** Schutte Self-Report Inventory | [16] | A self-report inventory designed, in part, to map onto the initial ability-based model of EI [1] | Overall EI, emotion perception ability, emotion utilization ability, self-relevant emotion-management ability, other-relevant emotion-management ability |

| | | | |
|---|---|---|---|
| **TECI-2** Emotional Competency Inventory | [17] | A 360° survey to be completed by target individuals in addition to several relatively close observers of said targets (e.g., supervisors); separate *self* and *other* assessment scores can be computed | Self-awareness, self-management, social awareness, social skills (each cluster includes both *self* and *other* components); further, each cluster includes multiple competencies with 18 competencies in all |
| **EQ-i** Emotional Quotient Inventory | [18–19] | An index of EI that requires participants to describe themselves (using a Likert scale) in terms of several emotion-relevant judgments pertaining to Bar-On's model of EI | Interpersonal skills, interpersonal skills, stress management, adaptability, general mood (as with the ECI, the EQ-i includes subscales tapping each of these five broader dimensions with 15 total subscales) |
| **SREIS** Self-Rated Emotional Intelligence Scale | [9] | A self-rated inventory designed to map onto the MSCEIT | Self-rated ability to perceive emotion in faces, use emotion to facilitate thought, understand emotions, and manage emotions |

## MSCEIT

Research by Mayer and his colleagues [7], [24] has resulted in two performance tests that measure the four emotion-related abilities captured by Mayer and Salovey's [4] EI theory (i.e., the perception, use, understanding, and management of emotion). The first such test was the Multifactor Emotional Intelligence Test (MEIS [24]). Although the MEIS was reliable, distinctive, and related to important outcomes, the test was quickly improved upon, leading to a briefer EI test that was produced professionally, the Mayer-Salovey-Caruso Emotional Intelligence Test (MSCEIT, v. 2.0 [7]).

The MSCEIT assesses the four-domain model of EI with 141 items that are divided among eight tasks (two for each domain). The test yields seven scores: one for each of the four domains, two area scores, and a total EI score. The two area scores are termed: Experiential EI (domains 1 and 2 combined) and Strategic EI (domains 3 and 4 combined). Experiential EI indicates the degree to which an individual "takes in" emotional experiences, whereas strategic EI indicates the degree to which an individual understands and uses emotion skills strategically for planning and self-management. The first domain of EI, *perceiving emotions*, is measured by asking individuals to identify the emotions expressed in photographs of people's faces ("faces") as well as the feelings suggested by artistic drawings and landscapes ("pictures"). The second domain of EI, *use of emotion to facilitate thought*, is measured by two tests that assess people's ability to describe emotional sensations and their parallels to other sensory modalities using a nonfeeling vocabulary ("sensations"), and to identify the feelings that might facilitate or interfere with the successful performance of various cognitive and behavioral tasks ("facilitation"). The third domain of EI, *understanding emotion*, is measured by two tests that pertain to a person's ability to analyze blended or complex emotions ("blends") and to understand how emotional reactions change over time or follow up on one another ("changes"). Finally, the fourth domain of EI, *managing emotion*, has two subtests that assess how participants manage their own emotions ("emotion management") and how they would regulate the emotions of others ("social management").

The MSCEIT is a performance-based test because there are better and worse answers on it, as determined by consensus or expert scoring. Consensus scores reflect the proportion of people in the normative sample (over 5000 people from various parts of the world) who endorsed each MSCEIT test item. In consensus scoring, responses are tallied from the normative sample, and respondents are given credit for "correct" answers to the extent that their answers match those provided by the normative sample (i.e., a representative sample from the general public).

Response scores are weighted by the proportion of the normative sample that also provided that answer. Norms can also be calculated for certain subgroups, including college students and mental health professionals. Expert norms were obtained from a sample of 21 members of the International Society Research on Emotions (ISRE) who provided their expert judgment on each of the test's items. In both scoring methods respondents receive credit for correct answers to the extent that they match those of the normative sample or experts. For example, if 65% of the expert samples say that there is a moderate amount of happiness in a face and a person chooses that answer that person's score is incremented by .65. The correlations among the domain, area, and total scores based on the two scoring methods are quite high across studies, $rs > .90$ [7], [25] and correlations with objective criteria such as social deviance (e.g., number of physical fights, stealing behavior) are also replicated across the two scoring methods [20].

The MSCEIT is reliable at the full-scale level and at the area and branch levels [25]. In a recent study using a large portion of the MSCEIT standardization sample (approximately 2000 individuals), Mayer et al. [25] reported full-test split-half reliabilities greater than .90 for both consensus and expert scoring. Reliabilities for the two area scores (experiential and strategic EI) were also above .86 for both scoring methods. The reliabilities of the four domain scores (perceiving, using, understanding, and managing emotions) for both methods of scoring were between .76 and .91. The reliabilities of the task scores, which the test authors do not recommend using, were somewhat lower (.55–.88). The test–retest reliability of the full-test over a 3-week period was .86 [20].

The MSCEIT also has a factor structure congruent with the four-domain model of EI. Using a large portion of the standardization sample, Mayer et al. [25] performed confirmatory factor analyses on the eight tasks measured by the MSCEIT. They tested for one-, two-, and four-factor models to examine the range of permissible factor structures. The best fit was the four-factor solution as evidenced by the following goodness-of-fit indices (NFI = .98, .97; TLI = .96, .97; RMSEA = .05, .04). The findings were the same for both consensus and expert scoring methods.

Although research is still in its early stages, a number of studies have shown that the MSCEIT is valid measure of EI. First, it appears to show appropriate discriminant validity from measures of analytic intelligence and personality. MSCEIT scores are related to, but not redundant with a range of intelligence measures ($rs$ in the .30–.45 range), including verbal SAT scores [26], the WAIS-III vocabulary subscale [27], and the Wonderlic Personnel Test [28–29].

With respect to personality, the MSCEIT is significantly related to, but not redundant with the Big Five personality traits. Mayer et al. [15]

summarized research with over 1500 participants that examined correlations between MSCEIT scores and Big Five traits. All of the weighted mean correlations were below $r = |.21|$. MSCEIT scores are also unrelated to social desirability or mood, and personality scales such as public and private self-consciousness, and self-esteem [27].

MSCEIT scores also are related to important psychological variables, including psychological health and well-being, particularly perceived personal growth and positive relations with others ($rs = .36, .27$, respectively [20], [27]). Moreover, MSCEIT scores are negatively related to indices of depression and anxiety ($rs = -.25, -.31$, respectively [28]). With respect to everyday life behaviors, lower MSCEIT scores, for men in particular, are related to maladaptive outcomes, including illegal drug and alcohol use, deviant activity, and poor relations with friends, $rs = -.28$ to $-.45$ [26].

MSCEIT scores (especially the managing emotions subscore) also are associated with various indicators of positive social relations, including global self-perceived quality of interpersonal relationships, supportive relationships with parents, and less antagonistic and conflictual relationships with close friends ($rs$ in the .20–.30 range [27]). In addition, MSCEIT scores are positively related to peer reports of relationship quality outcomes, including emotional support and less conflict [30]. Two studies examining whether MSCEIT scores were related to couples' relationship quality also have shown that couples with partners who were both low in EI tended to have poorer quality relationships than couples who were both high in EI [31–32].

Research on EI in the workplace suggests that the MSCEIT positively contributes to some, but not all aspects of job performance. Individuals with higher MSCEIT scores appear to exhibit better vision formulation and articulation, $r = .23$ [33], receive better supervisor ratings of job performance, $r = .22$ [34], and obtain higher ratings of customer satisfaction, $r = .46$ [35]. MSCEIT total and branch scores are also related to merit increases ($r = .36$) and peer ratings of positive work environment ($r = .48$) [36] as well as higher leadership effectiveness [37]. However, in one study, MSCEIT managing emotions scores were significantly lower for the highest ranked and highest paid among 59 senior executives in a large international organization [38]. Because the sample sizes in the above workplace studies were small, the results should be interpreted as preliminary.

The relation between MSCEIT scores and school grades is still undetermined. Studies have found associations in the .20–.25 range among college students; see [20], [39], but the correlations drop to nonsignificance when verbal ability is statistically controlled for. One study in Spain, however, using a sample of 80 high school students reported a zero-order correlation of .46 between MSCEIT scores (assessed at the beginning of the academic year) and end-of-the-year grades [40]. This association remained statistically significant after controlling for general intelligence ($r = .36$). It is possible that association between EI and grades is stronger for high school students than for college students because academic grades are less restricted in high school samples. Nevertheless, more research is needed to examine the role of EI in academic contexts.

In sum, according to Mayer et al. [24–25] the MSCEIT meets classical criteria for an intelligence test because: (a) its factor structure is congruent with the four domains of the theoretical model; (b) the four abilities show unique variance and are meaningfully related to other mental abilities such as verbal intelligence; (c) scores on the test develop with age and experience, (d) the four abilities are objectively measured, and (e) the test predicts important behavioral criteria.

Overall, the MSCEIT shows considerable promise as a performance measure of EI. However, more research is necessary to examine its psychometric properties and validity. For example, Day [41] calls for an examination of the scoring of the MSCEIT. Because scores on the test are determined by matching individual scores to those of the normative sample, there is concern that one's EI score on the MSCEIT measures the "norm" rather than high EI. Other concerns are that the test measures culturally shaped emotional knowledge as opposed to emotion abilities as they function during actual usage [3]. Finally, it will be necessary to test whether the MSCEIT total score and the individual domain scores predict a wide range of theoretically related outcomes in various settings.

## Self-Report Measures of EI

As mentioned earlier, self-report measures of EI require participants to describe themselves on Likert-scale items. These scales rely on the individual's self-understanding. Thus, if the person's self-concept is accurate, then such scales can be used as accurate measures of emotion-relevant traits or EI ability. However, one problem with self-report indices of mental skills is that people are generally poor at assessing their own mental abilities [42–43]. Self-report scales may also be modified to a 360° format. In this case, a particular target's score is based separately on his or her own self-report in addition to reports provided by observers (informants) who are highly familiar with the target, including peers, direct reports, and supervisors. Informant reports generally measure a person's reputation.

In this section we review the three best-known self-report measures of EI, including the Schutte Self-Report Inventory (SSRI [16]), the Emotional Quotient Inventory (EQ-i [5]), and the Emotional Competency Inventory (ECI [44]; see also [17]), which employs a 360° measurement strategy. We also review a new measure, the Self-Rated Emotional Intelligence Scale (SREIS [9]). As noted earlier, this instrument was developed to map onto the MSCEIT so the direct relationship between self-rated and ability EI could be examined. We direct the reader elsewhere [21] for a review of other well-known measures that assess perceived emotion-related abilities and traits captured by mixed or trait-based models of EI. These measures include the Trait-Meta-Mood-Scale (TMMS [45]) and the Toronto Alexithymia Scale (TAS-20 [46]).

## *SSRI*

The SSRI is a brief self-report measure developed by Schutte et al. [16]. The authors originally wrote a pool of 62 items that were largely based on their understanding of Salovey and Mayer's [1] model of EI. For example, they included items such as, "I am aware of my emotions as I experience them" to measure emotion perception. Factor analysis of the initial 62 items resulted in a single-factor 33-item scale. The internal and test–rest reliabilities of the SSRI total score are high, $\alpha_s = .93$ and .73, respectively [16].

The structural validity of the SSRI is questionable, however. Petrides and Furnham [8] assert that the SSRI is not unidimensional and that the scale does not map onto Salovey and Mayer's [1] model of EI, as claimed by the authors of the scale [16]. Petrides and Furnham [8] prefer the results of their own exploratory factor analysis, which divided the SSRI into four provisional factors (optimism and mood regulation, appraisal of emotions, social skills, and utilization of emotion). The reliability of some subscales (e.g., utilizing emotions) is quite low, however [47]. Other researchers prefer a three-factor solution [48]. Finally, Brackett and Mayer's [20] factor analysis of the SSRI resulted in only one interpretable factor pertaining to the perception or appraisal of emotions.

A few studies have examined the discriminant validity of the SSRI with respect to conventional personality inventories and measures of well-being. The test is significantly related to each of the Big Five traits (extraversion, agreeableness, conscientiousness, neuroticism, and openness to experience) in predictable directions (e.g., negatively correlated with neuroticism). The magnitudes of these correlations are not large enough to suggest construct redundancy [20], [48]. The SSRI does appear to overlap greatly with other conceptually related constructs, including psychological well-being and alexithymia. For example, the correlation between the SSRI and alexithymia is −.65 [16], and when Ryff's [49] scales of psychological well-being were regressed onto the SSRI total score, the multiple $R$ was .70 [20]. These findings suggest that the SSRI has high semantic overlap with conventional self-report measures of well-being and does not assess much beyond these measures.

A number of studies have tested the validity of the SSRI in relation to both psychological and behavioral outcomes. For instance, scores on the SSRI have been related to emotion-relevant outcomes such as attention to feelings and impulse control [16]. In the original study, the SSRI predicted end of the year GPA and discriminated between groups expected to be higher and lower in EI. Specifically, women scored higher than men, and therapists scored higher than both prisoners and psychotherapy patients. The association between the SSRI and college GPA was not replicated, however [20].

The SSRI also correlates with measures of interpersonal relationship quality, including empathic perspective taking, social skills, marital satisfaction, and supervisor ratings of student counselors who worked at mental health agencies [50]. For example, Schutte et al. [50] found that the SSRI correlated with reports of marital satisfaction ($r = .51$). These studies, however, did not examine the incremental validity of the SSRI after controlling for established measures, such as well-being. Finally, one study found that the SSRI was not predictive of maladaptive behavior (e.g., drug use) in a large sample of college students [20].

Based on our review of the literature, the utility of the SSRI as a self-report measure of EI is questionable. Independent factor analyses of the measure have resulted in one-, three-, and four-factor solutions, indicating that the test does not directly map onto Salovey and Mayer's [1] original model of EI. Also, the SSRI is unrelated to important life criteria, including smoking, drug use, alcohol use, and social deviance. Finally, the scale is redundant with existing measures of psychological functioning (e.g., well-being, alexithymia). These findings indicate that the SSRI may not have additional predictive power above and beyond already established measures.

## EQ-i

The Emotional Quotient Inventory (EQ-i [5]) is one of the most widely used and studied self-report indices of EI. Indeed, the test has been translated into more than 30 languages [19]. This scale evolved out of the author's question, "Why do some people have better psychological well-being than others? And, why are some people able to succeed in life over others?" [5, p. 1]. The EQ-i contains 133 items and employs a five-point response scale similar to most self-report measures that employ Likert-type scales. The EQ-i measures five constructs that are a composite of specific competencies, including *interpersonal skills* (i.e., self-regard, emotional self-awareness, assertiveness, independence, and self-actualization), (b) *interpersonal skills* (i.e., empathy, social responsibility, and interpersonal relationships), (c) *stress-management* (i.e., stress tolerance and impulse control), (d) *adaptability* (i.e., reality-testing, flexibility, and problem-solving), and (e) *general mood* (i.e., happiness and optimism). However, Bar-On [18] described the general mood factor as a facilitator of EI rather than a part of it. Thus, total EQ-i scores are now computed by summing the first four scales alone. The correlation between these scoring methods is rather high, however ($r$ = .98 [20]). Finally, the measure includes validity subscales to tap issues regarding item omission rate, within-subject inconsistency, socially desirable responding, and socially undesirable responding.

Conceptually the EQ-i has the qualities resembling a mixed model of EI (as per [6]). However, while this index includes constructs that pertain to both perceived traits and abilities, the mechanism of measurement does not directly access abilities due to its self-report method. As such, empirically, it may be appropriate to call the EQ-i a trait model as opposed to a *mixed* model (as indices of abilities are filtered through self-reports). Bar-On [19, p. 113] currently refers to the EQ-i as "a self-report measure of emotionally and socially intelligent behavior which provides an estimate of one's emotional and social intelligence."

The reliability and validity of the EQ-i have been assessed across several empirical studies (see [19, p. 115] for a summary of the development of this index). Generally, the subscales for the EQ-i have demonstrated strong internal reliability, yielding alpha coefficients that are consistently greater than .90. Further, test–retest coefficients have been reasonable in size across 2-week, 1-month, 2-month, 4-month, and 6-month intervals.

Regarding the validity of the EQ-i, Bar-On [19] has presented data speaking to the factorial, convergent, discriminant, and predictive validity of the test. Separate factor analyses (both exploratory and confirmatory) of the measure have yielded different results, including solutions with 6, 10, 13, and 15 factors [19], [51], calling into question the structural validity of the test.

Much of the information on the convergent/discriminant validity of the EQ-i originally appeared as unpublished data in the technical manual [5]. These reports and some recently published studies have shown that the EQ-i correlates highly with a number of personality measures including anxiety, depression, and alexithymia, as well as the Big Five traits (neuroticism in particular) [20], [52–54]. Independent reviews of the EQ-i [55–56] also have consistently stated that the items on the measure appear to have considerable semantic overlap with the Big Five personality traits. Indeed, empirical investigations suggest that EQ-i may in fact be too strongly intercorrelated with personality traits than is optimal. For example, Brackett and Mayer [20] reported a multiple $R$ of .75 when the Big Five traits were regressed onto the EQ-i total score. In that study, all of the Big Five traits significantly contributed to the prediction of the EQ-i.

Aside from concerns regarding the discriminant validity of the EQ-i, Bar-On [19] has provided evidence regarding the predictive validity of the measure in domains ranging from business/industry to education. For example, the EQ-i has discriminated between successful and unsuccessful Air Force recruiters (Handley, cited in [57]) and academically successful and unsuccessful students ([58], cited in [5]). The positive correlation with academic performance, however, has not been replicated [20], [53]. The EQ-i also appears unrelated to fluid intelligence [5], [59]. Finally, with respect to maladaptive behavior, the EQ-i was predictive of excessive alcohol consumption in one study after controlling for personality and well-being [20].

We have the same concerns about the EQ-i as we did for the SSRI. First, it will be important to determine the best factor structure of the test. Second, future research could benefit from addressing the degree to which EQ-i scores empirically provide unique information separate from data provided by personality trait and well-being measures. The most central concern is that the EQ-i has considerable semantic overlap with measures that have been used for decades. Therefore, future studies must demonstrate that the EQ-i is incrementally valid across multiple outcomes (with multiple control variables).

## *ECI*

The Emotional Competency Inventory (ECI) and its recent descendant, the ECI-2, were developed to address the popular model of EI put forth by Goleman and his collaborators at the Hay Group (see [17], [60]). In addition to being a self-report inventory, this index was explicitly designed to be a 360° measure, meaning that for any given target person, multiple scores are yielded as a result of the target's self-report and the reports provided by relevant observers of the target (e.g., a target's supervisor). Importantly, the ECI was developed in part to assess competencies in work-related contexts. This is evidenced in the authors' definition of EI. According to Boyatzis and Sala an "emotional intelligence competency is an ability to recognize, understand, and use emotional information about oneself or others that leads to or causes effective or superior performance" [17, p. 145].

The ECI-2 as described by Boyatzis and Sala [17] contains 72 items, which cluster into four broad competencies, including: (a) *self-awareness* (i.e., knowing one's internal states, preferences, resources, and intuitions), (b) *self-management* (i.e., managing one's internal states, impulses, and resources), (c) *social awareness* (i.e., handling relationships, awareness of others' feelings, needs, and concerns), and (d) *relationship management* (also called social skills; i.e., skill or adeptness at inducing desirable responses in others). Similar to the EQ-i, the ECI was designed to measure 18 specific competencies that are divided among the four higher order clusters. For example, the self-management cluster is comprised of subscales that tap self-control, trustworthiness, conscientiousness, adaptability, achievement orientation, and initiative. As noted earlier, many of the ECI subscales also assess competencies in work-related contexts. The social skills cluster speaks directly to this point. This cluster includes such competencies as perceived leadership and teamwork ability, the ability to influence others, and inspirational leadership. In an important critique of ECI, Matthews et al. write that "it is difficult not to be cynical of the [ECI], given the lack of publicly accessible data supplied by its creators and the constellation of old concepts packaged under its new label" [3, p. 218].

Since the publication of Matthews et al.'s [3] critique, Boyatzis and Sala [17] have provided information bearing on the psychometric properties of the ECI-2. They have provided data on thousands of workers across multiple organizations to address issues regarding the reliability and validity of this measure. Generally, alpha coefficients suggest relatively strong internal reliability for the informant reports (all but one of the alphas are above .71); however, for the self-assessments, about half of the 18 scales have reliability coefficients below .65. The results from their factor analysis suggest that a general EI factor emerges. However, the overall structural validity of the full-scale ECI is not strongly supported by the authors' factor analysis, which resulted in only nine factors with eigenvalues greater than 1.0. Thus, the degree to which the ECI empirically matches their underlying model of EI (i.e., four clusters that are comprised of 18 competencies) is questionable.

In spite of issues regarding the structural validity of the ECI, Boyatzis and Sala [17] provide some evidence that the ECI has discriminant validity because scores on the scale are not redundant with personality traits such as the Big Five. In one study, the strongest association between any ECI cluster and any of the Big Five traits, for instance, was between self-awareness and extraversion, $r = .47$ ([61], cited in [17]).

The ECI also appears to predict work-related outcomes reasonably well. For example, in a small sample of Turkish finance professionals, ECI scales correlated with salary ($rs = .30–.43$ across all four clusters). However, the scales did not correlate significantly with position in the company or number of promotions. ECI scores also were correlated positively with several indices of job performance in a sample of firefighters from Britain ([62], cited in [17]). However, in that study, the large correlations between the ECI informant ratings and objective performance ratings (e.g., teamwork and collaboration correlated highly with interpersonal ability), may be due to the conceptual overlap between the measures or to both measures having been completed by the same informants. In addition, Boyatzis and Sala review other interesting validation studies using the ECI, but many of the studies were conducted with very small sample sizes (Ns <30) [17]. Finally, there is little evidence that the ECI is incrementally valid.

In sum, the ECI shows some promise regarding its ability to predict relevant outcomes in work-related settings. There is a dearth of research, however, on the general psychometric properties of the measure, including its structural and incremental validity. As noted earlier, the ECI was designed to assess 18 competencies that are conceptually organized according to four broad clusters; however, factor analysis of the scale's 72 items indicates that there are nine factors [17]. Moreover, there are no reports of the intercorrelations of these nine factors or the four conceptual clusters. It would be important to know whether the nine factors are themselves hierarchically organized according to four clusters or one overall ECI factor. Future research needs to address these issues to provide empirical support for the latent model that this index was designed to measure.

## SREIS

The Self-Rated Emotional Intelligence Scale (SREIS [9]) was designed to measure people's self-reported ability to perceive, use, understand, and manage emotions, the four emotion-related abilities that are assessed by the MSCEIT. The measure was developed for the purposes of directly testing the relationship between people's self-reported beliefs about their emotion-abilities and their actual abilities. For example, do individuals who report having a rich emotions vocabulary actually have this lexicon?

On the SREIS, *emotion perception* is assessed with statements such as, "I am good at reading people's facial expressions." The *use of emotion to facilitate thought* is measured by statements such as, "When making decisions, I listen to my feelings to see if the decision feels right." *Understanding of emotion* is measured by statements including, "I have a rich vocabulary to describe my emotions." Finally, *management of emotion* is measured by statements such as, "I know how to keep calm in difficult or stressful situations."

Brackett et al. [9] addressed the factor structure of the SREIS. In two studies, the structure of the measure was examined using both exploratory (EFA) and confirmatory factor analytic (CFA) techniques. As predicted, the four-factor solution in the EFA was optimal. Moreover, the CFA model, which tested the four-domain solution with two subcomponents on the managing emotions domain (self management and social management), provided a good fit to the data (NFI = .91, TLI = .94, and RMSEA = .04). The reliabilities of the four subscales ($\alpha$s = .64–.84) and the SREIS total score ($\alpha$ = .77) were not all optimal, but in an acceptable range. Thus, these findings indicate that people's self-rated EI can be measured with some degree of reliability. Further, the results of CFA suggest that the basic dimensions of EI can be detected with a self-report scale such as the SREIS in addition to a performance-based measure such as the MSCEIT.

Brackett et al. [9] also examined (a) the relationship between the SREIS and the MSCEIT, (b) the discriminant validity of the SREIS, and (c) the incremental validity of the SREIS. As expected, the correlation between the SREIS and MSCEIT total scores were rather low ($rs < .25$ across three studies). Additional analyses showed that the relationship between self-reported EI and ability EI operates in the same way as other abilities [43]. That is, relative to actual performance, those with lower MSCEIT scores overestimated their EI, whereas those with higher MSCEIT scores underestimated their EI. The discriminant validity of the SREIS in relation to the Big Five personality traits and measures of well-being also was examined. With respect to the Big Five, SREIS scores correlated with all of the five Big Five traits (all $rs < .42$), except for agreeableness. With respect to measures of well-being, SREIS scores correlated with psychological well-being ($r = .47$) and with life satisfaction ($r = .23$). These results indicate that the relationship between the SREIS and well-studied personality attributes is not as strong as it was for the SSRI and the EQ-i.

Finally, Brackett et al. [9] examined the predictive and incremental validity of the SREIS (compared to the MSCEIT). The MSCEIT, but not the SREIS, was significantly related to self-perceived quality of interpersonal relationships (Study 2) and interpersonal competence in a lab-based social interaction (Study 3) after personality and well-being were held constant.

The results of this research suggest that measuring EI with performance-based tests such as the MSCEIT in contrast to self-report measures such as the SREIS makes it possible to analyze the degree to which emotion-related abilities contribute (independently) to a person's social behavior. Therefore, the utility of the SREIS as a self-report measure of EI is questionable. Future research, however, might examine whether discrepancy scores between self-report and ability measures, which tap the same underlying construct theoretically, predict behavior. For example, what are the implications for individuals who grossly overestimate or underestimate their EI?

# ☐ Intercorrelations Among Different EI Measures

Research indicates that ability tests of EI such as the MSCEIT do not correlate highly with self-report tests of EI, including the SSRI, EQ-i, or SREIS. For example, in one study, the MSCEIT correlated .21 with the EQ-i and .18

with the SSRI [20]. Even when self-report measures were designed to correspond with ability measures (e.g., MSCEIT and SREIS), the correlations between the measures were quite low [9], as noted above. The relationships among self-report measures of EI tend to be somewhat higher. For example, the correlation between the EQ-i and SSRI was .43 in one study [20] and .66 in another [63]. Ultimately, these findings suggest that self-report and performance tests of EI are empirically distinct.

The weak findings between ability and self-report EI scales can be interpreted in a number of ways. First, self-report and performance measures tap different mental systems (beliefs versus abilities) about the person, which may develop independently. Second, there is, in general, low variance in self-ratings because individuals rarely see themselves as "below average" [64]. Third, even though it seems the individual would be in the best position to make an assessment of his or her own mental ability, researchers are reluctant to use self-report indices because they contain a great deal of unwanted variance, mostly in the form of social desirability and self-deception [42], [65]. Fourth, a person's overall mental capacity also could influence his or her predictions. For example, it is likely individuals with low EI would not be in the position to self-report on their actual EI skills because they lack the metacognitive skills to do so [43]. Finally, the relationship between self-report and performance measures of EI may be especially weak because Western culture presents little opportunity for explicit feedback in this domain. That is, we do not have institutions to teach us about our emotion-related abilities as we do for our intellectual abilities. In school, for example, we receive objective feedback on our academic performance through grades and standardized test scores, which may help us to gauge our intellectual ability. There is no readily available criterion for EI, however, which would make it difficult for individuals to make accurate self-judgments about these skills.

# ☐ Conclusions Regarding Utility of Different EI Indices

There are now three general ways to assess EI. Performance tests such as the MSCEIT, which are based on Mayer and Salovey's [4] ability model, self-report tests such as the EQ-i and SSRI, which are based on trait- or mixed models of EI (e.g., [5], [19]), and self-report measures such as the SREIS that map onto ability tests [9].

Preliminary findings with the MSCEIT suggest that EI as a mental ability exists as a distinct, clearly defined construct that has evidence of incremental validity. The MSCEIT, however, measures only a select number of emotion-related abilities. For example, it would be important to test whether facial recognition of emotion as assessed by the MSCEIT correlates with real-time emotion recognition tasks. The factor structure and validity of the MSCEIT (and the other EI measures) also needs to be examined in different cultures. For example, the strategies deemed effective for the management of others' emotions in the United States might not be effective in India or China.

In regard to trait or mixed models, most of the attributes measured by the EQ-i and SRRI overlap substantially with existing constructs, which suggests that these scales have a breadth of coverage that is not very different from well-studied personality and well-being scales. These models and the tests that stem from them also are somewhat misleading because they suggest that there is a new, integrated, single psychological entity called EI that combines diverse traits such as stress tolerance, persistence, and good interpersonal skills. The utility of self-report measures such as the SREIS, which maps onto ability measures, is also questionable. The SREIS did not correlate with objective tests of EI or outcomes of social importance.

## ☐  Conclusion

As we learn more about EI, both the theories and tests will need to be updated. Research on EI is still in its beginning stages and there is much of to be learned about its various subcomponents and the best way to assess it. For example, it is unclear how EI abilities develop. That is, how much of EI is genetically based, learned or both? What are the parental and peer influences on the development of emotion skills? It is also unclear whether EI skills can be taught and who will benefit most from such interventions. A number of researchers [66] have developed and are currently testing whether the integration of emotional competencies into standard school curricula such as language arts and history will have an impact on children's socioemotional development. Finally, once the associations are confirmed, it will be necessary to explain the mechanisms by which EI predicts behavior.

What we know thus far suggests that broad definitions (and tests) of EI, which do not refer exclusively to skills associated with the terms *emotion* and *intelligence,* are probably improper uses of the term. When EI is not confined to emotion or intelligence, it is difficult to decide what list of traits, skills, and perceived abilities it encompasses. This is becoming increasingly evident as new models and tests of EI are continuously emerging in the literature. Although the traits covered by mixed or trait-based models such as optimism and stress tolerance, and the self-report scales that they empirically correlate with such as neuroticism and well-being are all important and predictive of real-life criteria, they are better addressed directly and as distinct from EI. There is a general consensus that performance tests are the gold standard in intelligence research because they measure the actual capacity to perform well at mental tasks, not just one's self-efficacy about certain mental tasks [6], [67]. Keeping the measurement of EI restricted to performance tests makes it possible to develop content valid ability measures and to analyze the degree to which EI skills specifically contribute to a person's behavior [6], [14], [68].

# ☐ References

1.  Salovey, P., & Mayer, J. D. (1990). Emotional intelligence. *Imagination, Cognition, and Personality, 9,* 185–211.
2.  Mayer, J. D., DiPaolo, M., & Salovey, P. (1990). Perceiving affective content in ambiguous visual stimuli: A component of emotional intelligence. *Journal of Personality Assessment, 54,* 772–781.
3.  Matthews, G., Zeidner, M., & Roberts, R. D. (2002). *Emotional intelligence: Science and myth.* Cambridge, MA: MIT Press.
4.  Mayer, J. D., & Salovey, P. (1997). What is emotional intelligence? In P. Salovey & D. J. Sluyter (Eds.), *Emotional development and emotional intelligence: Educational implications.* In R. J. Sternberg (Ed.), *Handbook of intelligence* (pp. 3–34). Cambridge, UK: Cambridge University Press.
5.  Bar-On, R. (1997). *The Bar-On Emotional Quotient Inventory (EQ-i): Technical manual.* Toronto, Canada: Multi-Health Systems, Inc.
6.  Mayer, J. D., Salovey, P., & Caruso, D. R. (2000). Models of emotional intelligence (pp. 396–420). In R. J. Sternberg (Ed.), *Handbook of human intelligence* (pp. 396–420). New York: Cambridge University Press.
7.  Mayer, J. D., Salovey, P., & Caruso, D. R. (2002). *Mayer-Salovey-Caruso Emotional Intelligence Test user's manual.* Toronto, Canada: Multi-Health Systems.
8.  Petrides, K.V., & Furnham, A. (2001). Trait emotional intelligence: Psychometric investigation with reference to established trait taxonomies. *European Journal of Personality, 15,* 425–448.
9.  Brackett, M. A., Rivers, S. E., Shiffman, S., Lerner, N., & Salovey, P. (2005). What is the best way to measure emotional intelligence? A case for performance measures. *Manuscript under review.*
10. Geher, G., Warner, R. M., & Brown, A. S. (2001). Predictive validity of the Emotional Accuracy Research Scale. *Intelligence, 29,* 373–388.
11. Mayer, J. D., & Geher, G. (1996). Emotional intelligence and the identification of emotion. *Intelligence, 22,* 89–113.
12. Barchard, K. A., & Russell, J. A. (2004). Psychometric issues in the measurement of emotional intelligence. In G. Geher (Ed.), *Measuring emotional intelligence* (pp. 51–70). Hauppauge, NY: Nova Science Publishing.
13. Geher, G., & Renstrom, K. L. (2004). Measurement issues in emotional intelligence research. In G. Geher (Ed.), *Measuring emotional intelligence: Common ground and controversy* (pp. 1–17). Hauppauge, NY: Nova Science Publishing.
14. Brackett, M. A., & Salovey, P. (2004). Measuring emotional intelligence with the Mayer-Salovey-Caruso Emotional Intelligence Test (MSCEIT). In G. Geher (Ed.),

*Measuring emotional intelligence: Common ground and controversy* (pp. 179–194). Hauppauge, NY: Nova Science Publishing.

15. Mayer, J. D., Salovey, P., & Caruso, D. (2004). Emotional intelligence: Theory, findings, and implications. *Psychological Inquiry, 15*, 197–215.

16. Schutte, N. S., Malouff, J. M., Hall, L. E., Haggerty, D. J., Cooper, J. T., Golden, C. J., & Dornheim, L. (1998). Development and validation of a measure of emotional intelligence. *Personality and Individual Differences, 25*, 167–177.

17. Boyatzis, R. E., & Sala, F. (2004). The Emotional Competence Inventory (ECI). In G. Geher (Ed.), *Measuring emotional intelligence: Common ground and controversy* (pp. 143–178). Hauppauge, NY: Nova Science Publishing.

18. Bar-On, R. (2000). Emotional and social intelligence: Insights from the Emotional Quotient Inventory. In R. Bar-On & J. D. Parker (Eds.), *The handbook of emotional intelligence: Theory, development, assessment, and application at home, school, and in the workplace* (pp. 363–388). San Francisco: Jossey-Bass/Pfeiffer.

19. Bar-On, R. (2004). The Bar-On Emotional Quotient Inventory (EQ-i): Rationale, Description, and Summary of Psychometric Properties. In G. Geher (Ed.), *Measuring emotional intelligence: Common ground and controversy* (pp. 111–142). Hauppauge, NY: Nova Science Publishing.

20. Brackett, M. A., & Mayer, J. D. (2003). Convergent, discriminant, and incremental validity of competing measures of emotional intelligence. *Personality and Social Psychology Bulletin, 29*, 1147–1158.

21. MacCann, C., Matthews, G., Zeidner, M., & Roberts, R. D. (2004). The assessment of emotional intelligence: On frameworks, fissures, and the future. In G. Geher (Ed.), *Measuring emotional intelligence: Common ground and controversy* (pp. 19–50). Hauppauge, NY: Nova Science Publishing.

22. Lane, R. D., Quinlan, D. M., & Schwartz, G. E. (1990). The Levels of Emotional Awareness Scale: A cognitive-developmental measure of emotion. *Journal of Personality Assessment, 55*, 124–134.

23. Nowicki, S., & Duke, M. P. (1994). Individual differences in the nonverbal communication of affect: The Diagnostic Analysis of Nonverbal Accuracy Scale. *Journal of Nonverbal Behavior, 18*, 9–35.

24. Mayer, J. D., Caruso, D., & Salovey, P. (1999). Emotional intelligence meets traditional standards for an intelligence. *Intelligence, 27*, 267–298.

25. Mayer, J. D., Salovey, P., Caruso, D., & Sitarenios, G. (2003). Measuring emotional intelligence with the MSCEIT V2.0. *Emotion, 3*, 97–105.

26. Brackett, M. A., Mayer, J. D., & Warner, R. M. (2004). Emotional intelligence and its relation to everyday behaviour. *Personality and Individual Differences, 36*, 1387–1402.

27. Lopes, P. N., Salovey, P., & Straus, R. (2003). Emotional intelligence, personality, and the perceived quality of social relationships. *Personality and Individual Differences, 3*, 641–659.

28. David, S. A. (2002). *Emotional intelligence: Developmental antecedents, psychological and social outcomes.* Unpublished doctoral dissertation, University of Melbourne, Australia.

29. Schulte, M. J., Ree, M. J., & Carretta, T. R. (2005). Emotional intelligence: Not much more than g and personality. *Personality and Individual Differences, 37*, 1059–1068.

30. Lopes, P. N., Brackett, M. A., Nezlek, J. B., Schütz, A., Sellin, I., & Salovey, P. (2004). Emotional intelligence and social interaction, *Personality and Social Psychology Bulletin, 30*, 1018–1034.

31. Brackett, M. A., Cox, A., Gaines, S. J., & Salovey, P. (2005). Emotional intelligence and relationship quality among couples. *Manuscript under review.*

32. Brackett, M. A., Warner, R. M., & Bosco, J. (2005). Emotional intelligence and relationship quality among couples. *Personal Relationships, 12*, 197–212.

33. Coté, S., Lopes, P. N., & Salovey, P. (2005). Emotional intelligence and vision formulation and articulation. *Manuscript under review.*
34. Janovics, J., & Christiansen, N. D. (2002). *Emotional intelligence in the workplace.* Paper presented at the 16th annual conference of the Society of Industrial and Organizational Psychology, San Diego, CA.
35. Rice, C. L. (1999). *A quantitative study of emotional intelligence and its impact on team performance.* Unpublished master's thesis, Pepperdine University, Malibu, CA.
36. Lopes, P. N., Cote, S., Grewal, D., Kadis, J., Gall, M., & Salovey, P. (2005). Emotional intelligence and positive work outcomes. *Manuscript under review.*
37. Rosete, D., & Ciarrochi, J. (in press). Emotional intelligence and its relationship to workplace performance outcomes of leadership effectiveness. *Leadership and Organization Development Journal.*
38. Collins, V. L. (2001). *Emotional intelligence and leadership success.* Unpublished doctoral dissertation, University of Nebraska, Lincoln, NE.
39. Barchard, K. A. (2003). Does emotional intelligence assist in the prediction of academic success? *Educational and Psychological Measurement, 63*(5), 840–858.
40. Gil-Olarte, M., Palomera, M. R., & Brackett, M. A. (in press). Emotional intelligence, social competence, and academic success among high school students. *Psicothema.*
41. Day, A. (2004). The measurement of emotional intelligence: The good, the bad, and the ugly. In G. Geher (Ed.), *Measuring emotional intelligence: Common ground and controversy* (pp. 239–264). Hauppauge, NY: Nova Science Publishing.
42. Paulhus, D. L., Lysy, D. C., & Yik, M. S. M. (1998). Self-report measures of intelligence: Are they useful as proxy IQ tests? *Journal of Personality Psychology, 66,* 525–554.
43. Dunning, D., Johnson, K., Ehrlinger, J., & Kruger, J. (2003). Why people fail to recognize their own incompetence. *Current Directions in Psychological Science, 12,* 83–87.
44. Boyatzis, R. E., Goleman, D., & Rhee, K. (2000). Clustering competence in emotional intelligence: Insights from the Emotional Competence Inventory (ECI). In R. Bar-On & D. A. Parker (Eds.), *Handbook of emotional intelligence* (pp. 343–362). San Francisco: Jossey-Bass.
45. Salovey, P., Mayer, J. D., Goldman, S. L., Turvey, C., & Palfai, T. P. (1995). Emotional attention, clarity, and repair: Exploring emotional intelligence using the Trait Meta-Mood Scale. In J. W. Pennebaker (Ed.), *Emotion, disclosure, and health* (pp. 125–154). Washington, DC: American Psychological Association.
46. Bagby, R. M., Taylor, G. J., & Parker, J. D. A. (1994). The twenty-item Toronto Alexithymia Scale: Convergent, discriminant, and concurrent validity. *Journal of Psychosomatic Research, 38,* 33–40.
47. Ciarrochi, J., Chan, A., & Bajgar, J. (2001). Measuring emotional intelligence in adolescents. *Personality and Individual Differences, 31,* 1105–1119.
48. Saklofske, D. H., Austin, E. J., & Minski, P. S. (2003). Factor structure and validity of a trait emotional intelligence measure. *Personality and Individual Differences, 34,* 707–721.
49. Ryff, C. D. (1989). Happiness is everything, or is it? Explorations on the meaning of psychological well-being. *Journal of Personality and Social Psychology, 57,* 1069–1081.
50. Schutte, N. S., Malouff, J. M., Bobik, C., Coston, T. D., & Greeson, C. (2001). Emotional intelligence and interpersonal relations. *Journal of Social Psychology, 141,* 523–536.
51. Palmer, B. R., Manocha, R., & Gignac, G. (2003). Examining the factor structure of the Bar-On Emotional Quotient Inventory with an Australian general population sample. *Personality and Individual Differences, 35,* 1191–1210.
52. Dawda, D., & Hart, S. D. (2000). Assessing emotional intelligence: Reliability and validity of the Bar-On Emotional Quotient Inventory (EQ-i) in university students. *Personality and Individual Differences, 28,* 797–812.
53. Newsome, S., Day, A. L., & Catano, V. M. (2000). Assessing the predictive validity of emotional intelligence. *Personality and Individual Differences, 29,* 1005–1016.

54. Parker, J. D., Taylor, G. J., & Bagby, R. (2001). The relationship between emotional intelligence and alexithymia. *Personality and Individual Differences, 30,* 107–115.

55. Hedlund, J., & Sternberg, R. J. (2000). Too many intelligences? Integrating social, emotional, and practical intelligence. In R. Bar-On & J. D. A. Parker (Eds.), *Handbook of emotional intelligence* (pp. 136–167). New York: Jossey-Bass.

56. McCrae, R. R. (2000). Emotional intelligence from the perspective of the five-factor model of personality. In R. Bar-On & J. D. A. Parker (Eds.). *The handbook of emotional intelligence* (pp. 263–276). San Francisco: Jossey-Bass.

57. Bar-On, R. (2005). The Bar-On emotional quotient inventory (EQ-i): Rationale, description, and summary of psychometric properties. In. G. Geher (Ed.), *Measurement of emotional intelligence* (pp. 115–145). Hauppauge, NY: Nova Science Publishers.

58. Swart, A. (1996). *The relationship between well-being and academic performance.* Unpublished master's thesis, University of Pretoria, South Africa.

59. Derksen, J., Kramer, I., & Katzko, M. (2002). Does a self-report measure for emotional intelligence assess something different than general intelligence? *Personality and Individual Differences, 32,* 37–48.

60. Goleman, D. (1998). *Working with emotional intelligence.* New York: Bantam Books.

61. Murensky, C. L. (2000). *The relationship between emotional intelligence, personality, critical thinking ability, and organizational leadership performance at upper levels of management.* Unpublished dissertation, George Mason University, Fairfax, VA.

62. Stagg, G., & Gunter, D. (2002). *Emotional intelligence in the fire service* (Working paper). London: London Fire Brigade.

63. Kohan, A., & Mazmanian, D. (2003). *Emotional intelligence: Construct validity in an organizational context.* Poster presented at the annual conference of the Canadian Psychological Association.

64. McCrae, R. R. (1990). Traits and trait names: How well is openness represented in natural languages? *European Journal of Personality, 4,* 119–129.

65. DeNisi, A. S., & Shaw, J. B. (1977). Investigation of the uses of self-reports of abilities. *Journal of Applied Psychology, 51,* 316–317.

66. Maurer, M., Brackett, M. A., & Plain, F. (2004). *Emotional literacy in the middle school: A six-step program to promote social, emotional, and academic learning.* Portchester, New York: National Professional Resources.

67. Carroll, J. B. (1993). *Human cognitive abilities: A survey of factor-analytic studies.* New York: Cambridge University Press.

68. Thingujam, N. S. (2004). Current trend and future perspective on emotional intelligence. *National Academy of Psychology, India, 49,* 155–166.

CHAPTER 3

Maureen Buckley
Carolyn Saarni

# Skills of Emotional Competence: Developmental Implications

Recent research highlights the key role that emotional processes and competencies play in both normal and atypical development [1]. In this chapter, we begin with a review of the construct of emotional competence, as articulated by Saarni [2]. We then address the processes by which the skills of emotional competence develop, and the consequences these skills, or lack thereof, have for the adaptation and well-being of young people. With regard to the implications of emotional competencies for development, we first review how the skills of emotional competence may contribute to positive development, including peer relationships, academic achievement, and health-related behaviors. We then explore how deficits in these skills may contribute to various problematic outcomes, including emotional difficulties and behavior problems. We do so by examining the five emotional competence domains commonly associated with child and adolescent behavioral difficulties: (a) difficulty in regulating anger and other negative affects, (b) low levels of positive affect, (c) lack of empathy, (d) misperception of other's emotions, and (e) poor frustration tolerance [3].

## ☐ Overview of Emotional Competence

Before providing an overview of emotional competence, we find it necessary to distinguish the construct from that of emotional intelligence.

The two concepts overlap in some notable ways, yet there are also some significant differences. As illustrated in the quotation below, emotional intelligence has been articulated in a way that emphasizes *ability*:

> Emotional intelligence involves the ability to perceive accurately, appraise, and express emotion; the ability to access and/or generate feelings when they facilitate thought; the ability to understand emotion and emotional knowledge; and the ability to regulate emotions to promote emotional and intellectual growth [4, p. 10].

Mayer, Caruso, and Salovey [5] have emphasized that emotional intelligence involves reasoning about emotion-related phenomena such as expressive displays, conventionally agreed upon elicitors of emotional responses, and effective ways of managing emotional arousal in oneself and other. Their goal has been to delineate emotional intelligence as a specific mental capacity and differentiate it from other kinds of measured intelligences (e.g., cognitive, spatial, or social intelligence). Given that they also wish to measure individual differences in this mental capacity to reason about emotion-related constructs, they have devoted much of their research to measurement concerns. Their measure, the MSCEIT, presumes that an individual scoring "high" on this test will apply his or her emotional intelligence "ability" across contexts. Although Mayer, Salovey, and Caruso use a definition of emotion that is very close to our perspective, namely, "emotions have the functional purpose of signaling relationships and changes in relationships . . . between people and their environments (including other people)" [6, p. 250], we contend that their emphasis on emotional intelligence as a mental ability that resides within a person has the effect of underestimating the role that outside influences, such as culture and context, play in our day-to-day emotional functioning. Furthermore, we propose that viewing emotional intelligence as an ability downplays the developmental processes through which our affective adaptations unfold. Lastly, the definition of emotional intelligence does not take into account how values—or what has been called a "moral sense"—inform our emotional experience. In so far as we endorse a view of emotion that emphasizes the dynamic yet functional relationship between individual and context for the generation of emotion [7], then the individual's goals, informed by her or his values, will necessarily play a pivotal role in emotional experience.

In contrast to the construct of emotional intelligence, Saarni's notion of emotional competence emphasizes emotional skills [2]; more specifically, the skills that we need to successfully adapt and cope within our immediate social environment. These skills can include reasoning, but the emphasis is on adaptive emotional functioning. The skills of emotional competence are learned; their acquisition is influenced by family, peers, school, media, societal scripts, and folk theories of how emotion "works."

However, the developing child also contributes to how the skills of emotional competence manifest themselves in a given social transaction, most notably through the influence of temperamental style, cognitive maturity, and developmental history. The eight skills of emotional competence, listed in Table 3.1, fall into three broad categories: emotion expression, emotion

---

**TABLE 3.1. Skills of emotional competence**

1. Awareness of one's emotional state, including the possibility that one is experiencing multiple emotions, and at even more mature levels, awareness that one might also not be consciously aware of one's feelings due to unconscious dynamics or selective inattention.

2. Skills in discerning and understanding others' emotions, based on situational and expressive cues that have some degree of consensus as to their emotional meaning.

3. Skill in using the vocabulary of emotion and expression in terms commonly available in one's subculture and at more mature levels to acquire cultural scripts that link emotion with social roles.

4. Capacity for empathic and sympathetic involvement in others' emotional experiences.

5. Skill in realizing that inner emotional state need not correspond to outer expression, both in oneself and in others, and at more mature levels the ability to understand that one's emotional-expressive behavior may impact on another and take this into account in one's self-presentation strategies.

6. Capacity for adaptive coping with aversive or distressing emotions by using self-regulatory strategies that ameliorate the intensity or temporal duration of such emotional states (e.g., "stress hardiness").

7. Awareness that the structure or nature of relationships is in part defined by both the degree of emotional immediacy or genuineness of expressive display and by the degree of reciprocity or symmetry within the relationship; e.g., mature intimacy is in part defined by mutual or reciprocal sharing of genuine emotions, whereas a parent–child relationship may have asymmetric sharing of genuine emotions.

8. Capacity for emotional self-efficacy: the individual views her- or himself as feeling, overall, the way he or she wants to feel. That is, emotional self-efficacy means that one accepts one's emotional experience, whether unique and eccentric or culturally conventional, and this acceptance is in alignment with the individual's beliefs about what constitutes desirable emotional "balance." In essence, one is living in accord with one's personal theory of emotion when one demonstrates emotional self-efficacy that is integrated with one's moral sense.

---

*Note.* From Saarni [8, pp. 77–78]. Copyright 2000 by Jossey-Bass. Reprinted by permission of the author.

understanding, and emotion regulation. Emotion expression refers to the range of affect a person communicates, both verbally and nonverbally, during social interactions. Emotion understanding encompasses the knowledge people have about emotional experience, both their own and that of others. Finally, emotion regulation refers to managing one's emotional reactivity in the service of engaging with others and coping with challenging circumstances.

While the skills are listed separately, they are, in fact, mutually dependent. For example, the ability to understand another's emotions is shaped by the range and complexity of an individual's emotion vocabulary, which in turn, facilitates or constricts how an individual conceptualizes another's emotional experience. These interconnected skills assist us in reaching goals by facilitating constructive coping and problem solving. They also aid social functioning in that they allow us to determine what others feel, to recognize the impact of our emotion communication on relationships and to use this information to determine an appropriate response to the situation. These eight skills were derived from empirical developmental research that has been primarily undertaken with Western European acculturated children and youth, and the last two skills may especially reflect this cultural bias. This is not to say that these eight skills do not apply to non-Western societies but they may be understood differently in relation to the values and beliefs of the local community.

In each emotional-laden encounter, our functioning is partially determined by the combined effects of individual factors (e.g., temperament) and past social learning. Yet, these factors alone do not account for our emotional functioning. The demonstration of emotional competence is also influenced by the immediate social context in which emotions are evoked. To illustrate, consider how one's empathy for victims of a natural disaster is evoked and perhaps differently nuanced in comparison with how one might feel about the desperate lives of heroin addicts. In short, our emotional reactions are closely linked with our particular motivations, values, and desired goals, and we regulate both our emotional experiences and our approach/avoidance of situations in order to maximize the likelihood of desired outcomes. It is this combination of individual and contextual factors that give meaning to our emotional reactions. For example, an individual knowingly lets down a dear friend (e.g., breaking a commitment to go out in order to pursue a more appealing invitation); yet assume this individual was raised to honor obligations and possesses the capacity to take the perspective of another person. The emotional outcome will likely include feeling guilt, and this experience of guilt will more likely motivate him or her to take action *vis-à-vis* the friend (e.g., make reparations).

Furthermore, in articulating emotional competence as a set of skills, rather than as an ability that resides within a person, it is understood that the skills of emotional competence are learned, but not always applied, to dynamic encounters with the environment. An individual with well-developed skills of emotional competence may indeed experience emotional incompetence during a given social interaction. In the example described immediately above, if the offending individual missed the engagement because she was stressed and overextended, feelings such as irritation or anger may come to the forefront, while energy to self-monitor and appropriately regulate these emotions may be limited. A possible result of these combined factors would be an angry outburst at the friend for placing demands on her. A competence approach implies that any given instance of actual behavior has only a probabilistic relationship to the skills a person may have learned. Research has yet to show us what that probability is between one's emotional competence and one's emotional performance in a given emotion-eliciting context.

Because the skills of emotional competence promote effective adaptation and coping, the definition of emotional competence as a superordinate construct includes the demonstration of self-efficacy in social transactions [9]. With development, a child learns that her or his efforts to understand emotional experience and to regulate emotional arousal and expression help to achieve interpersonal goals. These incremental experiences of being emotionally effective influence our sense of self-efficacy, in that we begin to believe that we can reach our goals when engaging in emotion-laden interactions with others. Rather than being preoccupied with perceived threats and self-defeating attitudes, a person with well-developed skills of emotional competence is able to mobilize the resources to gather new information, to acquire new insights, or develop further his or her talents. Thus, an emotionally competent child will succeed in developing friendships despite occasional conflict with peers, or will persist in a sporting competition in the face of defeat. As these examples illustrate, emotional competence is not necessarily feeling happy or content. A child facing either of the two previous scenarios may experience a variety of feelings, including anger, frustration, sadness, or regret. Yet, if they are able to use the skills of emotional competence to remain focused on personal goals, problem-solve, and adapt to the challenge, they are likely to emerge with a recognition that they coped effectively in difficult circumstances.

## The Development of Emotional Competence

Emotional competence is not solely about cognitive understanding of emotional experience, but subsumes a set of affect-oriented behavioral, cognitive, and regulatory skills that emerge over time as a person develops in a social context. In other words, how our emotional functioning develops and how it is revealed in our everyday life depends on the ongoing exchange between a person and her environment. Individual factors, such as cognitive development and temperament, do indeed influence the development of emotional competencies. Yet, skills of emotional competence are also influenced by past social experience and learning, including an individual's relationship history, as well as the system of beliefs and values in which the person lives. Thus, we actively create our emotional experience, through the combined influence of our cognitive developmental structures and our social exposure to emotion discourse. Through this process, we learn what it means to feel something and to do something about it.

The attachment relationship with a caregiver is the primary context in which a child's emotional life unfolds. An infant's survival depends on the ability to elicit a caregiving response through behaviors such as crying or smiling. The caregiver responds to cues from the baby, creating a cycle of reciprocal interaction. The cycle typically begins when the infant experiences discomfort and communicates this to the caregiver by crying. Ideally, the response from the caregiver calms the baby, which reinforces both caregiver and baby. This cycle is repeated thousands of times and, if the caregiver typically meets the infant's needs, the infant comes to internalize the notion that the world is a safe place and that others are trustworthy and responsive. The infant is then secure in his attachment to the caregiver.

Yet, there are times when the caregiver is unable to effectively respond to the infant's needs. This may occur due to a range of factors, including lack of skill, depression, substance abuse, or attributes of the infant, such as an undiagnosed medical condition or a particularly difficult temperament. Failure to establish the attuned cycle of soothing may result in the infant adopting a view of world as an unresponsive and unsafe place in which others cannot be trusted. Anger may take the place of need and/or the infant may stop trying to engage with others.

The caregiver–child relationship establishes the foundation for the development of emotional skills, and sets the stage for future social relationships. A secure attachment leaves the child free to explore the world and engage with peers. Affirmation that the world is responsive, predictable and reliable aids in the child's developing ability to self-regulate. In a study of preschoolers, Denham and her colleagues [3] found a positive association between security of attachment to mothers and security of attachment to teachers. Furthermore, security of attachment to both mother and teacher related positively to emotion understanding and regulated anger.

In contrast, a child who experiences the world as unpredictable, unresponsive and/or hostile must expend a tremendous amount of energy self-managing emotional arousal. Insecure attachment is associated with emotional and social incompetence, particularly in the areas of emotion understanding and regulated anger [3]. Furthermore, perceptions of an indifferent or unfriendly social world influence subsequent interpersonal behavior. For example, a child who experiences maltreatment may develop primary emotional responses such as anxiety or fear. Ever vigilant for signs of threat, the child may display aggressive or submissive behaviors as a means of self-protection, and such behaviors may place the child at risk for future status as a bully or victim [10]. Cognitive-affective structures associated with maltreatment may promote emotional constriction or peculiar emotional responsiveness, interfering with a child's ability to engage successfully with peers [10]. Maltreated children face a number of impediments to emotional competence, including angry, reactive and irritable affect, regulatory difficulties, and deficits in emotion understanding, communication, and recognition skills [11]. However, maltreatment contributes especially to problems with emotional regulation, specifically emotional lability and angry reactivity, which in turn incite aggressive reactions in others [11].

As outlined above, the emergence of emotional competence skills is a developmental process. As such, the presence and expression of these skills varies as a young person matures (see Table 3.2). With young children, emotion knowledge is more concrete, with heightened focus on observable factors. Young children's emotion expression and emotion regulation are less well-developed, requiring support and reinforcement from the social environment. Elementary school children advance in their ability to offer self-reports of emotions, and to use words to explain emotion-related situations [12–13]. As children mature, their inferences about what others are feeling integrate not only situational information, but also information regarding prior experiences and history (e.g., [14]). Older children are also more able to understand and express complex emotions such as pride, shame, or embarrassment. By adolescence, issues of identity, moral character, and the combined effects of aspiration and opportunity are more explicitly acknowledged as significant by youth.

The skills of emotional competence do not develop in isolation from each other and their progression is intimately tied to cognitive development. For example, insight into others' emotions grows in interaction with expanding awareness of one's own emotional experience, with one's ability to empathize, and with the capacity to understand causes of emotions and their behavioral consequences. Furthermore, as children learn about how and why people act as they do, they grow in their ability to *infer* what is going on for themselves emotionally.

# ☐ Developmental Implications

## Positive Development and Emotional Competence

Competent children and youth do not experience lives free of problems, but they are equipped with both individual and environmental assets that

**TABLE 3.2. Noteworthy markers of emotional development in relation to social interaction**

| Age period | Regulation/coping | Expressive behavior | Relationship building |
|---|---|---|---|
| Infancy 0–12 months | Self-soothing and learning to modulate reactivity. Regulation of attention in service of coordinated action. Reliance on caregivers for supportive "scaffolding" during stressful circumstances. | Behavior synchrony with others in some expressive channels. Increasing discrimination of others' expressions. Increasing expressive responsiveness to stimuli under contingent control. Increasing coordination of expressive behaviors with emotion-eliciting circumstances. | Social games and turn-taking (e.g., "peek-a-boo"). Social referencing. Socially instrumental signal use (e.g., "fake" crying to get attention). |
| Toddlerhood 12 months–2½ years | Emergence of self-awareness and consciousness of own emotional response. Irritability due to constraints and limits imposed on expanding autonomy and exploration needs. | Self-evaluation and self-consciousness evident in expressive behavior accompanying shame, pride, and coyness. Increasing verbal comprehension and production of words for expressive behavior and affective states. | Anticipation of different feelings toward different people. Increasing discrimination of others' emotions and their meaningfulness. Early forms of empathy and prosocial action. |
| Preschool 2½–5 years | Symbolic access facilitates emotion regulation, but symbols can also provoke distress. Communication with others extends child's evaluation of and awareness of own feelings and of emotion-eliciting events. | Adoption of pretend expressive behavior in play and teasing. Pragmatic awareness that "false" facial expressions can mislead another about one's feelings. | Communication with others elaborates child's understanding of social transactions and expectations for comportment. Sympathetic and prosocial behavior toward peers. Increasing insight into others' emotions. |

| Age | | | |
|---|---|---|---|
| Early elementary school 5–7 years | Self-conscious emotions (e.g., embarrassment) are targeted for regulation. Seeking support from caregivers still the prominent coping strategy, but increasing reliance on situational problem-solving evident. | Adoption of "cool emotional front" with peers. | Increasing coordination of social skills with one's own and others' emotions. Early understanding of consensually agreed upon emotion "scripts." |
| Middle childhood 7–10 years | Problem-solving preferred coping strategy if control is at least moderate. Distancing strategies used if control is appraised as minimal. | Appreciation of norms for expressive behavior, whether genuine or dissembled. Use of expressive behavior to modulate relationship dynamics (e.g., smiling while reproaching a friend). | Awareness of multiple emotions toward the same person. Use of multiple time frames and unique personal information about another as aids in the development of close friendships. |
| Pre-adolescence 10–13 years | Increasing accuracy in appraisal of realistic control in stressful circumstances. Capable of generating multiple solutions and differentiated strategies for dealing with stress. | Distinction made between genuine emotional expression with close friends and managed displays with others. | Increasing social sensitivity and awareness of emotion "scripts" in conjunction with social roles. |
| Adolescence 13+ years | Awareness of one's own emotion cycles (e.g., guilt about feeling angry) facilitates insightful coping. Increasing integration of moral character and personal philosophy in dealing with stress and subsequent decisions. | Skillful adoption of self-presentation strategies for impression management. | Awareness of mutual and reciprocal communication of emotions as affecting quality of relationship. |

Note. From Saarni [8, pp. 74–75]. Copyright 2000 by Jossey-Bass. Reprinted by permission of the author.

help them cope with a variety of life events. The skills of emotional competence are one set of resources that young people bring to life's diverse challenges. As with development in other domains, mastery of early skills related to emotional development, such as affective regulation, impacts a child's ability to navigate future developmental challenges [11].

Strengths in the area of emotional competence may help children and adolescents cope effectively in particular circumstances, while also promoting characteristics associated with positive developmental outcomes, including feelings of self-efficacy, prosocial behavior, and supportive relationships with family and peers. Furthermore, emotional competence serves as a protective factor that diminishes the impact of a range of risk factors. Research has isolated individual attributes that may exert a protective influence, several of which reflect core elements of emotional competence, including skills related to reading interpersonal cues, solving problems, executing goal-oriented behavior in interpersonal situations, and considering behavioral options from both an instrumental and an affective standpoint [15].

## Peer Relationships

Measured as early as the preschool years, emotional competence is associated with the social success of preschoolers, as well as to their later socioemotional functioning [3], [16]. As Denham and her colleagues point out, a key task during the preschool years is the ability to successfully initiate peer relationships, and preschoolers who succeed at this task have a solid foundation from which to negotiate their larger social world as they develop. Overall, research supports an ongoing link between children's social effectiveness and their emotion understanding, emotion appraisal skills and affective expressivity [17–19].

Bullying and victimization research provide a rich area from which to glean evidence of the protective influence of emotional competence. One area of bullying research explores why some children who are bullied progress relatively unfazed by the experience, whereas other children suffer severely or are subject to repeated victimization. To help address this question, Kochenderfer-Ladd [20] studied the role of emotions in elementary school students' coping with peer victimization. As might be expected, children experiencing peer aggression showed different emotional reactions, including anger, fear, or embarrassment. Kochenderfer-Ladd [20] found that a child's emotional response affected the coping strategy used by the child to deal with the aggression. Scared or embarrassed children were more likely to seek advice. Children who responded with anger were less likely to ask for help and more likely to seek revenge.

Kochenderfer-Ladd's research [20] further indicates that this connection between emotional reaction and chosen coping strategy helps explain why some children fare worse than others in the face of peer aggression. For example, the advice seeking shown by children who reacted with fear or embarrassment predicted prosocial attempts at conflict resolution (e.g., giving an "I" message, telling the perpetrator to stop, taking time to cool down, etc.). Such attempts to engage with the bully with the aim of stopping the behavior were, in turn, associated with decreased victimization. Furthermore, conflict resolution and advice seeking corresponded with fewer difficulties with internalizing problems such as loneliness, anxiety, and depression. In contrast, children who reacted to peer aggression with anger were more likely to endorse ineffective coping strategies such as revenge seeking, which were, in turn, related to increased victimization and risk for loneliness, anxiety, and depressive symptoms.

## Academic Success

During childhood and adolescence, young people are challenged to negotiate the demands of not just social relationships, but also the academic arena. Just as emotional competence is influential in social success, it plays a notable role in academic functioning. Emotion regulation and understanding impact school adjustment [21]. For example, emotional distress is associated with lower grade point average [22]. In a study of students in Hong Kong, elements of emotional functioning facilitated adjustment to the unique challenges facing gifted students [23]. Among these 12- to 16-year-olds, several skills in particular (assessed via an adapted form of the Emotional Intelligence Scale; EIS [24]) corresponded with adaptive social coping strategies. Although a measure of emotional intelligence, the EIS assesses emotion appraisal, expression, regulation, and utilization, domains relevant for the construct of emotional competence as well. Students higher in emotional intelligence favored coping by valuing peer acceptance and involvement in activities, and were less likely to cope using avoidance behaviors. The most salient skill, managing others' emotions, reflects the capacity to interact with others and shape others' emotions, with a focus on positive emotions (e.g., "compliment others for doing something well," "present to make a good impression," "share emotions with others," "aware of others' nonverbal messages"). A second skill, utilizing emotions, reflects constructive use of emotions to allow for self-evaluation, awareness, and generation of new ideas (e.g., "aware of nonverbal messages one sends," "see new possibilities when mood changes"). These skills appeared to encourage coping through valuing peer acceptance and activity involvement.

A third skill, managing one's own emotions, appeared to protect against less adaptive avoidance behaviors.

In a study of British secondary school students, emotional self-efficacy, or what the authors refer to as "trait emotional intelligence," played a particularly important role in the academic success of low IQ students [25]. The construct of trait emotional intelligence (trait EI) was assessed using a self-report questionnaire comprised of items that examined behavioral characteristics and self-perceptions regarding participant's facility with discerning, processing, and using affective information; these attributes all have relevance for emotional competence, as does the overarching notion of emotional self-efficacy. The impact of trait EI varied by academic subject, exerting no significant effect on science or math performance, but moderating the impact of IQ on English and overall performance. For students in the low IQ group, high trait EI corresponded with greater academic achievement, a relationship that did not hold true for students in the high IQ group. The authors postulate that low IQ students may be more taxed by their coursework, experiencing more stress and anxiety. In this case, attributes such as emotional self-efficacy may prove particularly valuable in coping with academic demands. That is, students with fewer cognitive resources may need to employ other competencies, including those in the emotional realm, to achieve success.

For students making the transition from high school to university, several skills of emotional competence may predict academic success. In particular, a study using a self-report measure of emotional intelligence (EQ-i [26]) found a modest but significant association between first-year grade point average and elements common to definitions of both emotional competence and emotional intelligence, namely, intrapersonal intelligence, stress management, and adaptability [27]. Differentiating students based on their level of academic success increased the strength of this relationship. That is, these three elements of emotional functioning served as strong predictors in detecting highly successful (first-year GPAs of 80% or better) and unsuccessful (first-year GPAs of 59% or less) students.

The sense of self-efficacy associated with emotional competence bolsters academic success, and motivational processes, including a belief in oneself as academically efficacious, may serve as a protective influence for young people struggling with challenging life circumstances or emotional difficulties [28]. In a sample of middle school students, a notable relationship existed between self-esteem, emotional difficulties (e.g., anxiety, depression, withdrawal, behavioral difficulties), and academic efficacy beliefs, and the self-reported tendency for mood states to interfere with learning. Specifically, students with decreased self-esteem, lower academic self-efficacy, and heightened emotional problems were more likely to describe their negative moods as hindering learning [28].

In another study of middle school students, emotion regulation and mood-related disposition toward academic activities predicted grade point average [29]. Young adolescents who reported more negative affect regarding ordinary academic routines obtained lower grade point averages, even when controlling for cognitive ability.

## *Resistance to Smoking*

The emotion-related skills that young people bring to face challenging life events most certainly impact their ability to manage these hurdles. Research related to one health-related behavior, smoking, demonstrates how specific emotional skills may contribute to positive outcomes. An initial study of seventh and eighth grader students found that emotional intelligence reduced the likelihood of smoking behavior [30]. A subsequent study looked at the psychosocial risk factors associated with smoking and explored the protective influence of a heightened ability to process social information, a factor associated with strong emotional competence [31]. While emphasizing the construct of emotional *intelligence*, the researchers used a competence-based measure that assesses one's ability to identify, understand and manage emotion in oneself and others (Multifactor Emotional Intelligence Scale [5]), components of emotional functioning with relevance to emotional *competence*.

In this sixth grade sample, high emotional intelligence functioned as a protective factor against psychosocial risk factors for smoking [31]. More specifically, these researchers discovered that students with high emotional intelligence showed heightened awareness of harmful social consequences of smoking and self-reported a sense of self-confidence in declining a cigarette offer. The authors suggest that these students might be clearer about their own beliefs about smoking and thus more confident in effectively communicating a refusal response. They also noted that these students might be better able to manage anxiety that might come with asserting a refusal. In addition, students with higher emotional intelligence were less likely to report an intention to smoke in the next year, perhaps, the authors suggest, because they were able to manage their emotions in a way that resulted in employment of a greater range of coping strategies.

As detailed above, strong emotional competence skills aid young people in maintaining a positive developmental trajectory across social, academic and health-related domains. Conversely, research suggests that deficits in social and emotional competencies, particularly effective problem-solving and relationship skills, are associated with problematic outcomes such as aggression [32–33]. In the following section, we examine existing knowledge regarding particular emotional competence skills and their links to various developmental challenges.

## Behavior Problems and Emotional Competence

While well-developed skills of emotional competence promote social functioning, academic success, and a sense of self-efficacy, correspondingly, deficits in these skills place children at risk. Children with underdeveloped emotion-related skills experience a variety of problematic behavioral outcomes, including both externalizing and internalizing behavioral issues. Externalizing behavior problems encompass actions directed toward others, and include verbal and physical aggression, hyperactivity, defiance, substance use and other acting-out behaviors. In contrast, internalizing problems include inwardly directed difficulties, such as anxiety and depression. In the subsequent section, we discuss the relationship between emotional competence and both internalizing and externalizing behavioral problems.

It stands to reason that children who lack skills of emotional competence will have greater difficulty interacting positively with their peers. Young people who frequently respond with negative affect, or who cannot adequately control their emotional responses, are likely to be less appealing to their peers. They will also struggle to accomplish tasks that require emotional and behavioral control. Likewise, children who fail to effectively read other's emotional cues will be less likely to interact in ways that draw age mates to them. This sets children on a negative social developmental trajectory. Indeed, deficits in emotional competence at as young as 3 years of age are associated with social difficulties in kindergarten [3]. The connection between emotional competence and social/behavioral outcomes appears to persist into adolescence and early adulthood. For example, among male college students, lower emotional intelligence corresponds with problematic relationships with friends, deviant social behaviors (e.g., physical fights), and alcohol consumption [34].

Research suggests that several emotional factors have a distinct impact on child and adolescent behavioral difficulties. These factors include: (a) anger and other negative affect, (b) lack of positive affect, (c) lack of empathy, (d) misperception of other's emotions, and (e) poor frustration tolerance [3]. In the following section, we will explore each of these factors in turn, including research findings and discussing their relevance for emotional competence.

## Anger and Other Negative Affect

The expression of a predominance of negative affect, particularly uncontrolled anger, relates to several skills of emotional competence (see Table 3.1), often in an interdependent manner. In terms of Skill 3, children prone to excessive outbursts of negative emotion have difficulty in verbalizing their negative emotion; with an inadequately developed lexicon of emotion to be able to communicate their distress more appropriately, they "blow up" or display tantrum behavior (see [35] for a review of relevant research). Regarding Skill 5, young people who fail to restrain excessive emotional negativity are unable to muster self-presentation strategies that work in their best interest. Either the child fails to understand the impact of her emotional-expressive behavior on others, or the drive to express unregulated anger supercedes that knowledge. It may also be that the child lacks the proficiency to adaptively cope with aversive emotions by using self-regulatory strategies (Skill 6). A child prone to unbridled outbursts of negative emotion is also unlikely to develop a sense of self-efficacy regarding emotion-laden transactions (Skill 8) (e.g., [36]).

Young people prone to unrestrained episodes of intense negative emotion are vulnerable in the social arena. Their peers dislike children who express predominantly negative affect, and their teachers find them less friendly and more aggressive than their more emotionally balanced peers [18]. Children prone to oppositional behavior, who struggle across a variety of social relationships, show increased levels of negative emotion [37].

Negative affect is also linked to compromised coping in the form of aggressive behavior and vulnerability to repeated peer victimization. Among preschoolers, negative affect and expression of anger are associated with increased risk for aggressive behavior [38–39]. A similar link between aggression and chronic, intense expression of anger has also been found among school-age youth [40]. In addition a tendency toward intense negative emotions also characterizes reactively aggressive children [41] and is associated with victimization by peers [20].

Angry children are less likely to choose effective coping strategies, preferring revenge seeking, a strategy linked to heightened victimization and subsequently increased risk for loneliness, anxiety and depressive symptoms [20]. Children who respond to peer aggression with strong negative emotion, for example, crying or fighting back, are more likely to experience chronic victimization [42]. It appears that bullies experience such displays of emotional distress as reinforcing [43], increasing the likelihood of revictimization.

## Poor Frustration Tolerance

Poor frustration tolerance is linked to the capacity for adaptive coping with aversive or distressing emotions (Skill 6). Even as early as the preschool years, children's styles of affective regulation are closely linked to their everyday anger-related actions [36]. For example, a child may engage in strategies such as self-comforting, distraction, or seeking external support in order to manage intense emotional arousal. Individuals who can cope with frustration and other strong, negative emotions demonstrate self-regulatory strategies that minimize the strength or duration of such emotional states. The combination of intense negative emotionality and trouble regulating these emotions interferes with socially competent behavior [44–46], as well as school adjustment [21], [47].

Aggressive behavior appears to be related to poor emotional regulation skills [48]. Children who bully others evidence emotion regulation difficulties including displays of inappropriate affect and a propensity toward displays of anger [10]. Difficulty controlling intense negative emotion is a distinguishing feature of peer-victimized youth [49]. Victimized children show emotion dysregulation in terms of heightened anxiety and arousal [10], which may lead to disorganized, maladaptive responding to peer aggression [50]. Such responses may, in turn, increase the likelihood that the child will be victimized again.

Although bullied children are often conceptualized as submissive and passive, there exists a subgroup that engages in aggressive and hostile behaviors [51], [46], [49]. These aggressive victims are particularly at risk in the social arena, due to their provocative, irritable, agitated, and oppositional presentation [51]. Their off-task and off-putting behaviors may lead to negative encounters with peers that quickly escalate into emotionally intense conflicts due to the child's difficulty regulating emotional arousal. Both the nonvictimized bully and the aggressive victim engage in hostile behavior. Yet, the nonvictimized bully is able to effectively control emotion in the service of goal attainment, and is less likely to show observable signs of anger or emotional agitation [52]. In contrast, the aggressive victim's poor emotional regulation skills result in behavior that interferes with achieving desired outcomes. These children are especially vulnerable to social rejection, poor academic performance, depression, and anxiety [53–54].

A notable body of research highlights the difficulty with emotion regulation among maltreated children [55]. For maltreated youth, poorly regulated emotional responses may be consistent with their caregiving experiences [10]. For example, the hypervigilance needed for survival in abusive homes may cooccur with heightened anxiety. While adaptive in the abusive home environment, such anxiety and arousal may hinder appropriate interactions with peers, placing them at risk for peer victimization [10]. The poor emotional control of the aggressive victim corresponds to a home environment marked by violence, abuse, and parents who are punitive and rejecting [46]. Children who grow up in such an environment may develop an interpersonal style characterized by anger, intense alertness to signs of danger or threat, and a tendency to make hostile attributions regarding others' behavior. In contrast, nonvictimized bullies tend to come from home environments in which aggression is modeled as a means of achieving goals, but they typically do not experience abuse or parental rejection themselves [46].

More recently, researchers have tried to more clearly delineate the relationship between affective regulation and behavior. Accordingly, Eisenberg and her colleagues [56] distinguish between effortful control and reactive control. Effortful control, or the ability to voluntarily inhibit or activate behavior, is considered an essential element of emotion regulation [57]. It encompasses attentional control (capacity to focus or shift attention and to persevere on task), as well as abilities related to activating or inhibiting behavior as required for adaptive responding [56]. Reactive control relates to a purportedly temperament-linked and thus less voluntary tendency to be either overly inhibited or impulsive. Problems in adjustment may occur due to propensity toward either overcontrolled or undercontrolled behavior. A disposition toward excessive control may render an individual overly inhibited, with associated internalizing difficulties such as anxiety [58], whereas proclivity to insufficient control may lead to maladaptive impulsivity and externalizing problems [59].

Recent research suggests that a combination of negative emotionality and ability to sustain attention predicts later behavioral outcomes. In a study that followed children over a 2 year period, Eisenberg et al. [56] examined how effortful control and reactive undercontrol were related to children's internalizing and externalizing problems. Impulsivity and deficient effortful control directly predicted externalizing problems, particularly if the children ranked high in dispositional anger. An earlier study by Eisenberg and colleagues found that, among 4- to 6-year-olds, those who frequently demonstrated high intensity negative emotions were also more likely to be distractible and to exhibit less constructive coping [60]. These children were also viewed as less desirable playmates by their peers and less socially mature by their teachers. Lawson and Ruff [61] found that the "double hazard" of negative emotionality and ability to sustain attention predicted later behavioral outcomes. More specifically, maternal ratings of their toddler's emotional lability and proneness to irritability at age 2, and trained observers' ratings of attentiveness during frustrating episodes, combined to predict cognitive function (IQ) and problem behavior ratings at age 3.5 years.

## Lack of Positive Affect

Emotional competence entails an awareness of emotional complexity; that we may feel a variety of feelings simultaneously, even if we are not consciously aware of it (Skill 1). It also involves being able to draw upon a diverse range of emotion vocabulary and expression (Skill 3). Displays of positive emotion play an important role in establishing and maintaining social interactions. The display of positive emotion is associated with perceptions of likeability and friendliness [16]. In other words, there is significant social value in the capacity to experience and express affirmative emotions.

Yet, as noted previously, some children lean towards emotional negativity. A sullen, gloomy, or hostile presentation does little to endear a child to his or her peers, and research indicates that school-related social competence is lower for children prone to negative emotionality [44]. In contrast, children who display a preponderance of positive emotions show more prosocial behavior and less aggression; they are also more accepted by their peers [38].

Range of emotional expression is important, and recognizing the value of positive emotion is not meant to obscure the importance of the ability to genuinely experience and express a range of feeling. We can engage more fully with those with whom we can establish an emotional connection, and breadth of affective experience may play a central role. Constrained emotional expression may impede this process. In a series of studies comparing children diagnosed with externalizing and internalizing disorders and their nondiagnosed peers, differences in emotional expression existed between the groups [37]. Children meeting the diagnostic criteria for Attention Deficit Hyperactivity Disorder (ADHD) displayed the most facial affect and showed the most changes in facial displays. They also exhibited more positive emotional displays than did children diagnosed with either Oppositional Defiant Disorder (ODD) or depression, whereas children diagnosed with ODD demonstrated more negativity in their vocal expression. Depressed children exhibited less facial display than children diagnosed with externalizing disorders, as well as their nondiagnosed peers.

Other research indicates that aggressive children display a limited range of emotional expression [10–11]. For children with a history of maltreatment, constricted emotional expression may function as a method of coping with overwhelming traumatic experiences. Yet, this form of affective regulation may contribute to the lack of empathy found among bullying children [10].

## Lack of Empathy

Empathy plays a prominent role in emotional competence. Optimal emotional functioning depends on skills in discerning other's emotions

(Skill 2) and the capacity for empathic involvement in other's emotional experience (Skill 4). Yet, children at risk for behavioral difficulties often display deficits in their capacity to read and empathically respond to others. This holds true for children who bully or behave aggressively toward others [10–11], [62], as well as youth identified as conduct disordered [63]. Lack of empathy interferes with a child's ability to connect meaningfully with others, and heightens their risk of engaging in maladaptive behaviors such as bullying [10], [62]. Strayer and Roberts [64] explored the link between children's anger and aggression and their empathy. Observing the play behavior of 5-year-olds, they found that empathic children were less angry, less verbally and physically aggressive, and involved in fewer object struggles with their peers. A meta-analytic review by Miller and Eisenberg revealed a moderate, negative relationship between empathic/sympathetic responding and externalizing behaviors [65]. In other words, across studies that measured empathy using questionnaires, children lower in empathy tended to show more aggression and antisocial behaviors. A link also existed between low levels of empathy/sympathy and a history of child abuse.

## Misperception of Others' Emotions

Research highlights the important relationship between children's ability to negotiate social interaction and their developing capacity discerning and understanding how others think and feel [66–67]. Competence in reading and understanding the emotional cues of others (Skill 2) is essential to productive interpersonal interactions. Young people who struggle with emotion understanding have difficulty responding to their peers in prosocial ways, and are also viewed by their peers as less likable [18], [68].

Young children with behavioral difficulties, as well as those with a history of maltreatment, possess deficits in emotion understanding and appraisal [55], [67], [69–70]. More specifically, research indicates that these children show deficits in their understanding of links between facial expression and emotion, in producing facial expressions, and in discriminating emotion expressions (e.g., [37], [71–73]).

For example, first and second grade students described by their parents as exhibiting behavior problems struggled to articulate their own emotional experience, whether discussing simple feelings (e.g., happy, sad, mad) or more complex feelings (e.g., proud, nervous). Similarly, when faced with an emotionally arousing situation, aggressive school-aged children showed relatively weak emotion understanding, particularly in terms of their ability to articulate the causes of emotion [40]. Pollack and colleagues [72] found that neglected children had difficulties in discriminating emotions, whereas physically abused children presented a bias toward seeing angry facial expressions.

Difficulty reading social and emotional cues is prevalent among aggressive and antisocial children [38], [41], [63]. More specifically, research with aggressive children indicates that they are prone to misreading ambiguous social situations in a manner that presumes hostile intent [74–76]. Among male preschoolers a connection has been found between aggression and the tendency to ascribe anger [77]. This same study found that for both boys and girls, over attribution of anger was related to peer rejection. A link between hostile attribution bias and poor peer relationships also exists among older children. Barth and Bastiani [78] explored children's biases in labeling their classmates' facial expressions in photos. Children who exhibited a bias toward reading angry facial expression in photos of classmates who were not, in fact, trying to look angry, also had less satisfactory peer relationships.

There is also evidence that within the category of externalizing behavior, different patterns of misperception exist for children diagnosed with ADHD, ODD, or depression [37]. When partnered with a peer for an experimental activity, only 11% of children diagnosed with ADHD were able to accurately assess either their own emotion or a peer's emotion expression. The appraisal errors of these children favored attribution of positive emotion. With marginally better, but still weak, appraisal skills, children diagnosed with ODD erred on the side of negative attribution or failure to recognize the emotion expression of their partners. This same pattern of errors existed for children diagnosed with Major Depressive Disorder (MDD). Yet, compared with their externalizing peers, children diagnosed with MDD were most accurate in judging their own and others' emotions. This research illustrates how issues of emotion appraisal vary for children with different types of difficulties, opening the door for more targeted intervention efforts.

# ☐ Summary and Conclusion

The construct of emotional competence involves affect-related skills that bolster adaptation and coping. Emotional competence integrates skills in the areas of emotion expression, emotion understanding, and emotion regulation. These skills emerge according to a developmental process, through the combined influence of factors such as learning, temperament, cognitive maturity, and developmental history. The manifestation of these skills is not static; that is, their expression is contingent on the immediate social context in which emotions are evoked.

The skills of emotional competence enhance our ability to successfully navigate the demands of living, particularly in the social realm. Thus, they promote a sense of self-efficacy. In this chapter, we explored the implications of emotional competence for a range of developmental outcomes, including the social, academic, and behavioral domains. The researched reviewed in this chapter suggests that strengths in the skills of emotional competence bolster social relationships and academic functioning, while potentially protecting against maladaptive behaviors such as smoking. The research also indicates that deficits in the capacities associated with emotional competence are associated with problematic developmental outcomes including aggression, peer-violence victimization, and social rejection.

While our review isolated five variables associated with these problematic outcomes (negative affect, lack of positive affect, lack of empathy, misperception of other's emotions, and poor frustration tolerance), emerging research attends to the complex interplay among these factors. Perhaps most promising to date is the increasing body of evidence suggesting that a combination of negative emotionality and ability to sustain attention predicts later behavioral outcomes. We look forward to future efforts to further specify the relationship between various emotional competence skills and adaptive functioning.

The research reviewed in this chapter provides valuable information for those interested in prevention and intervention efforts. For example, the data may inform public policy about early intervention, which may include parent guidance as well as appropriately structured preschool education for addressing the needs of children who are faced with the "double hazard" of low attentiveness and proneness to negative emotionality at a young age. These research findings also support a renewed emphasis on the role of emotion in treatment programs. As noted by Southam-Gerow and Kendall [1], the increasing movement toward a cognitive and behavioral focus in mental health treatment and prevention programs corresponds with a relative neglect of the contribution of emotion. Integration of research findings related to emotional competence and emotional intelligence would likely enhance our treatment efforts.

We would like to conclude with an acknowledgement that most children do acquire the skills of emotional competence, assuming that they have supportive families and healthy peer groups, live in nonviolent communities, and have access to a good education. The challenge, then, is working to ensure that societies can and will provide such opportunities and support for children and their families.

# ☐ References

1. Southam-Gerow, M. A., & Kendall, P. C. (2002). Emotion regulation and understanding: Implications for child psychopathology and therapy. *Clinical Psychology Review, 22,* 189–222.
2. Saarni, C. (1999). *The development of emotional competence.* New York: Guilford.
3. Denham, S., Blair, K. A., Schmidt, M., & DeMulder, E. (2002). Compromised emotional competence: Seeds of violence sown early? *American Journal of Orthopsychiatry, 72,* 70–82.
4. Mayer, J. D., & Salovey, P. (1997). What is emotional intelligence? In P. Salovey & D. Sluyter (Eds.), *Emotional development and emotional intelligence* (pp. 3–31). New York: Basic Books.
5. Mayer, J. D., Caruso, D. R., & Salovey, P. (1999). Emotional intelligence meets traditional standards for an intelligence. *Intelligence, 27,* 267–298.
6. Mayer, J. D., Salovey, P., & Caruso, D. R. (2004). A further consideration of the issues of emotional intelligence. *Psychological Inquiry, 15,* 249–255.
7. Saarni, C. S., Campos, J. J., Camras, L., & Witherington, D. (in press). Emotional development: action, communication, and understanding. In W. Damon (Series Ed.) & N. Eisenberg (Vol. Ed.), *Handbook of child psychology: Vol. 3. Social, emotional and personality development.* New York: John Wiley.
8. Saarni, C. (2000). Emotional competence: A developmental perspective. In R. Bar-On & J. D. A. Parker (Eds.), *Handbook of emotional intelligence: Theory, development, assessment, and application at home, school, and in the workplace* (pp. 68–91). San Francisco: Jossey-Bass.
9. Saarni, C. (1990). Emotional competence: How emotions and relationships become integrated. In R. Thompson (Ed.), *Nebraska Symposium on Motivation: 36. Socioemotional development* (pp. 115–182). Lincoln, NE: University of Nebraska Press.
10. Shields, A., & Cicchetti, D. (2001). Parental maltreatment and emotion dysregulation as risk factors for bullying and victimization in middle childhood. *Journal of Clinical Child Psychology, 30,* 349–363.
11. Shields, A., & Cicchetti, D. (1998). Reactive aggression among maltreated children: The contributions of attention and emotion dysregulation. *Journal of Clinical Child Psychology, 27,* 381–395.
12. Selman, R. L. (1981). What children understand of the intrapsychic processes. In E. K. Shapiro & E. Weber (Eds.), *Cognitive and affective growth* (pp. 187–215). Hillsdale, NJ: Lawrence Erlbaum Associates, Inc.
13. Trabasso, T., Stein, N., & Johnson, L. (1981). Children's knowledge of events: A causal analysis of story structure. In G. Bower (Ed.), *The psychology of learning and motivation* (Vol. 15, pp. 237–282). New York: Academic Press.
14. Gnepp, J., & Gould, M. E. (1985). The development of personalized inferences: Understanding other people's emotional reactions in light of their prior experiences. *Child Development, 55,* 1455–1464.
15. Consortium on the School-based Promotion of Social Competence. (1996). The school-based promotion of social competence: Theory, research, practice, and policy. In R. J. Haggerty, L. R. Sherrod, & N. Garmezy (Eds.), *Stress, risk, and resilience in children and adolescents: Processes, mechanisms, and interventions* (pp. 268–316). New York: Cambridge University Press.
16. Denham, S., Blair, K. A., DeMulder, E., Levitas, J., Sawyer, K., Auerbach-Major, S., et al. (2003). Preschool emotional competence: Pathways to social competence? *Child Development, 74,* 238–256.
17. Cassidy, J., Parke, R., Butkovsky, L., & Braungart, J. (1992). Family–peer connections: The roles of emotional expressiveness within the family and children's understanding of emotions. *Child Development, 63,* 603–618.

18. Denham, S. A., McKinley, M., Couchoud, E. A., & Holt, R. (1990). Emotional and behavioral predictors of peer status in young preschoolers. *Child Development, 61,* 1145–1152.
19. Walden, T., & Field, I. (1988). *Preschool children's social competence and production and discrimination of affective expressions.* Unpublished manuscript, Vanderbilt University, Nashville, TN.
20. Kochenderfer-Ladd, B. (2004). Peer victimization: The role of emotions in adaptive and maladaptive coping. *Social Development, 13,* 329–349.
21. Shields, A., Dickstein, S., Seifer, R., Guisti, L., Magee K. D., & Spritz, B. (2001). Emotional competence and early school adjustment: A study of preschoolers at risk. *Early Education and Development, 12,* 73–96.
22. Roeser, R. W., Eccles, J. S., & Sameroff, A. J. (1998). Academic and emotional functioning in early adolescence: Longitudinal relations, patterns, and prediction by experience in middle school. *Development and Psychopathology, 10,* 321–352.
23. Chan, D. W. (2003). Dimensions of emotional intelligence and their relationships with social coping among gifted adolescents in Hong Kong. *Journal of Youth and Adolescence, 32,* 409–418.
24. Schutte, N. S., Malouff, J. M., Hall, L. E., Haggerty, D. J., Cooper, J. T., Golden, C. J., et al. (1998). Development and validation of a measure of emotional intelligence. *Personality and Individual Differences, 25,* 167–177.
25. Petrides, K. V., Frederickson, N., & Furnham, A. (2004). The role of trait emotional intelligence in academic performance and deviant behavior at school. *Personality and Individual Differences, 36,* 277–293.
26. Bar-On, R. (1997). *Bar-On Emotional Quotient Inventory: Technical manual.* Toronto, Canada: Multi-Health Systems.
27. Parker, J. D. A., Summerfeldt, L. J., Hogan, M. J., & Majeski, S. A. (2004). Emotional intelligence and academic success: Examining the transition from high school to university. *Personality and Individual Differences, 36,* 163–172.
28. Roeser, R. W., van der Wolf, K., & Strobel, K. R. (2001). On the relation between social-emotional and school functioning during early adolescence: Preliminary findings from Dutch and American samples. *Journal of School Psychology, 39,* 111–139.
29. Gumora, G., & Arsenio, W. (2002). Emotionality, emotion regulation, and school performance in middle school children. *Journal of School Psychology, 40,* 395–413.
30. Trinidad, D. R., & Johnson, C. A. (2002). The association between emotional intelligence and early adolescent tobacco and alcohol use. *Personality and Individual Differences, 32,* 95–105.
31. Trinidad, D. R., Unger, J. B., Chou, C. P., & Anderson Johnson, C. (2004). The protective association of emotional intelligence with psychosocial smoking risk factors for adolescents. *Personality and Individual Differences, 36,* 945–954.
32. Maguin, E., Zucker, R. A., & Fitzgerald, H. E. (1995). The path to alcohol problems through conduct problems: A family-based approach to very early intervention with risk. In G. M. Boyd, J. Howard, & R. A. Zucker (Eds.), *Alcohol problems among adolescents: Current directions in prevention research* (pp. 105–124). Hillsdale, NJ: Lawrence Erlbaum Associates, Inc.
33. Reese, L. E., Vera, E. M., Thompson, K., & Reyes, R. (2001). A qualitative investigation of perceptions of violence risk factors in low-income African American children. *Journal of Clinical Child Psychology, 30,* 161–171.
34. Brackett, M. A., Mayer, J. D., & Warner, R. M. (2004). Emotional intelligence and its relation to everyday behavior. *Personality and Individual Differences, 36,* 1387–1402.
35. Chambers, S. M. (1999). The effect of family talk on young children's development and coping. In E. Frydenberg (Ed.), *Learning to cope: Developing as a person in complex societies* (pp. 130–149). Oxford, UK: Oxford University Press.

36. Eisenberg, N., Fabes, R., Nyman, M., Bernzweig, J., & Pinuelas, A. (1994). The relations of emotionality and regulation to children's anger-related reactions. *Child Development, 65*, 109–128.

37. Casey, R. (1996). Emotional competence in children with externalizing and internalizing disorders. In M. Lewis & M. Wolan Sullivan (Eds.), *Emotional development in atypical children* (pp. 161–183). Mahwah, NJ: Lawrence Erlbaum Associates, Inc.

38. Arsenio, W. F., Cooperman, S., & Lover, A. (2000). Affective predictors of preschoolers' aggression and peer acceptance: Direct and indirect effects. *Developmental Psychology, 36*, 438–448.

39. Calkins, S. D., & Dedmon, S. E. (2000). Physiological and behavioral regulation in two-year-old children with aggressive/destructive behavior problems. *Journal of Abnormal Child Psychology, 28*, 103–118.

40. Bohnert, A. M., Crnic, K. A., & Lim, K. G. (2003). Emotional competence and aggressive behavior in school-age children. *Journal of Abnormal Child Psychology, 31*, 79–91.

41. Dodge, K. A., Lochman, J. E., Harnish, J. D., Bates, J. E., & Pettit, G. S. (1997). Reactive and proactive aggression in school children and psychiatrically impaired chronically assaultive youth. *Journal of Abnormal Psychology, 106*, 37–51.

42. Kochenderfer, B., & Ladd, G. (1997). Victimized children's response to peer's aggression: Behaviors associated with reduced versus continued victimization. *Development and Psychopathology, 9*, 59–73.

43. Perry, D. G., Williard, J. C., & Perry, L. C. (1990). Peer's perceptions of the consequences that victimized children provide aggressors. *Child Development, 61*, 1310–1325.

44. Eisenberg, N., Fabes, R. A., Shepard, S. A., Murphy, B. C., Guthrie, I. K., Jones, S., et al. (1997). Contemporaneous and longitudinal prediction of children's social functioning from regulation and emotionality. *Child Development, 68*, 642–664.

45. Perry, D. G., Perry, L. C., & Kennedy, E. (1992). Conflict and the development of antisocial behavior. In C. U. Shantz & W. W. Hartup (Eds.), *Conflict in child and adolescent development* (pp. 301–329). New York: Cambridge University Press.

46. Schwartz, D., Dodge, K. A., Pettit, G. S., & Bates, J. E. (1997). The early socialization of aggressive victims of bullying. *Child Development, 68*, 665–675.

47. Ladd, G. W., Kochenderfer, B. J., & Coleman, C. C. (1997). Classroom peer acceptance, friendship, and victimization: Distinct relational systems that contribute uniquely to children's school adjustment. *Child Development, 68*, 1181–1197.

48. Conduct Problems Prevention Research Group. (1999). Initial impact of the Fast Track prevention trial for conduct problems: I. The high risk sample. *Journal of Consulting and Clinical Psychology, 67*, 631–647.

49. Schwartz, D., Proctor, L. J., & Chien, D. H. (2001). The aggressive victim of bullying: Emotional and behavioral dysregulation as a pathway to victimization by peers. In J. Juvonen & S. Graham (Eds.), *Peer harassment in school: The plight of the vulnerable and victimized* (pp. 147–174). New York: Guilford.

50. Egan, S. K., & Perry, D. G. (1998). Does low self-regard invite victimization? *Developmental Psychology, 34*, 299–309.

51. Olweus, D. (1978). *Aggression in the schools: Bullies and whipping boys.* Washington, DC: Hemisphere.

52. Dodge, K. A., Price, J. M., Coie, J. D., & Christopoulos, C. (1990). On the development of aggressive dyadic relationships in boys' peer groups. *Human Development, 33*, 260–270.

53. Kumpulainen, K., Räsänen, E., Henttonen, I., Almqvist, F., Kresanov, K., Linna, S. L., et al. (1998). Bullying and psychiatric symptoms among elementary school-age children. *Child Abuse and Neglect, 22*, 705–717.

54. Schwartz, D. (2000). Subtypes of victims and aggressors in children's peer groups. *Journal of Abnormal Child Psychology, 28*, 181–192.

55. Camras, L. A., Sachs-Alter, E., & Ribordy, S. C. (1996). Emotion understanding in maltreated children: Recognition of facial expressions and integration with other emotion cues. In M. Lewis & M. Wolan Sullivan (Eds.), *Emotional development in atypical children* (pp. 203–225). Mahwah, NJ: Lawrence Erlbaum Associates, Inc.

56. Eisenberg, N., Spinrad, T. L., Fabes, R. A., Reiser, M., Cumberland, A., Shepard, S. A., et al. (2004). The relations of effortful control and impulsivity to children's resiliency and adjustment. *Child Development, 75,* 25–46.

57. Eisenberg, N., & Spinrad, T. (2004). Emotion-related regulation: Sharpening the definition. *Child Development, 75*(2), 334–339.

58. Biederman, J., Rosenbaum, J. F., Bolduc-Murphy, E. A., Faraone, S. V., Chaloff, J., Hirshfeld, D. R., & Kagan, J. (1993). Behavioral inhibition as a temperamental risk factor for anxiety disorders. *Child and Adolescent Psychiatric Clinics of North America, 2,* 667–684.

59. Schwartz, C. E., Snidman, N., & Kagan, J. (1996). Early childhood temperament as a determinant of externalizing behavior in adolescence. *Development and Psychopathology, 8,* 527–537.

60. Eisenberg, N., Fabes, R., Bernzweig, J., Karbon, M., Poulin, R., & Hanish, L. (1993). The relations of emotionality and regulation to preschoolers' social skills and sociometric status. *Child Development, 64,* 1418–1438.

61. Lawson, K. R., & Ruff, H. A. (2004). Early attention and negative emotionality predict later cognitive and behavioural function. *International Journal of Behavioral Development, 28*(2), 157–165.

62. Olweus, D. (1991). Bully/victim problems among schoolchildren: Basic facts and effects of a school based intervention program. In D. J. Pepler & K. H. Rubin (Eds.), *The development and treatment of childhood aggression* (pp. 411–488). Hillsdale, NJ: Lawrence Erlbaum Associates, Inc.

63. Cohen, D., & Strayer, J. (1996). Empathy in conduct-disordered and comparison youth. *Developmental Psychology, 32,* 988–998.

64. Strayer, J., & Roberts, W. L. (2004). Empathy and observed anger and aggression in five-year-olds. *Social Development, 13,* 1–13.

65. Miller, P. A., & Eisenberg, N. (1988). The relation of empathy to aggressive and externalizing/antisocial behavior. *Psychological Bulletin, 103,* 324–344.

66. Selman, R. L., & Schultz, L. H. (1990). *Making a friend in youth: Developmental theory and pair therapy.* Chicago: University of Chicago Press.

67. Selman, R. L., Schultz, L. H., Nakkula, M., Barr, D., Watts, C., & Richmond, J. B. (1992). Friendship and fighting: A developmental approach to the study of risk and prevention of violence. *Development and Psychopathology, 4,* 529–558.

68. Denham, S. (1986). Social cognition, prosocial behavior, and emotion in preschoolers: Contextual validation. *Child Development, 57,* 194–201.

69. Cook, E. T., Greenberg, M. T., & Kusche, C. A. (1994). The relations between emotional understanding, intellectual functioning, and disruptive behavior problems in elementary-school-aged children. *Journal of Abnormal Child Psychology, 22,* 205–219.

70. Hughes, C., Dunn, J., & White, A. (1998). Trick or treat? Uneven understanding of mind and emotion and executive dysfunction in "hard-to-manage" preschoolers. *Journal of Child Psychology, 39,* 981–994.

71. Camras, L. A., Grow, G., & Ribordy, S. C. (1983). Recognition of emotional expressions by abused children. *Journal of Clinical and Child Psychology, 12,* 325–328.

72. Pollack, S. D., Cicchetti, D., Hornung, K., & Reed, A. (2000). Recognizing emotion in faces: Developmental effects of child abuse and neglect. *Developmental Psychology, 36,* 679–688.

73. Shipman, K., Zeman, J., Penza, S., & Champion, K. (2000). Emotion management skills in sexually maltreated and nonmaltreated girls: A developmental psychopathology perspective. *Development and Psychopathology, 12,* 47–62.

74. Crick, N. R., & Dodge, K. A. (1994). A review and reformulation of social information-processing mechanisms in children's social adjustment. *Psychological Bulletin, 115*, 74–101.

75. Dodge, K. A. (1995). Attributional bias in aggressive children. In P. C. Kendall (Ed.), *Advances in cognitive behavioral research and therapy* (Vol. 4, pp. 73–110). Orlando, FL: Academic Press.

76. Zelli, A., Dodge, K. A., Laird, R. D., & Lochman, J. E. (1999). The distinction between beliefs legitimizing aggression and deviant processing of social cues: Testing measurement validity and the hypothesis that biased processing mediates the effects of belief on aggression. *Journal of Personality and Social Psychology, 77*, 150–166.

77. Schultz, D., Izard, C. E., & Ackerman, B. P. (1999). Children's anger attribution biases: Relations to family environment and social adjustment. *Social Development, 9*, 284–301.

78. Barth, J., & Bastiani, A. (1997). A longitudinal study of emotion regulation and preschool children's social behavior. *Merrill-Palmer Quarterly, 43*, 107–128.

Joseph P. Forgas
Carrie L. Wyland

**CHAPTER 4**

# Affective Intelligence: Understanding the Role of Affect in Everyday Social Behavior

## ☐ Introduction

It is a bright sunny day outside, and you are in an excellent mood. As you stop for a cappuccino on your way to work, a woman in the bar reminds you of a childhood friend, and happy memories about your school years come flooding back. At work, you are on a selection committee, and as you interview the first applicant, you notice with delight what a pleasant person he is. As you discuss your decision with your colleagues, you act in a cooperative and friendly way. What role does mood play in the way people think and act in such everyday situations? How and why do mild affective states influence our thoughts, memories and behaviors? This chapter reviews recent evidence documenting the pervasive influence of affect on social thinking and behavior, and argues that emotional intelligence necessarily involves knowing how, when and why such effects occur.

Surprisingly, affect remains perhaps the "last frontier" in our quest to understand the dynamics of human behavior. Although most of us intuitively know that our feelings and moods can have a crucial influence on our mental life and actions, until recently we did not fully understand how and why these influences occur. A critical—and so far rather neglected—component of "emotional intelligence" is to understand how affective states will influence our thoughts and behaviors. Most of these effects are subtle, subconscious and difficult to detect introspectively. It is only as a result of the recent impressive growth of experimental research on affect that we can begin to understand the multifaceted influence of feelings on everything that we think and do. To be "emotionally intelligent," we need to know how these affective influences function, and how to control and manage them. As we shall see, it is not simply a case of trying to be always in a good mood. Both negative and positive moods can have beneficial consequences for our thinking and behavior in certain situations. Knowing how, when and why these effects occur is what this chapter is about.

These issues are not only of interest to psychologists, but to everyone who wants to understand the complex role of affect in human affairs. This chapter will review past and present ideas about the role of everyday affective states and moods in how people think and behave in social situations. Moods, unlike emotions, are relatively low-intensity, diffuse and long-lasting affective states that are often subconscious and have no salient cause. Unlike more intense emotions, moods often escape our conscious attention. Paradoxically, their effects on social thinking and behavior tend to be potentially more insidious, enduring and subtle, and may impact on both individual and group behaviors [1].

The main message of this chapter is that affect may color everything we think and do. Affective influences on everyday thinking, judgments and behavior occur because the way we feel is inseparable with the way we think and process information. Understanding the nature of these affective influences has been the focus of intensive experimental research in recent years, and is an essential aspect of affective intelligence. This chapter will survey recent empirical evidence for affect infusion into thoughts, judgments and behaviors, and highlight the conditions that facilitate or inhibit these effects. In particular, we will review evidence showing that affect can influence both

1. the *content* of thinking, judgments and behavior (*what* we think and do), and also
2. the *process* of thinking (*how* we deal with social information).

## ☐ Understanding the Consequences of Affect: Why Is It so Difficult?

Since the dawn of human civilization, philosophers such as Aristotle, Socrates, Plato, St. Augustine, Descartes, Pascal and Kant have struggled to understand the role of affect in thinking and behavior. Plato was among the first who thought that affect constitutes a more primitive, animal aspect of human nature that is incompatible with reason. The idea that affect subverts rational thinking was perpetuated in the speculative ideas of Freud and others. Some writers such as Arthur Koestler [2] even thought that humans' inability to know and control their often violent affective reactions is due to a fatal "flaw" in the way our brains developed, an evolutionary mistake that may threaten the very survival of our species. Surprisingly, most of what we know about the role of affect in social cognition and behavior has only been discovered during the past two decades. Although feeling and thinking were often assumed to be separate faculties by early philosophers and psychologists, recent research suggests a fundamental interdependence between feeling and thinking.

For example, brain research suggests that affect is often a useful and even essential component of adaptive responses to social situations. People with isolated frontal lobe damage who cannot integrate affective reactions also tend to make disastrous social decisions and their social relationships suffer accordingly, even though their intellectual abilities are unimpaired. Indeed, Adolphs and Damasio believe "affective processing to be an evolutionary antecedent to more complex forms of information processing; . . . higher cognition requires the guidance provided by affective processing" [3, p. 45]. They suggest that the frontal lobes act as a "somatic marker" that allows us to use our emotions as a gauge for decision making and risk assessment and without intact frontal lobes, we are impaired in our ability to make wise choices [4].

The intimate link between thoughts and feelings is also nicely illustrated by research by Blascovich and Mendes [5], who found that even fundamental biological reactions to a difficult situation, such as increased heart rate and blood pressure, are dependent on the particular thoughts a person has about the situation, and whether they interpret it as representing a challenge or a threat. In turn, affective reactions often determine the way information about the world is stored and represented [6–7]. As we shall see, even mild mood changes can have a profound influence on the kind of memories we retrieve, the information we notice and learn, and the way we respond to social situations. Dominant and enduring moods may also permeate the lives of entire groups, impacting on individual group members in powerful and often uncontrollable ways [1].

Despite recent advances, there remains much confusion about the role of affect in human affairs. Is affect essential to adaptive responses in social situations? Or is affect a dangerous, invasive force that subverts rational thinking and produces judgmental errors and maladaptive responses? There is good evidence that people are not very good at recognizing and understanding the consequences of their affective states—we often seem to be blind to the role that feelings play in our thoughts and behaviors.

This kind of "affective blindness"—a profound inability to correctly understand affective states and their consequences—is nicely illustrated in some recent studies on affective forecasting, and emotional cascades.

## Affect and Predicting the Future

If you won the lottery today, how happy would you be, and for how long? And how devastated would you feel if your current romantic relationship ended? Many everyday choices are driven by expected emotional reactions to future events. For example, we may be hesitant to end a romantic relationship because we might forecast that the separation would be too aversive to bear. However, such "affective forecasting" can be seriously mistaken. Winning the lottery will not make you as happy and for as long as you expected, and the end of a relationship may not be as traumatic as anticipated. Most people overestimate the intensity and duration of their anticipated positive and negative reactions to future events. Daniel Gilbert at Harvard University coined the term "miswanting" to describe the common mistake of wanting things that will make us less happy than we hope, and avoiding things that will not be as bad as we fear [8]. Why do these mistakes of affective forecasting occur?

We can go wrong because we often focus on the wrong (non-representative) details when imagining a future event, and then misunderstand and misread our own likely reactions. When thinking about winning the lottery, we focus on having all that money—but don't think about the difficult investment decisions we'll have to take, how our relatives might react, and what being much richer than our friends might do to our relationships. Such *focalism* (focusing only on the salient features of emotional events and ignoring the rest) produces unrealistic expectations and subsequent disappointment. Many fervently desired consumer acquisitions leave us less happy than we expected. It is for such reasons that people keep on buying goods they will never use such as exercise equipment or dieting products. They focus on the positive feelings linked to having a beautiful body, but fail to forecast the pain, exhaustion and hunger that necessarily go with the purchase.

Similarly, negative events are often less traumatic than we expect. We have many spontaneous and subconscious cognitive strategies—a psychological "immune system"—for coping with problems, and people typically underestimate their ability to cope with adversity. Distraction, self-affirmation and rationalization are just some of the highly effective and spontaneous strategies that make up the psychological immune system. "Immune neglect"—ignoring the immune system—leads to an overestimation of negative affective reactions.

Numerous studies now suggest that affective "miswanting" is very common: people often desire the wrong things for the wrong reasons, and avoid activities that, if undertaken, would make them much happier [8]. For example, people often avoid effortful or strenuous activities (like exercising, or meeting a new person) in favor of less effortful, routine tasks (watching TV, meeting a familiar person). Yet these decisions are often mistaken: it turns out that individuals who choose to engage in more demanding tasks (exercise, meet a new person) enjoy it much more and feel happier than those who opt for the easy alternatives [9].

How can we avoid these mistakes? Emotional intelligence implies that we should always consider *all* features of a future event and not just its focal aspects, and try to take into account the proven efficacy of our psychological immune system. Many everyday decisions, such as consumer decisions should always be based on a skeptical assessment of real utility outcomes, rather than just subjective feelings that many advertisers prefer us to focus on. Of course, this is not to argue that quick, simple judgments based on "gut" feelings cannot sometimes produce perfectly acceptable judgmental outcomes. However, when, as in the case of marketing and advertising, powerful commercial forces combine against us to create "gut" feelings to purchase, then a more careful and skeptical analysis of our real needs may provide a much-needed antidote to these manipulative influences.

## Coping with Stress and the "Neurotic Cascade"

Another and perhaps more extreme example of "affective blindness"—an inability to correctly interpret and control affective influences—occurs when intense negative affective states produce debilitating consequences for our thinking. In some people, extreme stress and anxiety can produce a dangerous "neurotic cascade" of reverberating negative affect and negative thinking [10]. In such a state, even minor problems tend to be magnified out of all proportion. "Awfulization" refers to the tendency to overdramatize negative outcomes by highly stressed persons, leading to thoughts such as "I wouldn't cope if I lost this deal" or "I couldn't survive for a week without my girlfriend." "Overgeneralization" is another faulty thought pattern often found in this negative state. For example, the loss of a partner ("she doesn't love me") will be overgeneralized to indicate that "nobody loves me." In such a state, people sometimes set unrealistic and unreasonable goals for themselves, show decreased flexibility in adjusting their goals, and so inadvertently produce more negative experiences. One approach to breaking this cycle of negative affectivity is to become aware of, and critically analyze our thoughts, determine whether they are rational or not, and to discard irrational ones. It may also be useful to question how others might respond to the same situation, and ask ourselves whether it is helpful to maintain such negative ideas [11–12].

## ☐ Affect Congruence and Affect Infusion: Feeling Good, Thinking Good, and Acting Good

Perhaps the most universal influence of affect is that it colors our thoughts and responses in an affect-congruent manner. When we feel good, we tend to see the world through rose-colored glasses. When depressed, everything appears bleak and gloomy. Some 65 years ago Razran [13] showed that people who were made to feel bad by an aversive smell also made more negative judgments about unrelated issues than those who felt good after receiving a free lunch. Such spontaneous, and often unconscious "affect congruence" appears to be a very common and reliable everyday phenomenon [14]. Why exactly do these effects occur, and what can we do about them?

Psychoanalytic theories suggested that affective impulses may invade and color unrelated thoughts unless sufficient "pressure" is exerted to control them. Alternative, conditioning theories maintained that such dynamic assumptions are not necessary, as affect may spontaneously attach itself to unrelated thoughts and judgments simply due to temporal and spatial conditioning. For example, people who feel bad because of the excessive heat and humidity in a room will form more negative impressions of a person they meet in such a situation due to a conditioned association between their affect and the target person [15]. However, these effects are not universal, and neither psychoanalytic theories, nor theories based on "blind" conditioning principles can explain the apparent situation- and context-sensitivity of affect infusion.

In contrast, contemporary theories emphasize the role of affect in how our memory representations about the world are organized and activated, and it is this link that drives affect infusion into thinking and behavior. When in a positive mood, we are significantly more likely to access and recall positive information and information that was first encountered in a previous happy mood state (as did the happy hero in our introductory paragraph while reminiscing about happy childhood memories). In contrast, negative mood selectively facilitates the recall of negative information. According to the associative network model developed by Gordon Bower [16], affective states are closely linked to all information we store and recall. Recent neuroanatomical evidence provides strong convergent "evidence for the inseparable relation between emotion and other aspects of cognition. Our everyday experience also clearly shows that affective influences essentially color all other aspects of cognitive functioning, including memory, attention, and decision making" [3, p. 44]. In other words, affect congruence in memory has widespread consequences for the way people think and behave. This occurs because we need to rely on selective memory-based information to make sense of complex events. Surprisingly, the more complex or unusual a social event, the more likely that we will have to extensively search our memories to make sense of it, and the greater the likelihood that affect will influence the kind of ideas we access and the interpretations we make. Thus, affect infusion increases when an open, constructive thinking style is adopted to deal with difficult, unusual situations, as only this kind of thinking promotes the incidental use of affectively primed information [17]. For example, it turns out that people are much more influenced by their temporary mood when thinking about difficult personal problems in their romantic relationship, but mood effects are much weaker when easier issues are considered [18].

Mood effects on memory are not the only way that affect can color our thinking and judgments. Occasionally, people respond to situations without any careful elaboration and without relying on memory-based information [19]. When this happens, instead of "computing a judgment on the basis of recalled features of a target, individuals may . . . ask themselves: how do I feel about it?/and/in doing so, they may mistake feelings due to a pre-existing state as a reaction to the target" [20, p. 529]. Using temporary affect as an "heuristic" cue is most likely when people lack sufficient interest, motivation or resources to produce a more elaborate response. For example, in a street survey people will often give more positive responses immediately after they have just seen a happy movie, and make more negative responses when they saw a sad film [21]. The simplest way to respond in such a situation is to rely on a "how do I feel about it?" heuristic, using the affective state to infer a quick reaction. Thus, affective states can produce an affect-congruent bias and may color both elaborate, well considered responses (through facilitating the use of affect-congruent information), and quick, off-the-cuff reactions (when people mistakenly use their current affect to infer a reaction).

## ☐ Affect Congruence in Memory and Judgments

As we have seen, perhaps the most fundamental influence that affective states have is on our memories. People in a happy mood remember more positive memories from their childhood, recall more happy episodes from the previous week, and remember better the words they have learnt when in a matching mood state [16]. It is for this reason that in a positive mood all seems well with the world and we predominantly think about and remember happy, joyful experiences. Negative mood in contrast triggers a stream of negative thoughts and ideas, depressing us even further. Becoming aware of these subtle and unconscious memory effects is an important component of emotional intelligence. These effects are most likely to occur when the situation calls for an open, constructive thinking strategy that requires the extensive use of memory-based information. Mood-congruent effects can be quite easily eliminated and even reversed when people's attention is directed towards themselves [22]. Thus, simply becoming aware of such mood effects is in itself an important step towards increasing our emotional intelligence. Once we know how and why these effects occur, we are in a much better position to predict and manage their consequences.

Affective states can also influence many other tasks that require the use of memory-based processes. For example, when people are asked to look at pictures depicting ambiguous social scenes (such as two people having an animated conversation), happy people construct more cheerful, positive explanations (they are telling a joke), and sad people construct a more negative event (they are arguing [16]). Ultimately, affect can also impact on real social judgments about real people. Observing others and interpreting their actions is one of the most fundamental judgments we perform in everyday life. We explored affective biases in such judgments by asking happy or sad participants to observe and rate their own and their partner's behaviors in a videotaped social encounter [23]. Happy people "saw" far more positive, skilled and fewer negative, unskilled behaviors both in themselves and in their partners than did sad subjects. These effects occur because affect directly influences the kinds of memories and interpretations that come to mind as observers try to make sense of complex and inherently ambiguous social behaviors.

In other words, the same smile that is seen as warm and friendly by a person in a good mood can easily be judged as condescending or awkward by somebody in a bad mood. These kinds of mood effects also influence how we interpret our own behaviors and our successes and failures in real-life tasks such as passing an exam [24]. Part of the reason for these judgmental effects is that people tend to pay selective attention to affect-consistent rather than affect-inconsistent information [25]. Thus, affect appears to influence what we notice, what we learn, what we remember, and ultimately, the kinds of judgments and decisions we make. However, this kind of spontaneous affect infusion is rather a fragile process, and can be easily controlled once people become aware of their mood states. An important aspect of emotional intelligence is thus to know how, when and why these effects occur.

## ☐ A Paradoxical Effect: When More Thinking Produces More Affect Infusion

Surprisingly, affect infusion seems significantly greater when people engage in more extensive and elaborate thinking, as such a processing style increases the opportunity and the need to use mood-congruent memories. For example, we found that affect had a much greater mood-congruent effect on judgments about couples who were unusual and badly matched and so required more elaborate interpretation, rather than typical, well-matched couples who were easier to interpret [26–27]. Time measures showed that unusual, badly matched couples actually required more lengthy and extensive thinking, and it was this more elaborate thinking that increased affect infusion. The conclusion is clear: the more we need to think about something, the more likely that our affective state may unconsciously influence our thoughts, memories and, eventually, our responses.

This pattern has been confirmed in a number of other studies. For example, affect also had a greater influence on judgments about more unusual, mixed-race rather than same-race couples. In one study we simultaneously manipulated *both* the physical attractiveness and the racial match of observed couples, and so created well-matched (same race, same attractiveness), partly matched (either race, or physical attractiveness matched) and mismatched, unusual (different race, different attractiveness) couples. Affect had the greatest influence on judgments about the most mismatched couples, had a weaker effect when couples were partly matched, and the smallest effect when they were well matched [27]. The same kind of results are also obtained when people make judgments about themselves: affect has a greater influence when judging less familiar, peripheral aspects of the self, but these effects are reduced when central, familiar features are judged [28].

Do real-life judgments about important issues show the same kind of affective bias? What happens when we are thinking about our intimate partners and relationships? Commonsense suggests that such personal and highly familiar judgments should be more resistant to fleeting affective biases. In fact, the opposite seems to be the case. Surprisingly, when we asked people who were feeling happy or sad to think about their own intimate relationships, mood effects were consistently greater when more extensive thinking was required to deal with more serious rather than simple, everyday interpersonal issues [18]. In a way, the more we know about a person or an issue, the richer and more extensive the number of positive and negative memories we can call upon, and the more likely that affect may have a strong selective influence on what comes to mind and the kind of judgments we make.

This might explain the remarkable effect that people may make extremely positive or extremely negative judgments about the same personal relationship at different times, despite having very detailed and extensive knowledge about their intimate partners. When feeling good, we more easily access memories about happy, positive events and the relationship seems fabulous. When in a negative mood, all that comes to mind is problems and difficulties, and the same relationship seems hardly worth having. Such affective biases in relationship judgments can be very dangerous especially if couples get caught up in each other's affective states (see also Chapters 6 and 7 in this volume). It is an important component of emotional intelligence to realize that affect can have a profound influence even on very familiar memories and judgments. Becoming aware of these effects is a helpful first step in controlling and eliminating the cycle of negative affectivity that can otherwise often spiral out of control.

## ☐ Thinking Fast Versus Thinking Elaborately

In this review we repeatedly touched on the question of whether slow, deliberate or fast, simplified thinking will produce better results. We saw in the section on affective forecasting that simplified processes such as focalism and immune neglect can contribute to "miswanting," shortcomings in judgments about the future. Much of consumer advertising and marketing also aims to shortcircuit more deliberate, rational thinking often dealing in affective images designed to create needs and "gut feelings" to purchase a product. More careful, deliberate thinking can help to avoid such emotional pitfalls. However, we have also seen that sometimes, quick, fast, intuitive decisions based on simple "gut" feelings can produce better outcomes [29–30]. Conversely, as some of the experiments reviewed above showed, more elaborate and constructive thinking can in turn magnify affective influences on thinking and judgments.

Is there a contradiction here? Does short, simplified thinking, or slow, deliberate thinking provide the best defense against affective distortions in judgments? The brief answer is that both information processing styles have advantages and disadvantages. Knowing how they work, and understanding the way affective states may influence them is the key to better decision making and improved affective intelligence. It entirely depends on the particular situation as to which thinking style will produce superior outcomes. Quick, heuristic reactions to complex situations have distinct advantages in terms of conserving cognitive effort and producing good outcomes—as long as there is no artificial contamination of the situation. Commercially motivated persuaders, such as marketers and advertisers, often seek to create conditions that promote an affective desire to purchase goods and services that on closer inspection we should avoid. Systematic thinking is likely to be effective in avoiding such pitfalls, as well as other shortcomings associated with affective forecasting described above.

# ☐  Affect Infusion and Social Behavior

So far we have focused on affective influences on thinking and judgments. As social interaction necessarily involves many rapid and largely subconscious cognitive decisions about alternative actions, affect is also likely to influence how people behave in social situations. We may expect that people in a positive mood should behave in a more confident, friendly, skilled and constructive way than do those in a negative mood. This prediction was confirmed when we asked female undergraduates to interact with a confederate immediately after they were made to feel good or bad as a result of watching a mood induction film [31]. The interaction was subsequently rated by trained observers who were not aware of the mood manipulation. Happy students communicated more and did so more effectively, used more engaging nonverbal signals, were more talkative and disclosed more about themselves. They were seen as acting in a more poised, skilled and rewarding manner. Sad participants in contrast were judged as being less friendly, confident and relaxed than were happy participants. It seems then that affect will infuse not only people's thoughts and judgments, but also their real-life social interactions. Again, there are clear implications for our understanding of emotional intelligence: to be emotionally intelligent means realizing that even mild mood states can fundamentally alter the way we behave and appear to others. People are not usually aware of these effects. When questioned, students in this study did not realize that their behavior was in any way influenced by their moods. It requires a conscious effort and awareness to correct for these effects if we want to increase our "emotional intelligence."

# ☐  Affective Influences on Communication Strategies

Several studies now show that affect has a significant influence on the way people communicate in social situations. Asking people to do something for us—requesting—is one of the more difficult and problematic verbal tasks we all face in everyday life. Requesting usually involves psychological conflict, as people must phrase their request so as to maximize the chances of compliance (by being direct), yet avoid the danger of giving offence (by not being *too* direct). Affect may influence request strategies, as the greater availability of positive thoughts in a happy mood may produce a more confident, direct requesting style. It turns out that happy persons indeed interpreted request situations in a more confident, optimistic way, and used more direct, impolite requests, while sad persons used more cautious, polite request forms. Further, these mood effects on requesting were much stronger when the request situation was demanding and difficult, and so required more extensive thinking [32–33]. Again, these effects also occur in real-life tasks. In one study, we recorded the requests made by subjects who were asked to get a file from a neighboring office after receiving a mood induction [34, Exp. 2]. Even in this "real" situation, negative mood produced more polite, cautious and hedging requests than did positive mood.

The implications of such studies clearly extend to many real-life situations. Imagine that you are planning to ask for a raise from your boss, and are thinking about how to phrase your request. The particular form of words used—and their success—will partly depend on the current mood state: when happy, people might prefer more confident and direct approaches; when feeling down, more cautious and polite forms will be used. Emotional intelligence requires that we know about these effects if we want to increase our interpersonal effectiveness.

Another common communication task found to be affect sensitive is *self-disclosure*. It is through disclosing increasingly personal and intimate information about ourselves that personal relationships are developed and a sense of self and identity is created [35]. It turns out that being in a good or a bad mood significantly influences the extent to which individuals feel comfortable disclosing personal information about themselves. We found that people who were induced to feel good were more willing to disclose intimate information and did so sooner than did persons experiencing temporary negative affect. This effect was even stronger when the partner reciprocated with matching levels of disclosure [36].

In a way, it seems that by selectively priming positive thoughts, positive affect creates a sense of confidence and well-being that leads people to interpret their situation in an optimistic way, and allows them to act in a more open and confident manner. Some psychologists, like Yaacov Trope, suggested that positive affect can be considered a *psychological resource*. In their experiments, Trope and his colleagues [37] found that people experiencing positive mood were more willing to seek out and cope with negative and threatening information about themselves, as

long as they believed the threatening information to be potentially useful. Another example of the interpersonal benefits of good mood is in the
area of negotiation and bargaining.

## ☐ Feeling Good and Getting Your Way?
## Affect Infusion into Bargaining Behaviors

Bargaining and negotiation by definition involve a degree of unpre-
dictability and require careful planning and preparation. Several studies
found that happy persons set themselves higher and more ambitious
negotiating goals, expect to succeed more, and make plans and use strategies that are more optimistic, cooperative and integrative than do people
in a neutral, or negative mood [38]. Most interesting was the finding that
positive affect actually helped people to do better. They were more successful and achieved better outcomes for themselves than did sad participants. These results have striking implications for our understanding of
emotional intelligence. They suggest that even small changes in affective
state due to a completely unrelated prior event can have a marked influence on the way people plan and execute strategic interpersonal encounters, and their likely success.

Why do these effects occur? Uncertain and unpredictable social
encounters such as bargaining require open, constructive thinking.
Positive affect may selectively bring to mind (prime) more positive
thoughts and ideas that lead to more optimistic expectations and the
adoption of more cooperative and integrative bargaining strategies.
Negative affect in turn seems to bring to mind more negative and pes-
simistic memories and leads to the less cooperative and ultimately, less
successful bargaining. These effects are largely automatic and subconscious, and few people realize that they occur at all. Developing emotional intelligence involves becoming aware of, and being able to control
and manage these subtle mood effects on our thinking and actions.

So far we have focused on affect infusion, that is, the affect-congruent
influence of feelings on the *content* of thinking and behavior. It is now
time to turn to the other major consequence of affect on everyday behavior: affective influences on the *process* of thinking.

## ☐ Affect and How We Think:
## Affective Influences on Thinking Styles

Affect influences not only the content of cognition and behavior (what we
think and do), but also the *process* of cognition, that is, *how* individuals

think. It was initially thought that good mood simply produces a lazier, more relaxed and superficial thinking style, as feeling good "informs" us that the situation is safe and no particular effort is required. Bad mood in turn may function as warning signal to be more careful and attentive [39]. However, positive affect doesn't just make people "lazy" thinkers. Rather, feeling good seems to produce a thinking style that gives greater rein to our internal thoughts, dispositions and ideas. In this mode of thinking individuals tend to pay less attention to external information, and tend to assimilate external details into their preexisting knowledge about the world. Negative affect in contrast produces a more externally focused thinking style where accommodation to the demands of the external world takes precedence over internal ideas [40–41].

These differences in thinking style are consistent with evolutionary ideas that suggest that affect signals appropriate ways of responding to different situations. Positive affect tells us that the environment is benign and that we can rely on our existing knowledge in responding. Negative affect is more like an alarm signal, alerting us that the environment is potentially dangerous and that we need to pay close attention to external information. Understanding these subtle processing consequences of affect is again likely to be an important feature of emotional intelligence. We now know that feeling good and feeling bad does make us deal very differently with the same social situation, as the studies below show.

## Feeling Bad—But Thinking Well?

It is often assumed in everyday life that being in a good mood is not only more pleasant, but also has universally desirable consequences. Organizational psychologists often assume that happy employers work better, are more flexible and creative, and create more customer satisfaction [42]. Despite the many obvious benefits of positive affect, the kind of careful, vigilant and systematic attention to stimulus details typically recruited by negative moods can also be of considerable benefit in certain situations. For example, when responding to persuasive messages those in a negative mood tend to scrutinize the message more carefully and respond more in terms of message quality than do happy persons [43]. People in a happy mood also tend to rely more on their pre-existing stereotypes when forming impressions about outgroup members (although other negative affective states, such as anger can also increase the use of stereotypes [44]). Some clinical research also suggests that those feeling depressed are actually more realistic in how they see the world and themselves, and it is "normal" people who tend to distort reality in a positive direction [45].

## Negative Affect may Reduce Judgmental Biases

Other recent studies suggest that mild negative mood may also help us to avoid certain judgmental mistakes, such as the "fundamental attribution error" (FAE), a tendency to infer intention and internal causation even when observed behavior can be fully explained in terms of external, situational pressures. The FAE occurs because people often ignore external constraints on people's behavior, and mistakenly assume that observed actions are internally caused and reflect genuine dispositions. In several recent studies we found that mild negative moods reduce this judgmental bias. We asked happy or sad people to form impressions about the writers of essays advocating either popular or unpopular opinions, who were either coerced, or were free to choose their position [46]. Happy persons tended to ignore information about coercion, and simply assumed that the essay reflected the writer's attitudes, thus committing the FAE. Negative mood reduced this bias: those feeling bad paid better attention to the available information, and tended to discount coerced essays as indicative of the writer's real views.

## Negative Affect may Improve Eyewitness Accuracy

Another area where mild negative mood was shown to have significant beneficial effects is eyewitness memory. Remembering witnessed events accurately is not only important in everyday social behavior, but eyewitness accounts are also accorded special evidential status in the legal system. In several recent experiments, we evaluated mood effects on eyewitness accuracy [47]. We first allowed people to witness complex real-life or videotaped social events. Some time later, good or bad mood was induced before they received questions that either included, or did not include "planted," misleading information about the scenes. When the accuracy of eyewitness memory was later tested, those who were in a negative mood when exposed to misleading information were more accurate and did not incorporate "false" details into their memory. Positive mood reduced accuracy, and increased the tendency to confuse misleading details with the original event. In other words, the more careful and externally oriented thinking style produced by mild negative moods can produce significant cognitive benefits and improve the accuracy of memories and social judgments.

Emotional intelligence should clearly include some attention to, and awareness of these effects. Many judgments and decisions in everyday life—including important organizational decisions—are made in very similar circumstances. For example, in a series of studies Stephanie

Moylan [48] showed that negative mood tends to decrease the incidence of a variety of errors and distortions in performance assessment judgments. The emotionally intelligent individual understands that mild negative mood states are not always harmful and can indeed be beneficial and confer cognitive benefits in certain problem-solving tasks and in certain social situations.

## Affective Influences on the Quality of Persuasive Messages: When Sad is Better?

Mild everyday mood states may also influence how well we think, and how well we do in demanding interpersonal situations, such as when we are trying to persuade others. Imagine that you are trying to produce persuasive arguments either for, or against propositions such as (a) student fees should be increased, and (b) nuclear testing should not occur in the Pacific. When we asked subjects to do this immediately after a mood induction [36], those in a negative mood came up with higher quality persuasive arguments than did happy persons. The same effects were also obtained in a second study, when happy or sad people were asked to persuade a friend for or against Australia becoming a republic, and for or against a right-wing populist party. In a further experiment, individuals produced their persuasive arguments in interacting with a "partner" through a computer keyboard as if exchanging emails. Half the participants were promised a significant reward (movie passes) if they were successful. Those in a negative mood again produced and used higher quality arguments. However, the provision of a reward reduced the size of mood effects by imposing a strong motivational influence on how the task was approached. These results suggest that mild negative moods promote a more careful, externally oriented processing style that is more attuned to the requirements of a given situation. However, a strong motivation to do well can override these mood effects. The implications of such findings for emotional intelligence are intriguing. If a task is performed without any thought or awareness of mood effects, affect is likely to influence our thinking style and the quality of the response. However, becoming aware that these effects occur, and being motivated to overcome them is likely to be a highly effective control strategy.

## ☐ Individual Differences in Affect Sensitivity

Not all people are equally influenced by their affective states, however. For example, personality traits such as neuroticism seem to increase the intensity and duration of negative affective reactions in particular [10]. Other traits are also important. We found that people who scored high on personality measures such as Machiavellianism (indicating a highly manipulative approach to people) and need for approval were less influenced by their moods when bargaining. Affect infusion was reduced for these people, because they habitually approach tasks such as bargaining from a highly motivated, pre-determined perspective. It is almost as if high Machiavellians and those high in need for approval had their minds made up about what to do and how to behave even before they started. As they did not rely on open, memory-based thinking, affect had much less of an opportunity to influence their plans and behaviors.

Perhaps predictably, individuals who score high on personality tests measuring openness to feelings are more influenced by mood when making consumer judgments than are low scorers [49]. Trait anxiety can also influence affect infusion. Low anxious people when feeling bad respond more negatively to a threatening out-group. High trait anxious individuals seem to do exactly the opposite [50]. In general, it seems clear that differences in personality or "temperament" do play an important role in how people deal with affect.

Indeed, the very concept of "emotional intelligence" refers to such enduring differences between people in terms of affective style (see Chapter 1 in this volume; [14]). Much of the evidence considered here suggests that individual differences in affectivity operate through a habitual preference for different ways of thinking. People who score high on measures such as self-esteem, Machiavellianism, social desirability or trait anxiety seem to respond to social situations in a motivated, controlled and highly directed fashion that makes it less likely that they openly search for, and use affectively loaded information from their memory.

## ☐ Toward an Integration: The Affect Infusion Model

As this necessarily brief review suggests, emotional intelligence requires an awareness that affect can have a powerful influence on the way people think and behave in social situations. Two major kinds of influences have been identified. *Informational* effects occur because affect informs the content of memories, thoughts and judgments. *Processing* effects occur because affect also influences how people deal with social information. However, it is also clear that affective influences on judgments and behavior are highly context specific. A comprehensive understanding of these effects—that is, becoming more "emotionally intelligent"—requires that we can specify the circumstances that promote or inhibit affect congruence, and also define the conditions that lead to affect infusion or its absence.

A recent integrative theory, the Affect Infusion Model (AIM [17], [51]) sought to accomplish this task by specifying the circumstances that promote an open, constructive processing style that leads to affect infusion. According to this model, the thinking strategies people can use in social situations differ in terms of two basic features: (1) the degree of *effort* invested, and (2) the degree of *openness* and *constructiveness* of the thinking strategy. The combination of these two features, quantity (effort), and quality (openness) of thinking defines four distinct processing styles: *substantive processing* (high effort/open, constructive), *motivated processing* (high effort/closed), *heuristic processing* (low effort/open, constructive) and *direct access processing* (low effort/closed).

Many social responses are based on the low effort *direct access strategy*, or the simple and direct retrieval of a pre-existing response. This is most likely when the task is highly familiar, and there is little need to engage in more elaborate thinking. For example, if asked in a street survey to rate a well-known political leader, reproducing a previously computed and stored evaluation will be sufficient. People possess a rich store of pre-formed attitudes and judgments. Retrieving them requires no constructive thinking and affect infusion should not occur. The second, *motivated processing strategy* involves highly selective and targeted thinking that is dominated by a particular motivational objective. This strategy also precludes open information search, and should be impervious to affect infusion. For example, if in a job interview you are asked about your attitude towards the company you want to join, the response will be dominated by the motivation to produce an acceptable response. Open, constructive processing is inhibited, and affect infusion is unlikely. Depending on the particular goal, motivated processing may also produce mood-incongruent responses and a reversal of affect infusion.

Simplified, *heuristic processing* is most likely when the task has little personal relevance, and there is no reason for more detailed processing. This kind of fast, superficial processing is likely for example when people respond to an unexpected telephone survey [52] or a street interview [21]. Heuristic processing can lead to affect infusion, if people use the simple "how do I feel about it" strategy. Finally, *substantive processing* is used when people need to fully and constructively deal with a social situation. This is an inherently open and constructive thinking style that characterizes most of our most personally relevant and important decisions.

The AIM predicts greater affect infusion whenever more substantive thinking is required to deal with a more demanding task. This paradoxical effect has been confirmed in a number of studies, as we have seen above. Unfamiliar, complex and atypical tasks should recruit more substantive thinking. Affect itself can also influence processing choices; as we have seen, positive affect promotes a more internally driven, top-down thinking style, and negative affect triggers more externally focused, bottom-up thinking. An integrative model such as the AIM makes a useful contribution to our understanding of emotional intelligence because it helps to specify the circumstances leading to the *absence* of affect infusion when direct access or motivated processing is used, and the *presence* of affect infusion during heuristic and substantive processing.

Two of the thinking styles identified by the model may also be involved in how we manage our everyday moods. We have seen that substantive processing typically facilitates affect infusion and the maintenance and accentuation of an existing affective state. In contrast, motivated processing may produce affect-incongruent responses, and the attenuation of the affective state. Affect management can thus be achieved as people spontaneously switch their information processing strategies between substantive and motivated processing so as to calibrate their prevailing moods. In other words, these two thinking styles may jointly constitute a dynamic, self-correcting mood management system. Several studies support this account. When responses by happy and sad people are monitored over time, initial mood congruence spontaneously gives way to mood incongruent responses [53]. This switch from "first congruent, then incongruent" responses suggests the existence of a spontaneous affect regulation system, and emotional intelligence is likely to involve a ready ability to switch from substantive to motivated thinking.

# ☐ Summary and Conclusions

This chapter has argued that emotional intelligence necessarily requires a degree of awareness of how affective states infuse our memories, thoughts, judgments and interpersonal behaviors. The research reviewed here suggests that different information processing strategies play a key role in explaining these effects. Theories such as the Affect Infusion Model seek to explain when and how affect influences everyday judgments and behaviors [17], [51]. A number of studies showed that more constructive, substantive thinking reliably increases affect infusion into thinking. Further, affect infusion also impacts a range of interpersonal behaviors, such as the use of requests, persuasive communication and strategic bargaining. We have also seen that positive and negative mood also produce different thinking strategies, and as a result, positive mood often increases and negative mood decreases memory and judgmental errors.

In contrast, affect infusion is reduced or absent whenever a social task can be performed using a simple, well-rehearsed direct access strategy, or a highly motivated strategy. Frequently, the social situations we face impose strong motivational demands to act in required ways that override these subtle mood effects. Sometimes, the pressures to act in a particular manner come from within. We have seen that certain personality traits can strongly predict how people will act. When people do not rely on open, constructive thinking to figure out what to do, mood states are much less likely to influence their responses. These general principles have important consequences in many real-life situations, and our understanding of emotional intelligence must include an appreciation of these effects.

Affect is thus likely to influence many relationship behaviors, group behaviors, organizational decisions, consumer preferences and health-related behaviors, and emotional intelligence necessary involves knowing when and how these effects occur (see Chapters 6 and 7 in this volume). Individuals who experience negative moods report more and more severe physical symptoms and more negative attitudes and beliefs about their ability to manage their health (see Chapter 11 in this volume). Recent studies also confirm that affect has a highly significant influence on many organizational behaviors and decisions (see Chapters 9 and 10 in this volume). The evidence we discussed clearly illustrates the multiple influences that affect has on interpersonal behavior. Being "emotionally intelligent" requires a degree of awareness of how and when these processes operate, as a first step towards controlling our emotional responses. Hopefully, the work described here will contribute to a greater understanding of the role of affect in social life.

## ☐ Acknowledgement

This work was supported by an Australian Professorial Fellowship by the Australian Research Council, and the Bellagio Fellowship by the Rockefeller Foundation, New York, to Joseph Forgas.

## ☐ References

1.  Kelly, J. R., & Spoor, J. R. (in press). Affective influence in groups. In J. P. Forgas (Ed.), Hearts and minds: The role of affect in social thinking and behavior. New York: Psychology Press.
2.  Koestler, A. (1978). *Janus: A summing up*. London: Hutchinson.
3.  Adolphs, R., & Damasio, A. (2001). The interaction of affect and cognition: A neurobiological perspective. In J. P. Forgas (Ed.), *The handbook of affect and social cognition* (pp. 27–49). Mahwah, NJ: Lawrence Erlbaum Associates, Inc.

4. Damasio, A. R. (1994). *Descartes' error: Emotion, reason and the human brain*. New York: Avon Books.
5. Blascovich, J., & Mendes, W. B. (2000). Challenge and threat appraisals: The role of affective cues. In J. P. Forgas (Ed.), *Feeling and thinking: The role of affect in social cognition* (pp. 131–152). New York: Cambridge University Press.
6. Forgas, J. P. (1982). Reactions to life dilemmas: Risk taking, success and responsibility attribution. *Australian Journal of Psychology, 34*, 25–35.
7. Niedenthal, P. M., & Halberstadt, J. H. (2000). Grounding categories in emotional response. In J. P. Forgas (Ed.), *Feeling and thinking: The role of affect in social cognition* (pp. 131–152). New York: Cambridge University Press.
8. Gilbert, D. T., & Wilson, T. D. (2000). Miswanting: Some problems in the forecasting of future affective states. In J. P. Forgas (Ed.), *Feeling and thinking: The role of affect in social cognition* (pp. 178–200). New York: Cambridge University Press.
9. Dunn, E. W., & Laham, S. M. (in press). A user's guide to emotional time travel: Progress on key issues in affective forecasting. In J. P. Forgas (Ed.), *Hearts and minds: Affective influences on social thinking and behaviour*. New York: Psychology Press.
10. Suls, J. (2001). Affect, stress and personality. In J. P. Forgas (Ed.), *Handbook of affect and social cognition* (pp. 392–409). Mahwah, NJ: Lawrence Erlbaum Associates, Inc.
11. Beck, J. S. (1995). *Cognitive therapy: Basics and beyond*. New York: Guilford Press.
12. Ellis, A. (2001). *Overcoming destructive beliefs, feelings, and behaviors: New directions for Rational Emotive Behavior Therapy*. Amherst, NY: Prometheus Books.
13. Razran, G. H. S. (1940). Conditioned response changes in rating and appraising sociopolitical slogans. *Psychological Bulletin, 37*, 481.
14. Mayer, J. D. (2001). Emotion, intelligence, and emotional intelligence. In J. P. Forgas (Ed.), *The handbook of affect and social cognition* (pp. 410–432). Mahwah, NJ: Lawrence Erlbaum Associates, Inc.
15. Clore, G. L., & Byrne, D. (1974). The reinforcement affect model of attraction. In T. L. Huston (Ed.), *Foundations of interpersonal attraction* (pp. 143–170). New York: Academic Press.
16. Bower, G. H. (1981). Mood and memory. *American Psychologist, 36*, 129–148.
17. Forgas, J. P. (1995a). Mood and judgment: The affect infusion model (AIM). *Psychological Bulletin, 117*(1), 39–66.
18. Forgas, J. P. (1994). Sad and guilty? Affective influences on the explanation of conflict episodes. *Journal of Personality and Social Psychology, 66*, 56–68.
19. Clore, G. L., Schwarz, N., & Conway, M. (1994). Affective causes and consequences of social information processing. In R. S. Wyer & T. K. Srull (Eds.), *Handbook of social cognition* (2nd ed., pp. 221–259). Mahwah, NJ: Lawrence Erlbaum Associates, Inc.
20. Schwarz, N. (1990). Feelings as information: Informational and motivational functions of affective states. In E. T. Higgins & R. Sorrentino (Eds.), *Handbook of motivation and cognition: Foundations of social behavior* (Vol. 2, pp. 527–561). New York: Guilford Press.
21. Forgas, J. P., & Moylan, S. J. (1987). After the movies: The effects of transient mood states on social judgments. *Personality and Social Psychology Bulletin, 13*, 478–489.
22. Berkowitz, L., Jaffee, S., Jo, E., & Troccoli, B. T. (2000). On the correction of feeling-induced judgmental biases. In J. P. Forgas (Ed.), *Feeling and thinking: The role of affect in social cognition* (pp. 131–152). New York: Cambridge University Press.
23. Forgas, J. P., Bower, G. H., & Krantz, S. (1984). The influence of mood on perceptions of social interactions. *Journal of Experimental Social Psychology, 20*, 497–513.
24. Forgas, J. P., Bower, G. H., & Moylan, S. J. (1990). Praise or blame? Affective influences on attributions for achievement. *Journal of Personality and Social Psychology, 59*, 809–818.
25. Forgas, J. P., & Bower, G. H. (1987). Mood effects on person perception judgements. *Journal of Personality and Social Psychology, 53*, 53–60.

26. Forgas, J. P. (1993). On making sense of odd couples: Mood effects on the perception of mismatched relationships. *Personality and Social Psychology Bulletin, 19*, 59–71.

27. Forgas, J. P. (1995b). Strange couples: Mood effects on judgments and memory about prototypical and atypical targets. *Personality and Social Psychology Bulletin, 21*, 747–765.

28. Sedikides, C. (1995). Central and peripheral self-conceptions are differentially influenced by mood: Tests of the differential sensitivity hypothesis. *Journal of Personality and Social Psychology, 69*(4), 759–777.

29. Wilson, T. D., Kraft, D., & Dunn, D. S. (1989). The disruptive effects of explaining attitudes: The moderating effect of knowledge about the attitude object. *Journal of Experimental Social Psychology, 25*(5), 379–400.

30. Wilson, T. D., Lisle, D. J., Schooler, J. W., & Hodges, S. D. (1993). Introspecting about reasons can reduce post-choice satisfaction. *Personality and Social Psychology Bulletin, 19*(3), 331–339.

31. Forgas, J. P., & Gunawardene, A. (2000). *Affective influences on spontaneous interpersonal behaviors*. Unpublished manuscript, University of New South Wales, Sydney, Australia.

32. Forgas, J. P. (1998b). Asking nicely? Mood effects on responding to more or less polite requests. *Personality and Social Psychology Bulletin, 24*, 173–185.

33. Forgas, J. P. (1999a). On feeling good and being rude: Affective influences on language use and request formulations. *Journal of Personality and Social Psychology, 76*, 928–939.

34. Forgas, J. P. (1999b). Feeling and speaking: Mood effects on verbal communication strategies. *Personality and Social Psychology Bulletin, 25*, 850–863.

35. Forgas, J. P., & Williams, K. D. (Eds.). (2002). *The social self*. New York: Psychology Press.

36. Forgas, J. P. (2005). *On being sad but influential: Affective influences on the production of persuasive messages*. Unpublished manuscript, University of New South Wales, Sydney, Australia.

37. Trope, Y., Ferguson, M., & Raghunathan, R. (2001). Mood as a resource in processing self-relevant information. In J. P. Forgas (Ed.), *Handbook of affect and social cognition* (pp. 256–274). Mahwah, NJ: Lawrence Erlbaum Associates, Inc.

38. Forgas, J. P. (1998a). On feeling good and getting your way: Mood effects on negotiation strategies and outcomes. *Journal of Personality and Social Psychology, 74*, 565–577.

39. Clark, M. S., & Isen, A. M. (1982). Towards understanding the relationship between feeling states and social behavior. In A. H. Hastorf & A. M. Isen (Eds.), *Cognitive social psychology* (pp. 73–108). New York: Elsevier-North Holland.

40. Bless, H. (2000). The interplay of affect and cognition: The mediating role of general knowledge structures. In J. P. Forgas (Ed.), *Feeling and thinking: The role of affect in social cognition* (pp. 201–222). New York: Cambridge University Press.

41. Fiedler, K. (2001). Affective influences on social information processing. In J. P. Forgas (Ed.), *Handbook of affect and social cognition* (pp. 163–185). Mahwah, NJ: Lawrence Erlbaum Associates, Inc.

42. Forgas, J. P., & George, J. M. (2001). Affective influences on judgments and behavior in organizations: An information processing perspective. *Organizational Behavior and Human Decision Processes, 86*, 3–34.

43. Petty, R. E., DeSteno, D., & Rucker, D. (2001). The role of affect in attitude change. In J. P. Forgas (Ed.), *The handbook of affect and social cognition* (pp. 212–236). Mahwah, NJ: Lawrence Erlbaum Associates, Inc.

44. Bodenhausen, G. V., Mussweiler, T., Gabriel, S., & Moreno, K. N. (2001). Affective influences on stereotyping and intergroup relations. In J. P. Forgas (Ed.), *The handbook of affect and social cognition* (pp. 319–343). Mahwah, NJ: Lawrence Erlbaum Associates, Inc.

45. Alloy, L. B., & Abramson, L. Y. (1988). Depressive realism: Four theoretical perspectives. In L. B. Alloy (Ed.), *Cognitive processes in depression* (pp. 223–265). New York: Guilford Press.

46. Forgas, J. P. (1998c). Happy and mistaken? Mood effects on the fundamental attribution error. *Journal of Personality and Social Psychology, 75,* 318–331.
47. Forgas, J. P., Vargas, P., & Laham, S. (in press). Mood effects on eyewitness accuracy. *Journal of Experimental Social Psychology.*
48. Moylan, S. J. (2000). *Affective influences on performance evaluation judgments.* Unpublished PhD thesis, University of New South Wales, Sydney, Australia.
49. Ciarrochi, J. V., & Forgas, J. P. (2002). The pleasure of possessions: Affect and consumer judgments. *European Journal of Social Psychology, 30,* 631–649.
50. Ciarrochi, J. V., & Forgas, J. P. (1999). On being tense yet tolerant: The paradoxical effects of trait anxiety and aversive mood on intergroup judgments. *Group Dynamics: Theory, Research and Practice, 3,* 227–238.
51. Forgas, J. P. (2002). Feeling and doing: Affective influences on interpersonal behavior. *Psychological Inquiry, 13,* 1–28.
52. Schwarz, N., & Clore, G. L. (1988). How do I feel about it? The informative function of affective states. In K. Fiedler & J. P. Forgas (Eds.), *Affect, cognition, and social behavior* (pp. 44–62). Toronto, Canada: Hogrefe.
53. Forgas, J. P., Ciarrochi, J. V., & Moylan, S. J. (2000). Subjective experience and mood regulation: The role of information processing strategies. In H. Bless & J. P. Forgas (Eds.), *The message within: The role of subjective experience in social cognition* (pp. 167–199). Philadelphia: Psychology Press.

Moshe Zeidner
Gerald Matthews
Richard D. Roberts

CHAPTER 5

# Emotional Intelligence, Coping with Stress, and Adaptation

This chapter examines two prominent concepts in modern day psychological research, emotional intelligence (EI) and coping with psychological stress. EI may be defined as a set of inter-related abilities for identifying, expressing, understanding, and managing emotions (e.g., [1–3]). Coping refers to the process of managing various demands that are appraised as personally threatening, challenging, or otherwise demanding [4]. Spurred by Goleman's best-selling book [5] drawing parallels between the two concepts, researchers have posited that effective coping with the demands, pressures, and conflicts evident in the home, at work, and in social life is central to the EI construct [6]. Indeed, the scientific merit of EI plausibly rests in demonstrating that it is a coherent quality of the person that underpins adaptive coping.

Research on EI has often neglected the extensive, and well-established, literature on stress, emotion, and coping. A person's vulnerability to stress symptoms (such as negative emotion and worry) is already capable of being assessed, with a high degree of validity, using existing personality (or other self-report) scales (e.g., [3]). The danger is that researchers are simply reinventing the wheel in couching stress vulnerability (and related constructs) under the rubric of "emotional intelligence." Viewed from another perspective, however, existing stress research may actually have missed something important about individual differences, which is captured by emerging models and measures of EI.

In this chapter, we examine current thinking and research investigating both EI and adaptive coping. Specifically, we evaluate the prospects for establishing EI as an explanatory construct in the domain of stress and coping and, in particular, whether the concept of EI, as a master faculty for adaptive coping, is compatible with existing stress theory. We begin with a schematic overview of the two constructs under consideration (i.e., EI and coping), followed by discussion of the proposed pattern of relations found between them. This is followed by a review of recent empirical research focusing on the EI–coping interface. Noting limitations in theory and research practice, we then present an heuristic model relating EI to adaptive coping from a transactional perspective. We conclude with a brief summary of the present status of the EI–coping relationship, pointing throughout to potential research strategies for conceptualizing and validating the EI construct within the stress domain.

# ☐ Conceptualizations of EI and Coping as Scientific Constructs

## Emotional Intelligence

EI has been defined as: the competence to identify, monitor, and express emotions; to label, differentiate, and understand the complex nature, antecedents, and consequences of emotions; to assimilate emotions in thought and strategically use emotions to achieve one's adaptive goals; and to effectively regulate positive and negative emotions, both in self and others. It is commonly claimed that EI is predictive of important criteria, beyond the proportion of variance general mental ability (GMA) and/or personality predicts. High EI may facilitate the way that an individual deals with stressful events, through accurate perception, understanding, and regulation of the negative emotions of the self and others, leading to more effective coping. Indeed, EI may contribute to handling challenging events successfully in a wide array of domains, including education [7], clinical intervention [3], and the workplace [8].

Despite popular appeal, there are still troubling issues in the conceptualization, measurement, and body of evidence supporting the utility of EI in applied domains. With respect to conceptualization, although researchers are making a concerted effort to map out the nomological network of EI [9], there are major definitional confusions evident in the scientific literature [10]. Thus, as the current volume attests, the construct remains slippery, with researchers failing to reach consensus as to whether EI should be conceptualized as a cognitive ability, a personality trait, or, as in popular writing, a grab-bag of desirable personal characteristics. No decision rules exist that allow us to evaluate personal qualities, such as empathy, assertiveness, and optimism, as emotionally intelligent behaviors or not [11]. It is also generally agreed that EI can be split into multiple components, yet there is no consensus on the nature (or even the dimensionality) of these components.

With respect to assessment, although several tests have been developed, mirroring the lack of a consensus in definition, it remains uncertain whether EI should be measured using objective (i.e., maximum performance) or self-report (i.e., typical performance) techniques [12]. Unfortunately, questionnaire measures of EI have proved to be highly confounded with existing personality (especially neuroticism) and stress symptom measures (see [13–16]). Current objective measures, such as the Mayer-Salovey-Caruso Emotional Intelligence Test (MSCEIT [17]), are perhaps more promising, but remain beleaguered by concerns, including problematic evidence for the proposed factor structure, low subscale reliabilities, and the biasing effects of cultural values and norms on the scoring procedures employed [10], [18–19].

With respect to the practical utility of EI, many current propositions presented in both the popular and specialist literatures have little empirical substance [2]. In organizational psychology, for example, various suggestions that the predictive validity of "EQ" exceeds that of "IQ" remain unsubstantiated [8]. In a rather acerbic critique, Brody goes farther: "There is not a single study reported that indicates that EI has nontrivial incremental validity for a socially important outcome variable after controlling for intelligence and personality" [18, p. 237]. Nevertheless, ability tests for EI (in particular) show some promise with respect to criteria such as quality of interpersonal relationships and interactions [20–21], and deviant behavior such as drug abuse and bullying. Even so, further work is necessary to ensure that "emotional intelligence" accounts for these relations (rather than some confounding variable influencing social functioning directly). Although work on social-emotional learning in schools is more promising [22], it is unclear if reference to EI adds anything to existing notions of training specific skills such as impulse control [7].

In sum, it is presently unclear if there is anything to EI that psychologists working within the fields of differential and applied psychology do not know already. Stripped of scientific trappings, it remains plausible that EI is nothing but the latest in a long line of psychological fads. Alternatively, because scientific research is just beginning, as are the development of more sophisticated measures [23], EI may indeed mature into a construct that is theoretically meaningful, empirically cogent, and practically useful. It is with these caveats in mind that we turn to discussion of the research on stress and coping.

# Stress and Coping

Transactional models (e.g., [4]) view stress as a multivariate process involving inputs (person and environmental variables), outputs (immediate and long-term effects), and the mediating activities of appraisal and coping processes [24]. According to this perspective, stress responses reflect a developing series of transactions between person and environment that may change as the stressful encounter unfolds over time. Any evaluation of a stressful encounter must perforce consider the challenges, constraints, and affordances of a particular situation in relation to one's personal resources and competencies. Notably, the transactional approach adds to biological and information-processing accounts of emotion by relating stress to "knowledge-level" constructs such as personal goals, intentions, self-beliefs, and the like (e.g., [25]). According to this perspective, stress represents a misalignment between external demands and personal motivations and abilities (capacities) rather than some pre-defined neurological or information-processing state.

Coping refers to a person's efforts to manage, control, or regulate threatening or challenging situations that are appraised as taxing or exceeding a person's resources [4]. Coping behaviors can minimize the impact of stress and alleviate its negative consequences. Three major protective functions of coping have been identified: (a) eliminating, modifying, or avoiding conditions giving rise to problems, (b) perceptually controlling or reinterpreting meanings of experience in a manner that neutralizes stress, and (c) keeping emotional consequences of problems within manageable bounds [26]. Thus, handling the aversive cognitions and emotions invoked in a stressful encounter may be critical to negotiating it successfully [25].

The coping process entails cognitive appraisals, identification of potential coping strategies, and implementation of actual coping behaviors in a particular setting [27]. Appraisals, which often guide the choice of coping strategy, may be distinguished along two main dimensions [4]. Primary appraisals, such as threat, refer to the immediate personal significance of the stimulus, whereas secondary appraisals represent the person's evaluation of how they might cope with stressful demands or control antecedents and consequences. Lazarus and Folkman [4] further distinguish two broad categories of coping. Emotion-focused coping comprises sequences of self-referent cognitions that aim to regulate distressing emotions, channel negative affect, and reconceptualize the problem (e.g., by looking on the bright side). Problem-focused coping is directed towards changing external reality, and typically refers to behaviors intended to resolve the problem. Other authors discriminate avoidance of the problem (e.g., through distraction) as yet another basic type of coping (e.g., [28]).

Both the nature of the situation and various intrapersonal qualities influence appraisal and coping mechanisms. Controllable situations are more likely to elicit appraisals of challenge and task-focused coping, whereas uncontrollable situations elicit threat appraisals and emotion-focused coping [29–30]. In addition, personality factors are reliably associated with biases in appraisal and coping [31]. People have preferred styles of cognition, so that how a person copes in a particular situation depends on an interaction between habitual appraisals/coping preferences and the situation itself. GMA may also make some contribution to adaptive coping; evidence suggests that intelligence measures correlate with constructs related to confidence in one's own coping abilities, such as self-efficacy and ego resiliency (e.g., [32–34]). Persons high on GMA may handle stress more adaptively because they manage, for example, to perceive situations in more realistic ways [33]. At the same time, there is clearly more to successful coping than GMA; correlations between conventional ability measures and coping scales are modest, at best.

Plausibly, EI measures may be superior to intelligence tests in their capacity to predict how successfully individuals will handle stressful environments. Within this context, for EI to have explanatory power, it must be distinguished from stress outcomes, perhaps serving as a set of competencies that controls whether a person handles and copes with demanding events successfully. In other words, the level of a person's EI should tell us not just about his or her propensity to experience stress symptoms, but also the underlying causes of stress vulnerability, and how to measure these causal factors independently of assessments of distress. For example, if the key to EI is good emotion regulation, then we should be able to assess the person's emotion regulation under non-stressful conditions, and show that emotion regulation predicts lower distress when the person is under pressure.

## ☐ The EI Perspective on Coping

Proponents of EI have embraced the notion of adaptive coping as "emotional intelligence in action," supporting mastery of emotions, emotional growth, and both cognitive and emotional differentiation, allowing us to evolve in an ever-changing world (e.g., [5], [35]). Current thinking among these researchers suggests that "heeding the wisdom" provided by the emotional system determines effective coping behaviors and shapes adaptive outcomes. For example, Salovey et al. claim that EI helps individuals cope successfully because they "accurately perceive and appraise their emotional states, know how and when to express their feelings, and can effectively regulate their mood states" [35, p. 161].

According to such accounts, it is not just stressful environmental demands that call for coping resources, but also the aversive emotions evoked by external demands. Coping strategies that perpetuate negative moods and cognitions (or that over time exacerbate demands) may serve to turn a minor hassle into a major source of upset. For example, becoming angry, brooding, and eventually retaliating in response to a neighbor's annoying habits might generate a protracted feud or lead to a courtroom appearance. Thus, maladaptive coping may be a consequence of difficulties in processing emotional material (i.e., low EI; see [35]). Conversely, clarity of thought and experience seems to promote well-being and active regulation of mood, while emotional disclosure may promote adaptive self-transformation (e.g., [36]). Similarly, Epstein [37] views EI as a personal antecedent of adaptive coping, with EI operating through various causal processes (e.g., obtaining social support) that sustain effective handling of emotional challenges (see also [35]). However, the nature of these associations is nebulous; few studies have tested the mediating role of emotion-regulation in conferring hardiness under stress to the more emotionally intelligent individual.

The preceding account suggests that there may be several mediating mechanisms that might account for the proposed relationship between EI and coping. In the sections that follow, consideration is given to these accounts, posited in the main by researchers working with the construct of EI, along with supporting evidence. Because this research represents a relatively new domain of inquiry, we also highlight, where relevant, issues that need to be resolved in order to give these accounts more credibility.

## Avoidance of Stressful Encounters

Plausibly, the emotionally intelligent individual has less stress because they conduct their personal affairs in environments that produce fewer frustrating events. These individuals may be adept at identifying, and thus avoiding, potentially dangerous or harmful social contexts due to careful monitoring of the emotional cues that are available from social situations [37]. Although this is an attractive proposition, there is presently no hard empirical evidence supporting these claims. Moreover, contrary to this hypothesis, adaptive success may require engaging with, and successfully managing, aversive environments. For example, studies of social anxiety suggest that avoidance of stressful circumstances undermines self-confidence and hinders the acquisition of social skills [38]. Rather than avoiding stressful encounters it might therefore be hypothesized that the person high in EI learns more quickly in social and emotional situations relative to others. Similar to learning differences between people on GMA, emotionally intelligent individuals might make coping "mistakes" less often until an adaptive style is learned, whereas individuals low in EI might try the same maladaptive coping strategy (like rumination) over and over again. Clearly, an event sampling study, testing these rival hypotheses is warranted.

## More Constructive Perceptions and Situational Appraisals

Emotionally intelligent individuals, it is claimed, may be characterized by more constructive thought patterns. As a result, these individuals may find it easier to identify faulty appraisals and to correct maladaptive construals [37]. High EI individuals may also more faithfully observe the procession of their thoughts, and their impact on emotion, whereas low EI individuals may tend to ruminate unproductively about the antecedents and consequences of their problems. This, in turn, leads high EI individuals to interpret stressful conditions, if unavoidable, in a more benign and less stressful way, viewing them more as challenges than as threats [37]. Individuals who make sense out of their feelings have also been shown to have greater rebound from induced negative mood and reduced rumination [39]. However, there is a lack of direct evidence on whether EI actually exerts a causal influence on rumination, an issue that we return to shortly.

## Adaptive Regulation and Repairing of Emotions

Both clarity and repair of emotions are components of EI that are postulated to be essential ingredients for adaptive coping [40]. Those skilled at regulating emotions appear better able to repair negative emotional states, by engaging, for example, in pleasant activities as a distraction from negative affect. Furthermore, high EI individuals are thought not to be overly sensitive to disapproval and to worry less about things that are beyond control [37]. Another key emotional skill may be effective disclosure of past personal traumas. For example, Pennebaker [36] has shown that the simple act of disclosing emotional experience (through writing) improves a person's physical and mental health (e.g., improving immune functioning, decreasing depression). The disclosure process may restructure emotionally disturbing experiences, giving them a coherent and meaningful place in the person's life. Additional research is needed, however, to investigate whether measures of EI are associated with the use of more effective strategies for managing mood and emotionally charged memories.

## Richer Coping Resources

Emotionally intelligent individuals may have richer emotional and social coping resources compared to their less emotionally intelligent counterparts, leading to more positive appraisals of personal competence in handling stressful encounters [37]. In particular, EI has been hypothesized to work through social support [35]. Accordingly, EI has been claimed to equip the individual with the necessary skills and social connections required to build an extensive and supportive social network. In times of need, emotionally intelligent individuals are better able to rely on rich social networks to provide an emotional buffer against negative events [40]. Recent research by the present authors (see below) supports the mediating role of social support in the EI–coping relationship, but hard evidence for the importance of other personal resources in mediating the EI–coping interface is sparse and in need of further empirical instantiation.

## Use of Effective and Flexible Coping Strategies

It has also been claimed that individuals with high EI engage in active coping during stressful situations, whereas those low in EI tend to opt for less adaptive emotion-focused (or sometimes avoidance) responses in similar situations (e.g., [37]). Problem-focused coping has been associated with the competencies to clearly perceive, differentiate, and repair one's own emotions. According to this line of reasoning, people need to perceive their feelings clearly in a stressful situation and believe they are capable of managing their emotions in order for them to cope adaptively. In short, "a time-honored principle of effective coping is to know when to appraise a situation as uncontrollable and hence abandon efforts directed at altering the situation and turn to emotion-focused processes in order to tolerate or accept the situation" [41, p. 849]. However, much research has made unwarranted assumptions about the adaptiveness of coping strategies associated with EI; another issue that we take up in the sections that follow.

It is evident from these sections that the scope of individual differences in coping linked to EI is very broad. Some of the mediating mechanisms (e.g., adaptive regulation) refer directly to coping with emotion itself. Other mechanisms, such as managing exposure to stressors, are more likely to influence emotion indirectly, depending on the outcome of the encounter. However, it is unclear which of these various mechanisms should be related primarily to EI and which to other personality and ability factors; the place of EI in the nomological network connecting different stress-related constructs remains uncertain.

# ☐ Empirical Research on EI and Coping

Research devoted to uncovering relations between EI and effective coping strategies has generally touched on two related issues. The first, simpler, issue has involved determining how EI measures correlate with established coping scales. The second, more subtle, issue has involved ascertaining whether coping mediates associations between EI and well-being. In a study typical of the former approach, Brackett and Mayer [15] found that psychological well-being correlated at .54 and .69 with two questionnaire scales assessing EI, and .28 with the more objective measure, the MSCEIT. As we have noted elsewhere, there are a variety of explanations for the self-report correlations, including the confounding influence of personality traits, self-enhancing response biases, and "criterion contamination" in that some EI questionnaires contain items assessing well-being (e.g., [2], [10]). Published questionnaire-based studies have failed to test these competing hypotheses. Thus, findings based on objective assessments are arguably more compelling, although in the review that follows, we consider studies that follow both approaches.

Moreover, the hypothesis that EI leads to more effective coping, which in turn leads to more positive outcomes from social encounters, appears defensible. However, direct tests of the mediating role of coping are sparse. In surveying this literature, it is convenient to divide studies according to the EI measure used. These are: (1) overt EI questionnaires (i.e., studies using the Emotional Quotient Inventory, EQ-i [13]; and Schutte Self-Report Inventory, SSRI [42]), (2) mood-regulation questionnaires (which focus almost exclusively on the Trait Meta Mood Scale, TMMS [43]), and (3) quasi-objective tests (i.e., studies using the MSCEIT [17]). Treating these studies as though giving different insights into relations between EI and coping is of necessity; as noted from the outset, it is uncertain that these different scales converge on any common, core construct, such that they may be differentially related to coping and stress criteria.

An early empirical finding, using questionnaires, was that the EQ-i correlates moderately with high problem-focused coping and low emotion-focused coping [13]. Given that these coping strategies are commonly viewed as adaptive, this finding suggests that self-reported EI might be related to adaptive forms of coping. Exactly this result would be expected, however, based on the high correlation reported between the EQ-i and neuroticism, which is similarly related to coping [28]. Chan [44] reported that, in a sample of gifted adolescents in Hong Kong, the SSRI correlated with various aspects of social coping, including valuing peer acceptance and involvement in activities. Again, personality confounds were not addressed. Furnham, Petrides, and Spencer-Bowdage [45] showed that the SSRI was positively related to repressive coping; i.e., coping through suppressing feelings of anxiety and other negative emotions. They suggest that repressive copers may be better adapted than is usually supposed. Indeed, although repressors show relatively little grief following bereavement, they are no worse adjusted than nonrepressors in the long term [46].

In further investigations using the SSRI, Ciarrochi, Deane, and Anderson [47] examined components of EI and coping. Multiple regression analyses suggested that managing the emotions of others predicted lower levels of hopelessness and suicidal ideation more so than any other construct. Ciarrochi et al. [47] suggest that the effects of this factor may be mediated by more effective mood-regulation of others, leading to greater availability of social support. In another study exploring the factors comprising EI, Ciarrochi, Chan, and Bajgar [48] found that managing self-relevant emotions related to mood-regulation strategies, although the SSRI factors did not moderate emotional response to negative and positive mood inductions used in this study.

In a study designed to assess self-reported mood-regulation rather than EI *per se*, Salovey et al. [39] found that emotion repair related to greater active coping, less passive coping, less rumination, and the perception of laboratory stressors as being less threatening. Two additional scales comprising the TMMS—emotional clarity and attention to emotion—were related to psychophysiological indices of reduced response to stressors, including lowered cortisol responses. Gohm and Clore [49] used the TMMS and other scales relating to the experience and regulation of emotion to derive several latent factors including clarity, attention, and emotional expression, which were then correlated with a number of subscales of the COPE inventory [27]. Across two separate studies, attention and emotional expression were, consistently, significantly correlated with coping strategies, including seeking emotional social support and focusing and venting negative emotions, whereas clarity was most consistently associated with active, planful coping and positive reinterpretation. Gohm and Clore [49] also present some limited analyses of possible confounds with personality, suggesting that in some cases the emotion regulation factors showed incremental validity with respect to the Big Five personality factors. In these analyses, emotional expression and attention appeared to be more robust predictors of coping than clarity about one's own emotions.

The third group of studies, those using quasi-objective tests, offers somewhat indirect evidence on EI and coping. Ciarrochi et al. [20] found that high scorers on the MEIS were more likely than low scorers to retrieve positive memories during mood induction, suggesting an influence on mood regulation. Ciarrochi et al. [47] also found that an objective measure of emotion perception moderated the impact of hassles on depression, hopelessness, and suicidal ideation. Perhaps surprisingly, people good at emotion perception showed greater levels of depression when life hassles were high. This is in accordance with the finding that depressive people have a more realistic view of the world than nondepressives. The authors suggest that either emotional insensitivity may have a protective effect, or that individuals with poor perception may be unaware of their affective responses to stress. Finally, Ciarrochi, Caputi, and Mayer [50] showed that another objective test, the Levels of Emotional Awareness Scale [51], was weakly associated with perceived social support, but not with any mental health outcome measures. Self-report measures of social problem-solving ability and emotion control were more predictive of mental health in this study. Based on these results one might speculate that perceived EI, as operationalized by self-report measures, is sometimes more predictive of adaptive coping than objective EI, implying circumstances in which self-confidence is more important than actual competence.

Turning to the authors' own studies, we set out to explore the nexus of relations between EI and coping strategies, using both correlational and experimental designs [52]. Across four studies, EI was measured using the MSCEIT. The first study examined the EI–coping association, statistically controlling for personality and cognitive ability. The respondents were 163 college students (54% female) with a mean age of 26.67 ($SD$ = 6.91) years. As expected, a moderate positive correlation ($r$ = .28) was found between performance-based EI and problem-focused coping strategies, while a weak negative correlation ($r$ = –.22) was found between EI and emotion-focused coping strategies (with coping assessed by the Coping Inventory for Stressful Situations [28]). These relations were significant even when statistically controlling for the Big Five personality factors and intelligence level (assessed by the Ravens Progressive Matrices).

In a second study, we explored the potential mediating role of a number of factors in the EI–coping relation, including social support, rumination, and self-efficacy (cf. [35]). Participants included 187 students (61% female) at the University of Haifa, with a mean age of 23.37 ($SD$ = 2.98). Consistent with data reported by Gohm and Clore [49], EI was modestly correlated with a number of active coping tactics, including positive reinforcement and planning, seeking social support, and "emotional ventilation." Furthermore, EI was negatively correlated with a number of dysfunctional avoidant strategies, including alcohol use, denial, and behavioral disengagement. Analysis of the role of postulated mediating variables confirm the hypothesized role of social support in mediating the EI–coping relationship. This finding suggests that high EI individuals use their emotional competencies to create a rich supportive social network that may serve as a buffer against the aversive effects of stressful encounters.

The third study was designed to ascertain whether high EI individuals employ coping strategies more effectively (i.e., use problem-focused coping in situations viewed as controllable and emotion-focused coping in unalterable situations [4]; cf. [28]). To test these hypotheses, we assessed EI in a sample of 200 Israeli students, asking them to describe their coping behaviors under controllable versus uncontrollable stressful situations. In fact, high EI students were no more likely than their low EI counterparts to use problem-focused coping under controllable conditions, or emotion-focused coping strategies under uncontrollable conditions. The data, therefore, did not vindicate the hypothesis.

The Mayer et al. [1] model of EI predicts more effective coping and fewer disturbances of mood and cognition in challenging situations. To examine this proposition, we conducted a fourth study aimed at identifying individual differences in the processing of information under neutral and stressful conditions by means of the Emotional Stroop paradigm [9]. Participants were requested to name the color of a neutral word or stressful term related to the prolonged spate of terror attacks in Israel (e.g., "suicide bomber"), whilst their reaction time was being measured. It was hypothesized that people with high EI will effectively regulate their attention and emotions and will therefore not be negatively impacted by negative emotions when confronted with the lexical stimuli. The hypothesis was not confirmed; high and low EI participants responded at the same rate to negatively valenced stimuli.

A study of 200 college students, conducted at the University of Cincinnati, links the MSCEIT to coping and subjective stress response [53]. The study aimed to redress some of the weaknesses of existing research, by inducing stress experimentally, by assessing coping strategies applied to the specific situation, by controlling for the Big Five personality traits, and by taking objective behavioral measures (performance). Participants were randomly allocated to a control condition (reading magazines) or one of three stressful task conditions validated in previous research (see [54]). The Dundee Stress State Questionnaire was administered before and after performance. Results confirmed that the three stress conditions induced different patterns of subjective stress response, including increases in distress greater than one standard deviation relative to the control condition, across all three experimental manipulations. Participants also completed the Coping in Task Situations questionnaire [55], which assesses use of task-focused, emotion-focused, and avoidance strategies in performance settings. EI was associated with lower distress and worry, and with reduced use of emotion-focus and avoidance coping, strategies likely to be maladaptive in the performance context. The association with emotion focus was eliminated when the Big Five were controlled, with neuroticism emerging as the main predictor, but EI contributed uniquely, though weakly, to the prediction of avoidance. Further analysis showed, however, that distress and worry correlated with EI prior to any exposure to stress, and the task-induced elevation of distress actually tended to be higher in more emotionally intelligent individuals. In addition, EI failed to predict objective performance measures. Thus, the coping style of the higher EI participants did not, in fact, appear to produce more adaptive outcomes, at least over the short time-span of the study. These findings suggest that the MSCEIT does not predict tolerance of specific task stressors, but rather registers greater social involvement, and hence better mood, in general.

To summarize, correlations between EI and coping appear moderate to high, especially when EI is assessed using questionnaires. However, research has yet to establish that EI plays some unique role in the coping process. Thus, most self-report measures of EI have proved to be highly confounded with existing personality and stress symptom measures (e.g., [16]). Research using more narrowly focused mood-regulation questionnaires such as the TMMS appear promising, especially as (1) these measures may be less confounded with personality than are EI questionnaires [49], and (2) one study shows evidence for meaningful psychophysiological correlates [39]. Objective tests for EI appear to be more modest predictors of both coping and well-being/stress outcomes; our own work suggests, however, that the MSCEIT has some incremental validity with respect to personality and ability (e.g., [9]). One problem common to each approach is that the mechanisms linking EI constructs to coping and stress outcomes remain obscure. For example, our studies with the MSCEIT have failed to show that EI moderates stress response as expected. The most promising mediating mechanism, from all available studies, appears to be social support, which has been implicated both in the effects of self-reported [47] and performance-based EI [9].

## ☐ EI from the Perspective of Transactional Stress and Coping Theory

Much of the research reviewed thus far is limited by its relative neglect of the theory of stress offered by the transactional model [4], [25], [56]. The transactional model emphasizes the study of stress within specific situations and suggests that only limited conclusions may be drawn by correlating EI with scales for generic styles of coping; these are likely not predictive of how the individual negotiates specific stressful encounters. In the sections that follow, we discuss the meaning of "adaptive" coping, which is central to the transactional model. We also ascertain whether emotionally intelligent people tend to use specific coping styles. In an attempt to bridge the gap between current EI theory and the transactional model, avenues for future research are also suggested.

## The Transactional Model of Stress and Coping

The transactional model calls for a contextual definition of effectiveness in handling an emotionally laden situation. Thus, in a given situation, adaptive coping protects us by eliminating (or modifying) the conditions that produce stress or by keeping the emotional consequences within manageable bounds [57]. Within this situated context, "adaptive" refers to "the effectiveness of coping in improving the adaptational outcome" [56, p. 237]. Adaptive or functional coping behavior is seen as a "buffer" that absorbs the impact of stressful events, protecting the individual from the immediate, damaging effects of stress, including physiological disturbance and emotional distress. It also maximizes the chances of "rising to the challenge" and making the most of any opportunities for personal gain that the situation affords. Conversely, maladaptive coping fails to resolve the situation successfully, and may even exacerbate the problems that the individual is experiencing.

Many outcome criteria have been proposed for judging coping effectiveness including, reduction of physiological reactions and psychological distress, normative functioning, and perceived coping effectiveness (e.g., [58]). Ideally, successful coping should lead to satisfactory task completion with little additional residual outcomes while maintaining a positive emotional state [26]. In some instances, outcomes may be universally positive or negative. More typically, outcomes are mixed, and represented by some complex pattern of costs and benefits. So far, research has provided no metric for integrating mixed outcomes, so that there are no universal criteria for assessing coping effectiveness [24]. For example, it is unclear how we should gauge outcomes such as (1) failing to achieve a goal but still feeling good about oneself, (2) experiencing high distress and physiological disturbance but eventually prevailing, or (3) choosing to enjoy short-term gains at the expense of long-term losses in emotional state. Self-reports of preferred outcomes are limited to the extent that some personal goals (e.g., to get high on drugs) may prove to be destructive to the person's well-being and social status: people do not always avoid what is bad for them.

Most relevant research has employed limited outcome measures that may not fully capture adaptation. In general, such research provides only weak support for common assumptions about coping effectiveness, i.e., that task focus is better than emotion focus and avoidance (see [24]).

Determining the coping behaviors that are most effective in the short and long term, their contexts, and relevance to the individual poses a series of conceptual and empirical problems. Clearly, coping responses are not uniformly adaptive; some strategies work with modest effects, sometimes, for some people, although even here the magnitudes of effects are frequently disappointing. Work on "coping flexibility" [59] points towards one new avenue that might be relevant to EI.

In fact, a basic tenet of transactional theory is that we cannot prejudge particular strategies employed in dealing with managing stressful emotional encounters as being universally adaptive or maladaptive (see [24], [56]). Rather, the concern must be for whom and under what circumstances a particular mode of coping has adaptive consequences, requiring attention to the social and cultural context of coping, the specific time course of coping, and the manifold functions and consequences of particular coping behaviors [24] (see also [60]). Each coping strategy confers both benefits and costs; strategies often viewed as maladaptive (e.g., avoidance, distancing) may be adaptive under some circumstances, while even problem-focused strategies may sometimes be maladaptive. Thus, while correlating EI measures with coping scales helps us to integrate the construct with the wider world of stress research, cross-sectional correlational studies tell us little about whether more emotionally intelligent individuals do, in fact, obtain significant real-life benefits by virtue of their coping styles.

## Modeling EI and Coping from a Transactional Perspective

If coping is a more complex construct than some researchers have assumed, so too is EI. Within the present context, EI encapsulates various stable qualities of the person, represented in long-term memory, which bias the temporal unfolding of the cycle of interaction between person and external demands [60]. It is unclear, however, whether these various qualities relate to a single construct. Matthews, Zeidner, and Roberts [61] have distinguished four distinct conceptualizations of EI that may not necessarily be subsumed under an overarching, general EI factor. In the sections below, we consider these along with implications for a transactional model of stress and coping.

### *Temperamental Qualities*

This type of construct refers to biases such as sensitivity to positive and negative affect that may influence well-being. For example, the neuroticism personality trait correlates with a variety of stress processes and outcome measures, as well as with low EI, especially as assessed by self-report. Some researchers might wish to exclude temperament from the sphere of EI, although it may play a major role in current questionnaires.

## Information-Processing Components

This concept describes specific processing components such as those supporting the accurate perception of emotions. An acknowledged limitation of stress research is that it has tended to focus on broad classes of constructs (e.g., coping strategies), rather than focusing on objectively assessed processing constructs. Thus, the role that information processes (e.g., identifying emotion in faces) play in relation to stress and related outcomes has been neglected. Some research, however, suggests that attentional and interpretive biases may contribute to anxiety [62].

## Emotional Self-Regulation Mechanisms

This conceptualization of EI refers to processes such as maintaining self-esteem and confidence in demanding circumstances, and overlaps with constructs such as mood management, emotional clarity, and repair (e.g., [40]). Individual differences in emotional self-regulation potentially represent a unique contribution of EI research to understanding stress (see [47]).

## Emotional Knowledge

This conceptualization of EI refers to acquired, contextualized skills for handling specific encounters (e.g., calming an upset friend). As with cognitive skills, such emotional skills may be numerous, and highly specialized for specific problems. They may also be represented as either explicit knowledge, such as that assessed by the MSCEIT, or as implicit, procedural skills. The latter is currently underrepresented by extant measures of EI.

Figure 5.1 represents these different categories of construct within a framework suggested by Lazarus and Folkman's transactional model of stress [4], coupled with Wells and Matthews' account of self-regulation and emotion [30]. Following Lazarus [25], it is postulated that when a person is experiencing a stressful event (or indeed any event), processing of incoming stimuli produces appraisals, which guide subsequent attempts at coping. Coping may be realized either through reappraisal, or through overt behaviors, potentially influencing multiple adaptive outcomes, which may take any of the various forms indicated in Figure 5.1.

Maladaptation might be signaled by failure to attain a significant goal, subjective distress, health problems, or disruptions in the relationships

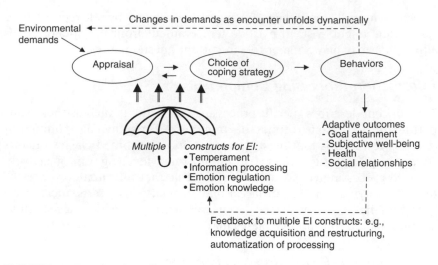

**FIGURE 5.1.** Emotional intelligence within the transactional model of stress.

that an individual has with others. The person remains in dynamic interaction with the external environment. Thus, feedback from outcomes may influence both the external demands themselves (e.g., exacerbation of the problem) and/or the person's own cognitions of the situation, which may change some of the more malleable aspects of EI, such as specific learned processing routines (e.g., associative memory retrieval) and the content of knowledge. Figure 5.1 groups together multiple, independent constructs under the umbrella heading of EI. We assume that there are multiple mechanisms that support biasing effects of these constructs on appraisal and coping, but we have little knowledge of the specific paths that influence coping.

Conventional accounts of EI (e.g., [14]) assume that people can be rank ordered in terms of their personal coping efficacy, reflecting a coherent set of underlying competencies for handling affectively loaded encounters. The simple causal chain is that emotional competence leads to more effective coping that, in turn, leads to more positive outcomes. However, the transactional perspective we have developed presents challenges for this position.

First, competencies may be largely independent of each other. If EI represents a coherent psychological construct, then different competencies should be correlated. With respect to stress, the various, distinct mechanisms for adaptive coping should intercorrelate. Thus, individuals who are effective at mood regulation should also possess a richer and more effective repertoire of coping strategies, and should be adept at resolving conflicts. However, competencies identified with EI might not be positively correlated. For example, a ruthless CEO might be highly effective in managing others' behaviors to attain corporate goals, but lack empathy. Conceivably, handling emotive situations might be influenced by a variety of unrelated competencies. If so, EI (like "stress") might be a useful umbrella label for a broad area of inquiry, but the term should not be assumed to identify a single, global construct.

Indeed, current research questions the conceptual coherence of a single, unifying EI construct. Measures related to the four different conceptualizations of EI shown in Figure 5.1 are often only weakly correlated (and differentially related to the various tests for EI). For example, self-reports of emotional competence often appear to have poor validity as predictors of objective behaviors, exemplified by Ciarrochi et al.'s finding [47] that objective and subjective emotion perception measures are independent, although it should be noted that objective measures tend to assess perceptions of others, whereas subjective measures refer to both self and others. A recent study suggests that the MSCEIT is a poor predictor of information-processing tasks such as perception of emotion in voices and faces, and the Emotional Stroop (see [63]). Furthermore, within each conceptual category, there are multiple constructs that may be differentially related to EI. For example, researchers on temperament and personality have found it essential to differentiate extraversion and neuroticism as separate influences on affect, possibly relating to different brain systems; they cannot be lumped together as a single emotionality dimension.

Consider for example, the competencies contributing to "managing emotions," one of the core abilities contributing to EI, which involves understanding one's feelings and managing their expression [1], [64]. Multiple factors might contribute to difficulties in emotional management (see also [65]), including one or more of the following:

1. Temperamental qualities leading to rapid escalation of emotions or tendencies to experience emotions intensely rather than mildly.
2. Deficiencies in information processing, such as selecting verbal descriptors for emotions and accessing memories of personal emotional experiences.
3. Deficiencies in regulating maladaptive emotions such as perpetuating negative moods and inability to improve mood.
4. Lack of knowledge relevant to handling specific contexts, such as recognition and coping with specific environmental triggers for mood disturbance.

Thus, a problem with anger at work might variously reflect temperamental irritability, misappraisals of others as hostile (information processing), brooding on themes of injustice and retaliation (self-regulation), or lack of skills for dealing with specific sources of frustration such as an uncooperative coworker (knowledge). It is far from clear that these different sources of dysfunctional anger management can be grouped together as lack of EI. In the larger context of person–environment interaction, the nature of the misregulation might also depend on the immediate impact of the person's style of behavioral expression on others (e.g., swearing when angry) and the longer term consequences of outcomes, such as health problems, acquiring a reputation for being antagonistic, or the development of a generally hostile work environment.

Second, coping strategies may not be universally adaptive or maladaptive. It is assumed that the coping strategies linked to EI, such as use of problem focus in place of emotion focus, are generally effective. However, as previously discussed, we cannot in general partition coping strategies into those that are adaptive and those that are not. In any case, the outcomes of coping are complex and multifaceted. In other words, operationalizations of EI may not signal overall adaptive advantages but qualitatively different patterns of costs and benefits related to the preferred mode of coping. Low EI may sometimes bring adaptive benefits as well as costs. For example, neuroticism (related to low EI) relates to coping through maintaining attention on potential threats and personal failings, a style of coping that depresses mood but also supports early anticipation of danger [3].

Third, adaptations may be situation-specific. People with high EI should express it in a variety of situations (cf. [24]). For example, individuals with good impulse control appear able to resist qualitatively different impulses. However, this need not be the case; consider, for example, the eating disorder patient who might be good at resisting all impulses except the desire to eat compulsively. Research on EI has neglected situational moderators by almost exclusively operationalizing coping and stress through global measures. Personality research suggests that each trait is adaptive in some contexts but not others [31]; for example, extraverts are equipped to handle demanding social encounters, whereas introverts fare better in unstimulating situations requiring sustained information processing. Existing research provides some clues that EI constructs too may not be universally adaptive. Baumeister, Smart, and Boden [66] identified a "dark side" of self-esteem, including denial of problems and excessive self-enhancement. Ciarrochi et al. [47] found that individuals with good objective emotion perception may be vulnerable to negative affective responses to daily hassles. Although some studies have shown beneficial effects of expressing or writing about personal emotions [36], Bonanno [46] points to data showing that focusing on and expressing of the negative emotions brought about by grieving is associated with delayed recovery; regulation or minimization of negative grief-related emotions is more effective.

In our research, we are beginning to find some contexts in which EI is not strongly adaptive (attention to terrorism threats, managing high work-loads), but there may be allied situations (dealing with grief over victims of terrorism, team performance) in which one or more of the EI constructs does moderate stress response. At this point, we simply do not know which contexts are most relevant, and there is an urgent need for studies focusing on the role of EI in facing specific types of challenge. Thus, it appears that interpreting EI as representing some global coping ability is misconceived. It is difficult to categorize coping strategies as generally adaptive or maladaptive (except, perhaps, in the case of dysfunctional strategies associated with clinical disorders). Likewise, individuals cannot be classified as more or less adapted in some generic sense: individual differences in adaptation to external demands and pressures appear to be context bound, and contingent upon the criteria used to define "adaptation." Adaptive coping in a given situation depends on a variety of independent competencies, and their interaction with unique features of the situation itself.

## ☐ Summary and Conclusions

EI researchers claim that successful coping depends on the integrated operation of rational as well as emotional competencies [40]. Accordingly, the entire hierarchy of emotional competencies referred to as "emotional intelligence," discussed throughout, may contribute to the successful regulation of emotion and coping. Furthermore, emotional competencies may impact adaptive coping through a number of mediating processes (i.e., coping resources, flexible coping strategies, and so forth).

Cross-sectional studies substantiate associations between EI and various coping scales. Studies converge in pointing to the positive association between EI and problem-focused strategies and a negative association between EI and emotion-focused and avoidance strategies. It is tempting to conclude that EI simply relates to greater use of more positively toned strategies and less use of strategies that focus on negative aspects of challenge (cf. [45]). The empirical data leave many issues unresolved, including the extent to which findings are simply a consequence of the well-known confounding of EI scales with personality. Biases towards positively framed coping strategies, and away from negatively framed strategies, are exactly what might be expected on the basis of the overlap between EI and (1) extraversion and (2) low neuroticism (e.g., [16]). Perhaps more promising than studies using global coping measures are those that have investigated EI, coping, and mood regulation within specific contexts (e.g., [47–48]). Nevertheless, the personality and situational factors that moderate the impact of EI on coping remain obscure, and it has yet to be established that the coping styles character-istic of high scorers on tests for EI actually confer any real benefits in terms of well-being, behavioral adaptation, or health.

Our review of the EI literature also demonstrates the vague construal of the conceptual relationship between EI and "adaptive coping." It is presently unclear whether adaptive coping is a subcomponent of the multidimensional structure of EI; whether EI, particularly emotion regu-lation, is part and parcel of the coping process; or whether EI is a major antecedent of adaptive coping. Furthermore, the mechanisms through which EI impacts on coping behaviors and adaptive outcomes are unclear. Do high EI individuals simply avoid stressful situations, have a more diverse repertoire of coping resources, or use more effective coping strategies?

The transactional theory of emotion and stress may provide a frame-work for addressing the viability of claiming that EI represents an index of individual differences in adaptation (or adaptability) to emotional demands. For EI to have explanatory power, it must be conceptualized as an aptitude for handling challenging situations, as opposed to an out-come variable, i.e., the successful resolution of emotional challenges. Thus, theories of EI should delineate the competencies that control whether or not a person handles demanding events successfully. Con-struct validation requires identifying the key processes and knowledge structures that support the effective analysis and regulation of emotions and emotive events.

In attempting to develop a transactional perspective on EI, we identi-fied three pivotal problems for conventional accounts of EI as an index of adaptive coping. First, multiple emotional competencies have been labeled as "EI." We have discriminated temperament, basic information processing, emotion regulation, and emotional knowledge as separate (though interacting) domains of emotional competence, each of which may have multiple, independent constructs nested within them. Furthermore, the processes that mediate effects of competencies on cop-ing and outcome are themselves complex and differentiated; hence, EI cannot reside exclusively in any single psychological source. A person may read the emotional connotations of a situation accurately, but still fail to choose and implement an effective coping strategy. Conversely, advanced behavioral coping skills may be rendered ineffective by a fun-damental misinterpretation of the situation. It follows that there may not be a single "emotional intelligence" process that controls adaptive success analogous to the "speed of processing" factor that is sometimes (contro-versially) claimed to control general intelligence.

Second, most coping strategies are neither universally adaptive nor mal-adaptive. The gains and losses consequent upon the use of a particular coping strategy depend on both personal and situational factors. Consequently, a notionally adaptive strategy such as problem-focused coping may fail, for example, because the event is outside personal control, because a short-term fix for the problem causes long-term harm, or because the individual lacks the expertise to implement their chosen strategy effectively. Furthermore, it is unclear (1) whether single "adaptational outcomes" can be scaled on some single continuum of success versus failure, and (2) whether there are consistent individual differences in success of outcome.

Third, the transactional model emphasizes the importance of situational factors and intra-individual variability in appraisal and coping across different situations. It is entirely possible that EI measures may be predictive of stress and coping in some contexts but not others [61]. It is possible too that constructs labeled as EI, like personality traits, in fact confer benefits in some situations but costs in others. Research to date has not only neglected the role of the situation, but has failed to place findings in the dynamic context described by the transactional model. Viewed thus, EI may involve various biases in processing and knowledge, as well as adaptive trajectories of person–situation interaction, such as building supportive social networks and acquiring experience of diverse social settings.

In conclusion, the existing research literature does not support the notion of a continuum of adaptive competence. Thus, there are no accepted criteria for rating the outcomes of events in terms of overall adaptive success or failure [60], while empirical studies suggest particular coping strategies are only weakly related to outcomes [24]. More generally, it is central to the transactional approach that emotions must be understood within the specific context in which they occur. Although the concept is superficially appealing, the bulk of the evidence suggests that we cannot identify EI with emotional adaptability. Thus, we are skeptical that EI will be shown to be an aptitude central to adaptive coping. Yet, we are not dismissive, in that specific constructs labeled as EI may prove to add to existing understanding of the stress process. Progress of this kind requires: (1) clearer conceptual and psychometric discrimination of the multiple constructs related to emotional competency, (2) a stronger focus on mediating mechanisms, (3) a stronger focus on situational moderators of EI constructs, and (4) a greater emphasis on building causal models using data from experimental and longitudinal studies.

# ☐ Note

The views expressed are those of the authors and do not necessarily reflect those of the Educational Testing Service.

☐ **References**

1. Mayer, J. D., Salovey, P., & Caruso, D. R. (2000). Models of emotional intelligence. In R. J. Sternberg (Ed.), *Handbook of intelligence* (pp. 396–420). New York: Cambridge University Press.
2. Matthews G., Roberts, R. D., & Zeidner, M. (2004). Seven myths about emotional intelligence. *Psychological Inquiry, 15,* 179–196.
3. Matthews, G., Zeidner, M., & Roberts, R. D. (2002). *Emotional intelligence: Science and myth.* Cambridge, MA: MIT Press.
4. Lazarus, R. S., & Folkman, S. (1984). *Stress, appraisal, and coping.* New York: Springer.
5. Goleman, D. (1995). *Emotional intelligence: Why it can matter more than IQ.* New York: Bantam Books.
6. Bar-On, R., & Parker, J. D. A. (Eds.). (2000). *The handbook of emotional intelligence.* San Francisco: Jossey-Bass.
7. Zeidner, M., Roberts, R. D., & Matthews, G. (2002). Can emotional intelligence be schooled? A critical review. *Educational Psychologist, 37,* 215–231.
8. Zeidner, M., Matthews G., & Roberts, R. D. (2004). Emotional intelligence in the workplace: A critical review. *Applied Psychology: An International Review, 53,* 371–399.
9. Zeidner, M., Matthews, G., & Roberts, R. D. (2005). *The emotional intelligence primer: Current theory, assessment and applications.* Cambridge, MA: MIT Press. Manuscript in preparation.
10. Zeidner, M., Matthews, G., & Roberts, R. D. (2001). Slow down you move too fast: Emotional intelligence remains an "elusive" intelligence. *Emotions, 1,* 265–275.
11. Matthews, G., Emo, A., Roberts, R. D., & Zeidner, M. (in press). What is this thing called emotional intelligence? In K. R. Murphy (Ed.), *The case against emotional intelligence: What are the problems and how can they be fixed?* Mahwah, NJ: Lawrence Erlbaum Associates, Inc.
12. MacCann, C., Matthews, G., Zeidner, M., & Roberts, R. D. (2003). Psychological assessment of emotional intelligence: A review of self-report and performance-based testing. *International Journal of Organizational Analysis, 11,* 247–274.
13. Bar-On, R. (1997). *Emotional Quotient Inventory (EQ-i): Technical manual.* Toronto, Canada: Multi-Health Systems.
14. Bar-On, R. (2000). Emotional and social intelligence: Insights from the Emotional Quotient Inventory. In R. Bar-On & J. D. A. Parker (Eds.), *The handbook of emotional intelligence* (pp. 363–388). San Francisco: Jossey-Bass.
15. Brackett, M. A., & Mayer, J. D. (2003). Convergent, discriminate, and incremental validity of competing measures of emotional intelligence. *Personality and Social Psychology Bulletin, 29,* 1147–1158.
16. Dawda, D., & Hart, S. D. (2000). Assessing emotional intelligence: Reliability and validity of the Bar-On Emotional Quotient Inventory (EQ-i) in university students. *Personality and Individual Differences, 28,* 797–812.
17. Mayer, J. D., Salovey, P., & Caruso, D. R. (2002). *Mayer-Salovey-Caruso Emotional Intelligence Test (MSCEIT) user's manual.* Toronto, Canada: Multi-Health Systems.
18. Brody, N. (2004). What cognitive intelligence is, and emotional intelligence is not. *Psychological Inquiry, 15,* 234–238.
19. Roberts, R. D., Zeidner, M., & Matthews, G. (2001). Does emotional intelligence meet traditional standards for an intelligence? Some new data and conclusion. *Emotion, 1,* 196–231.
20. Ciarrochi, J., Chan, A. Y. C., & Caputi, P. (2000). A critical evaluation of the emotional intelligence construct. *Personality and Individual Differences, 28,* 539–561.

21. Lopes, P. N., Brackett, M. A., Nezlek, J. B., Schutz, A., Sellin, I., & Salovey, P. (2004). Emotional intelligence and daily social interaction. *Personality and Social Psychology Bulletin, 30*, 1018–1034.
22. Greenberg, M. T., Weissberg, R. P., O'Brien, M. U., Zins, J. E., Fredericks, L., Resnik, H., & Elias, M. J. (2003). Enhancing school-based prevention and youth development through coordinated social, emotional, and academic learning. *American Psychologist, 58*, 466–474.
23. Roberts, R. D., Schulze, R., Zeidner, M., & Matthews, G. (2005). Understanding, measuring, and applying emotional intelligence: What have we learned? What have we missed? In R. Schulze & R. D. Roberts (Eds.), *International handbook of emotional intelligence* (pp. 311–341). Seattle, WA: Hogrefe & Huber.
24. Zeidner, M., & Saklofske, D. S. (1996). Adaptive and maladaptive coping. In M. Zeidner & N. S. Endler (Eds.), Handbook of coping (pp. 505–531). New York: John Wiley & Sons.
25. Lazarus, R. S. (1999). *Stress and emotions: A new synthesis.* New York: Springer.
26. Pearlin, L. I., & Schooler, C. (1978). The structure of coping. *Journal of Health and Social Behavior, 19*, 2–21.
27. Carver, C. S., Scheier, M. F., & Weintraub, J. K. (1989). Assessing coping strategies: A theoretically based approach. *Journal of Personality and Social Psychology, 56*, 267–283.
28. Endler, N., & Parker, J. (1990). Multi-dimensional assessment of coping: A critical review. *Journal of Personality and Social Psychology, 58*, 844–854.
29. Endler, N. S., Speer, R. L., Johnson, J. M., & Flett, G. L. (2000). Controllability, coping, efficacy, and distress. *European Journal of Personality, 14*, 245–264.
30. Wells, A., & Matthews, G. (1994). *Attention and emotion: A clinical perspective.* Hove, UK: Lawrence Erlbaum Associates Ltd.
31. Matthews, G., Deary, I. J., & Whiteman, M. C. (2003). *Personality traits* (2nd ed.). Cambridge, UK: Cambridge University Press.
32. Block, J., & Kremen, A. M. (1996). IQ and ego-resiliency: Conceptual and empirical connections and separateness. *Journal of Personality and Social Psychology, 70*, 349–361.
33. Zeidner, M. (1995). Personality trait correlates of intelligence. In D. Saklofske & M. Zeidner (Eds.), *International handbook of personality and intelligence* (pp. 299–319). New York: Plenum.
34. Zeidner, M., & Matthews, G. (2000). Personality and intelligence. In R. J. Sternberg (Ed.), *Handbook of human intelligence* (2nd ed., pp. 581–610). New York: Cambridge University Press.
35. Salovey, P., Bedell, B. T., Detweiler, J. B., & Mayer, J. D. (1999). Coping intelligently: Emotional intelligence and the coping process. In C. R. Snyder (Ed.), *Coping: The psychology of what works* (pp. 141–164). New York: Oxford University Press.
36. Pennebaker, J. W. (1997). Writing about emotional experiences as a therapeutic process. *Psychological Science, 8*, 162–166.
37. Epstein, S. (1998). *Constructive thinking: The key to emotional intelligence.* New York: Praeger.
38. Wells, A. (2000). *Emotional disorders and metacognition: Innovative cognitive therapy.* Chichester, UK: Wiley.
39. Salovey, P., Stroud, L. R., Woolery, A., & Epel, E. S. (2002). Perceived emotional intelligence, stress reactivity, and symptom reports: Further explorations using the trait meta-mood scale. *Psychology and Health, 17*, 611–627.
40. Salovey, P., Bedell, B. T., Detweiler, J. B., & Mayer, J. D. (2000). Current directions in emotional intelligence research. In M. Lewis & J. M. Haviland-Jones (Eds.), *Handbook of emotions* (pp. 504–520). New York: Guilford Press.
41. Folkman, S. (1984). Personal control and stress and coping processes: A theoretical analysis. *Journal of Personality and Social Psychology, 46*, 839–852.

42. Schutte, N. S., Malouff, J. M., Hall, L. E., Haggerty, D. J., Cooper, J. T., Golden, C. J., & Dornheim, L. (1998). Development and validation of a measure of emotional intelligence. *Personality and Individual Differences, 25,* 167–177.

43. Salovey, P., Mayer, J. D., Goldman, S. L., Turvey, C., & Palfai, T. P. (1995). Emotional attention, clarity, and repair: Exploring emotional intelligence using the Trait Meta-Mood Scale. In J. W. Pennebaker (Ed.), *Emotion, disclosure, and health* (pp. 125–154). Washington, DC: American Psychological Association.

44. Chan, D. W. (2003). Dimensions of emotional intelligence and their relationships with social coping among gifted adolescents in Hong Kong. *Journal of Youth and Adolescence, 32,* 409–418.

45. Furnham, A., Petrides, K. V., & Spencer-Bowdage, S. (2002). The effects of different types of social desirability on the identification of repressors. *Personality and Individual Differences, 33,* 119–130.

46. Bonanno, G. A. (2004). Loss, trauma, and human resilience: Have we underestimated the human capacity to thrive after extremely aversive events? *American Psychologist, 59,* 20–28.

47. Ciarrochi, J., Deane, F. P., & Anderson, S. (2002). Emotional intelligence moderates the relationship between stress and mental health. *Personality and Individual Differences, 32,* 197–209.

48. Ciarrochi, J., Chan, A. Y. C., & Bajgar, J. (2001). Measuring emotional intelligence in adolescents. *Personality and Individual Differences, 31,* 1105–1119.

49. Gohm, C. L., & Clore, G. L. (2002). Four latent traits of emotional experience and their involvement in well-being, coping, and attributional style. *Cognition and Emotion, 16,* 495–518.

50. Ciarrochi, J., Caputi, P., & Mayer, J. D. (2003). The distinctiveness and utility of a measure of trait emotional awareness. *Personality and Individual Differences, 34,* 1477–1490.

51. Lane, R. D., Quinlan, D. M., Schwartz, G. E., Walker, P. A., & Zeitlin, S. B. (1990). The Levels of Emotional Awareness Scale: A cognitive-developmental measure of emotion. *Journal of Personality Assessment, 55,* 124–134.

52. Zeidner, M., Cohen-Kloda, I., Matthews, G., & Roberts, R. D. (2005). *Emotional intelligence and coping with stress.* Manuscript in preparation.

53. Matthews, G., Emo, A., Funke, G., Zeidner, M., & Roberts, R. D. (in press). Emotional intelligence, personality, and task-induced stress. *Journal of Experimental Psychology: Applied.*

54. Matthews, G., Campbell, S. E., Falconer, S., Joyner, L., Huggins, J., Gilliland, K., et al. (2002). Fundamental dimensions of subjective state in performance settings: Task engagement, distress and worry. *Emotion, 2,* 315–340.

55. Matthews, G., & Campbell, S. E. (1998). Task-induced stress and individual differences in coping. In *Proceedings of the 42nd annual meeting of the Human Factors and Ergonomics Society* (pp. 821–825). Santa Monica, CA: HFES.

56. Lazarus, R. S. (1993). Coping theory and research: Past, present, and future. *Psychosomatic Medicine, 55,* 237–247.

57. Zeidner, M., & Hammer, A. (1990). Life events and coping resources as predictors of stress symptoms in adolescents. *Personality and Individual Differences, 11,* 693–703.

58. Taylor, S. E. (1986). *Health psychology.* New York: Random House.

59. Cheng, C. (2003). Cognitive and motivational processes underlying coping flexibility: A dual-process model. *Journal of Personality and Social Psychology, 84,* 425–438.

60. Matthews, G., & Zeidner, M. (2000). Emotional intelligence, adaptation to stressful encounters, and health outcomes. In R. Bar-On & J. D. A. Parker (Eds.), *The handbook of emotional intelligence* (pp.459–489). San Francisco: Jossey-Bass.

61. Matthews, G., Zeidner, M., & Roberts, R. D. (in press). Measuring emotional intelligence: Promises, pitfalls, solutions? In A. D. Ong & M. van Dulmen (Eds.), *Handbook of methods in positive psychology.* Oxford, UK: Oxford University Press.

62. Mathews, A., & MacLeod, C. (2002). Induced processing biases have causal effects on anxiety. *Cognition and Emotion, 16,* 331–354.
63. MacCann, C., Matthews, G., Zeidner, M., & Roberts, R. (2004). The assessment of emotional intelligence: On frameworks, fissures, and the future. In G. Geher (Ed.), *Measuring emotional intelligence: Common ground and controversy.* Hauppauge, NY: Nova Science Publishers.
64. Salovey, P., & Mayer, J. D. (1990). Emotional intelligence. *Imagination, Cognition, and Personality, 9,* 185–211.
65. Gross, J. J., & John, O. P. (2002). Wise emotion regulation. In L. F. Barrett & P. Salovey (Eds.), *The wisdom in feeling: Psychological processes in emotional intelligence* (pp. 297–318). New York: Guilford Press.
66. Baumeister, R. F., Smart, L., & Boden, J. M. (1996). Relation of threatened egotism to violence and aggression: The dark side of high self-esteem. *Psychological Review, 103,* 5–33.

PART

# APPLICATIONS OF EMOTIONAL INTELLIGENCE RESEARCH TO EVERYDAY LIFE

CHAPTER

Julie Fitness

# The Emotionally Intelligent Marriage

## ☐ Introduction

> there is little about a relationship that can be understood without under-
> standing . . . the emotions and feelings that partners experience in their
> association with each other [1, p. 858]

If ever there were a context in which one might expect emotional intelligence to matter it is marriage. Marriage is the source of some of our
deepest feelings and emotions, from love, hate, and anger, to fear, sadness,
and joy; and the extent to which spouses can understand, communicate,
and manage these and other powerful emotions plays a crucial role in
their marital happiness. However, although it makes intuitive sense to
argue for the importance of emotional intelligence in close relationships,
and to speculate that more emotionally intelligent people should have
longer and happier marriages, there has actually been very little scientific research specifically examining emotional intelligence in this context.
This is particularly surprising given the rapidly growing body of literature
emphasizing the central role of feelings and emotions in the initiation,
maintenance and dissolution of close relationships [2–3].

The overall aim of this chapter is to update the material published in
the first edition of this volume with respect to the most recent and relevant research on the experience, expression, and regulation of marital
emotion(s), and to highlight the implications of such research for
enhancing our understanding of emotional intelligence in marriage. In
particular, I will argue that, although emotional intelligence may be conceived as a set of skills or abilities that individuals bring to their close

**129**

relationships, over time successful marriages acquire a character of their own that may also be described as "emotionally intelligent."

# ☐ Emotional Intelligence: Four Primary Abilities

The emotional intelligence literature suggests that individuals may be more or less "intelligent" with respect to four, interrelated abilities: (a) the ability to perceive emotions, (b) the ability to use emotion to facilitate thought, (c) the ability to understand emotions, and (d) the ability to manage emotions [4]. All four abilities would appear to be important in the emotion-rich context of marriage, and there is, in fact, a growing body of research attesting to the crucial role played by each of them in promoting marital stability and happiness.

## The Ability to Perceive Emotion

Research on the perception of emotions and emotional signals in marriage has primarily been conducted via the videotaping of "live" couple interactions in the laboratory (e.g., see [5–7]). Overall, the results of these studies have been extremely consistent. First, they have demonstrated that marriage is, indeed, an emotion-rich context, and that high conflict marital discussions are emotionally arousing, as evidenced by physiological measures such as heart rate, skin conductance, and muscular activity. They have also demonstrated that individuals vary in their abilities to accurately perceive each other's emotions, with some spouses oblivious to their partners' emotion signals, or prone to misidentify even the most unambiguous of them (e.g., interpreting sadness as hostility).

Researchers have found reliable associations between these variations in people's abilities to accurately perceive and identify emotions, and marital happiness. For example, Koerner and Fitzpatrick found that for both spouses, the ability to accurately decode nonverbal expressions of relationship-related positive emotion (e.g., love for partner) and nonverbal expressions of non-relationship-related negative emotion (e.g., my partner is angry about work, not me) was associated with greater marital satisfaction [8].

It is important to note, however, that in the dyadic context, accurate emotion perception and decoding is only half the story. Emotions must also be clearly communicated and expressed, and this is an emotion-related skill that EI scholars have tended to overlook (though there is a growing body of research on managing and regulating emotions, as discussed later in this chapter). Marital researchers have demonstrated that individuals vary considerably in their abilities to clearly express emotions, and that the habitual expression of ambiguous or confusing emotion signals (e.g., simultaneously smiling and frowning) is reliably associated with marital distress [7].

One reason for this association derives from what has been referred to in the marital interaction literature as "negative affect reciprocity," or the tendency of interacting spouses to reciprocate the emotions they perceive (accurately or inaccurately) are being expressed to them (e.g., [6]). Researchers have found that unhappy spouses, who typically expect the worst from one another, tend to perceive neutral or only mildly negative emotional messages as hostile, and reciprocate with overtly hostile emotional messages. These messages are, in turn, perceived even more negatively than they were intended and trigger even more hostile responses. In this way, destructive emotion sequences or negative escalation spirals are established, from which couples find it difficult to escape. In fact, these kinds of negative escalations and tit-for-tat sequences typify unhappy marriages [6].

Another possible reason for the link between emotion miscommunication and marital distress is suggested by the results of a study that found no relationships between participants' perceptions of how well they communicated their own emotions nonverbally, and objective measures of their expressive abilities [8]. These findings suggest that individuals who are unrealistically confident about their abilities to clearly express their emotions may mistakenly attribute the causes of any marital communication problems to the stupidity or insensitivity of their spouses, rather than to their own ineptitude. Again, these types of self-excusing, partner-blaming attributions for upsetting or frustrating interactions are reliably associated with marital distress [9].

To summarize, marital interaction research has demonstrated that, just as Mayer et al. have argued [4], individuals differ in their abilities to perceive others' emotions accurately. It has also revealed that individuals differ in another, closely related emotional skill: the ability to clearly express emotions. Further, research has demonstrated that happy spouses tend to be better than unhappy spouses at both expressing and decoding verbal and nonverbal emotional messages.

What marital interaction studies have not revealed is the extent to which spouses' abilities to accurately identify their *own* emotions is important for marital happiness. However, there is a body of research in the clinical literature suggesting that individuals who lack the ability to identify their own emotions and distinguish amongst them (a condition called alexithymia) tend also to experience social and interpersonal difficulties [10]. Such individuals may, for example, interpret the physiological symptoms of anxiety as denoting physical illness, or they may be confused about whether they are feeling sad, angry, or fearful when interacting with others. Given the potential implications of alexithymia both for the accurate expression of emotions and for the ability to identify others' emotions, this is clearly an intriguing issue for further exploration in the context of marital stability and happiness.

## The Ability to Use Emotion to Facilitate Thought

The ability to use emotion to facilitate thought refers in part to people's capacity for empathy, such that they can imagine how others are feeling, and can appreciate the emotional nuances of complex interpersonal situations. In the marital context, for example, this might involve the ability to imagine how one's spouse is feeling after a stressful day at work, or to appreciate the underlying insecurity of a spouse who demands frequent reassurance that they are loved and valued. There has been a considerable amount of research on the role of empathy and empathic accuracy in close relationship functioning (see Chapter 7 in this volume), and will not be discussed further here.

It should be noted, however, that although this facet of emotional intelligence is potentially adaptive in marriage, someone who is skilled at reading other people's emotions could just as well use this ability for destructive as for constructive purposes [11]. For example, married partners could conceivably use their empathic awareness in a calculated way to identify their partners' vulnerabilities and insecurities, and exploit these for their own purposes (e.g., see [12]). Nevertheless, and regardless of the potentially positive or negative outcomes of such empathic abilities, it is clear that for individuals to be able to accurately perceive and utilize emotions in the marital context, they need to understand what emotions are all about—how they are caused, what they motivate people to do, and their likely consequences. This kind of detailed emotion understanding underpins the third ability involved in emotional intelligence.

## Understanding Emotions

People acquire knowledge as they are growing up about how emotions are caused, what they feel like, and what their outcomes are likely to be. Such emotion knowledge is both general (e.g., knowing what makes human beings angry) and context specific (e.g., knowing what makes spouses, in particular, angry with one another). Evidence suggests that most people have a minimum amount of context-specific emotion knowledge. For example, researchers have found that people's imaginary accounts of what would make spouses angry, loving, hateful, or jealous, and the consequences of these emotions, are consistent with recalled accounts of actual emotion instances in marriage [13–14]. However, people differ in the complexity and accuracy of their emotion knowledge; differences that may well influence spouses' abilities to understand and deal effectively with the emotional ups and downs of marriage.

The results of a study on marital forgiveness provide some support for the important role of emotion knowledge and understanding in marriage (see [12]). Ninety long-term married and seventy divorced men and women were asked to recall and write about either a forgiven or an unforgiven marital offense. They provided details of who had offended, what had happened, and how they and their partners had felt and behaved in relation to the offense. They also completed questionnaires about various aspects of their marriages and personalities, including one of the earliest published measures of emotional intelligence, the Trait Meta-Mood Scale [15]. This 30-item measure consists of three subscales measuring what were, in the early 1990s, considered to be the major dimensions of emotional intelligence: attention to feelings (e.g., "I pay a lot of attention to how I feel"); clarity of feelings (e.g., "I am rarely confused about how I feel"); and mood repair (e.g., "When I become upset I remind myself of all the pleasures in life").

The results of this study showed that only emotion clarity, or the ability to understand and reason about emotions, was an important factor in reported marital forgiveness. Specifically, individuals with higher emotion clarity reported significantly less difficulty in forgiving a partner-caused offense than lower emotion-clarity participants, regardless of how serious the offense had been, how much hurt it had caused, or how happily or unhappily married the individual was. In addition, individuals who reported higher emotion clarity also tended to report greater marital happiness, irrespective of age or sex. These findings suggest that the ability to understand the causes, features, and outcomes of emotions facilitates the constructive resolution of even the most hurtful marital transgressions, and contributes significantly to perceptions of marital satisfaction. Further, the results of a second study on aspects of marital forgiveness with newly wed participants also found a positive association between emotion clarity and marital happiness, so this appears to be a reliable finding [16].

The results of these studies are consistent with the hypothesis that the more finely tuned people's understanding of emotions, the more adaptively they may behave in the marital context. This brings us to the fourth ability involved in emotional intelligence: the ability to effectively manage emotions.

## Managing Emotions

As noted previously in this chapter, there is a growing body of research suggesting that emotion regulation and management is an integral aspect of emotional intelligence. Marital research, too, confirms the importance of effectively managing emotions (and in particular, their expression) in marriage. For example, researchers have found that, compared to unhappy spouses, happy spouses are more likely to inhibit their impulses to react destructively when their partners express anger, and to respond instead in a conciliatory manner (e.g., see [17]). Gottman, too, has argued that the tit-for-tat cycles of reciprocated negative emotions observed in the interactions of unhappy spouses may come about partly as a function of partners' inabilities to effectively soothe one another [18].

These findings do not, however, imply that emotionally "neutral" or inexpressive spouses have the happiest marriages. Feeney, for example, measured the extent to which married individuals reported suppressing anger, sadness, anxiety, happiness, love, and pride in their relationships, and found a positive association between insecure attachment and efforts to control the expression of all these emotions [19]. In fact, spouses generally regard emotional openness and expressiveness as both positive and desirable in marriage, and more emotionally expressive spouses tend to have happier partners [20].

There are several possible reasons for this. First, marriage is a relationship characterized by the expectation that spouses will care about each other's needs and desires. Emotional expressions of joy, sadness, anger, and love communicate spouses' needs and desires to one another and allow for the reciprocal fulfillment of such needs [2]. Second, and relatedly, the open expression of emotions reduces the possibility of misunderstandings between spouses. For example, Mongrain and Vettese found that women who were ambivalent about the expression of emotion (i.e., who may have wanted to express emotions but who feared the consequences of such expression) failed to communicate clearly during videotaped interactions and sent more "mixed messages" to their partners [21]. Further, Richards, Butler, and Gross found that instructing romantic partners to deliberately suppress emotional expression during a naturalistic interaction actually interfered with their memories of what was said during the interaction [22].

Emotional expressiveness, then, appears to be adaptive in marriage. However, there is an important caveat to this finding. Specifically, marital happiness appears to critically depend on the overall number of expressed positive emotions outweighing the number of expressed negative emotions (optimally, by 5:1, according to Gottman [6]). Studies of long-term marriages confirm the importance of predominantly positive emotional expression to marital happiness and stability. For example, in a large-scale study of middle-aged and older couples, Carstensen, Gottman, and Levenson found that although happy spouses still expressed negative emotions like anger and sadness in their interactions with one another, they more frequently expressed love, affection, and good humor in those interactions [23].

In summary, emotional intelligence in marriage involves the frequent expression of positive emotions and a willingness to engage with one's partner in a climate of trust and affection. In this respect, it may not be unreasonable to conceptualize emotional intelligence within the context of long-term marriages as an emergent property of happily married couples' interactions, rather than as a set of abilities residing within one spouse or the other. This points to the need for more research to help identify the nature and features of the "emotionally intelligent" marriage, and to explore the ways in which marital happiness itself may lead to more emotionally intelligent behavior over time.

## ☐ What is the Emotionally Intelligent Marriage Like?

Mayer et al. asked, "what is the high EI individual like?" Their prototype included features such as "able to manage emotions better than others . . . more open and agreeable than others . . . can solve emotional problems with less cognitive effort . . . less apt to engage in problem behaviors" [4, p. 210]. Based on the research reviewed in this chapter, it may also be feasible to ask what the "emotionally intelligent" marriage is like.

One reasonable assumption would be that a high EI marriage would require two, high EI spouses. However, this is not necessarily the case. For example, in a recent study, Brackett, Warner, and Bosco [24] examined the relationship between emotional intelligence and relationship quality with 86 heterosexual couples in romantic relationships. Emotional intelligence was measured with the Mayer-Salovey-Caruso Emotional Intelligence Test (MSCEIT [25]). The MSCEIT is an objective test of individuals' abilities to perceive, use, understand, and regulate emotions, as opposed to tests that rely on people's self-reported emotional abilities. Somewhat surprisingly, Brackett et al. [24] found that couples in which both partners were low on EI reported significantly poorer relationship outcomes than couples where either or both partners were high on EI. In other words, having one high EI partner appeared to be sufficient to keep a relationship "on track" but having two high EI partners made no appreciable difference to relationship quality. Whether this is the case for long-term happy marriages, however, is currently unknown. It may be the case, for example, that some long-term marriages succeed because initially low EI spouses do acquire skills over time.

The apparent links between the various facets of emotional intelligence and marital happiness may also not be entirely straightforward. For example, although accuracy in perceiving emotions is clearly an important factor in marital happiness, evidence suggests that a certain amount of perceptual *inaccuracy* is also important for a happy marriage. Researchers have found, for example, that happy spouses tend to perceive their partners through rose-colored spectacles—glossing over or simply not noticing their faults, and attributing charitable intentions to each other in the face of less than exemplary behavior [26]. Happy spouses also tend to expect the best from each other, as well as perceive the best.

A recent longitudinal study suggests that the positive association between optimistic expectations and marital happiness is, in part, a function of spouses' interpersonal skills. Using videotapes to record couple interactions, McNulty and Karney found that for spouses with good interpersonal skills, having positive expectations of each other, predicted more stable satisfaction over time [27]. However, less positive expectations predicted declines in happiness, presumably because interpersonal skills are less relevant in a relationship that is deteriorating or unhappy for other reasons. For spouses who were less interpersonally skilled, positive expectations predicted steeper declines in satisfaction over time, perhaps as a function of their general disappointment with relationship outcomes. Ironically, low skill levels coupled with low expectations actually predicted more stable satisfaction.

The finding that the impact of expectations on marital happiness interacts with the interpersonal skills spouses bring to their marriage is possibly one of the clearest empirical links to the emotional intelligence literature to date. However, and as mentioned earlier in the chapter, there is another, crucial element involved in long-term marital success. Specifically, happily married spouses tend to regard one another with admiration and fondness, as opposed to contempt and disdain, and they foster a "culture of appreciation" within their marriages [18], [28].

Ultimately, it may be this ability to generate a positive emotional climate that best distinguishes the emotionally intelligent marriage. As noted by Murray, Holmes, and Griffin, even in most well-established marriages spouses still want each other's admiration and approval, and individuals who feel cherished and valued by their partners are much better able to withstand the inevitable disappointments and hurts that arise in any long-term relationship [29]. The question then arises, how do spouses generate and maintain such a positive emotional climate?

One point to note is that positive emotion does not automatically arise in the mere absence of negative emotion—indifference and/or emotional disconnection are more likely outcomes of the emotionally "neutral" marriage [18]. Nor does a positive emotional climate arise through the chronic suppression of negative emotions, which, as discussed earlier, may lead to misperceptions and miscommunication. Rather, the capacity to actively generate positive emotions requires all the abilities hypothesized to constitute emotional intelligence, including empathy, emotion understanding, and emotion management. For the individual spouse, and in line with Mayer et al.'s [4] description of the emotionally intelligent individual, this implies openness, agreeableness, and self-control, along with optimism and a constructive coping style (see [30]). At the relationship level, generating positive emotions requires spouses to make active efforts to please one another and to exceed each other's expectations; to plan and implement pleasant surprises for one another; to share mutually rewarding activities; and to actively support each other through life's vicissitudes.

In short, it seems that emotional intelligence does increase the chances of maintaining a long-term, satisfying marriage. It should be noted, however, that emotional intelligence alone is not sufficient to guarantee marital happiness. Spouses must also want to be married, and be committed to the idea of being married. In addition, spouses must be committed to each other, look out for each other, care for and show compassion toward each other, and be willing to assume responsibility for each other's needs. Such motivations, goals and behaviors may ultimately have very little to do with emotional intelligence *per se*.

## ☐ Conclusions

The literature reviewed in this chapter reveals a relatively long-standing and rich tradition of psychological research on emotions in the context of marital relationships. The findings are consistent with the hypothesis, drawn from the emotional intelligence literature, that people differ in their abilities to accurately perceive emotions, use and understand emotions, and manage emotions. Further, these differences in emotion-related abilities are reliably associated with a highly desirable life outcome: marital happiness and stability.

As noted at the beginning of this chapter, emotions are profoundly interpersonal phenomena; people's emotional intelligence, then, may only really come to life within interpersonal and relational settings. Clearly, both emotion and close relationship scholars have much to offer one another with respect to theoretical insights and methodological expertise. Hopefully we are now witnessing the blossoming of a relationship between these two areas of scholarship that will flourish and endure for many years to come.

# ☐ References

1.  Reis, H. T., Collins, W. A., & Berscheid, E. (2000). The relationship context of human behavior and development. *Psychological Bulletin, 126,* 844–872.
2.  Clark, M., Fitness, J., & Brissette, I. (2001). Understanding people's perceptions of relationships is crucial to understanding their emotional lives. In G. J. O. Fletcher & M. Clark (Eds.), *Handbook of social psychology: Vol 2. Interpersonal processes* (pp. 253–278). Oxford, UK: Blackwell Publishers.
3.  Planalp, S., Fitness, J., & Fehr, B. (in press). Emotion in theories of close relationships. In D. Perlman & A. Vangelisti (Eds.), *Handbook of personal relationships.* New York: Cambridge University Press.
4.  Mayer, J. D., Salovey, P., & Caruso, D. (2004). Emotional intelligence: Theory, findings, and implications. *Psychological Inquiry, 15,* 197–215.
5.  Fletcher, G. J. O., & Thomas, G. (1999). Behavior and on-line cognition in marital interaction. *Personal Relationships, 7,* 111–130.
6.  Gottman, J. M. (1994). *What predicts divorce? The relationship between marital processes and marital outcomes.* Hillsdale, NJ: Lawrence Erlbaum Associates, Inc.
7.  Noller, P., & Ruzzene, M. (1991). Communication in marriage: The influence of affect and cognition. In G. J. O. Fletcher & F. Fincham (Eds.), *Cognition in close relationships* (pp. 203–233). Hillsdale, NJ: Lawrence Erlbaum Associates, Inc.
8.  Koerner, A., & Fitzpatrick, M. (2002). Nonverbal communication and marital adjustment and satisfaction: The role of decoding relationship-relevant and relationship-irrelevant affect. *Communication Monographs, 69,* 33–51.
9.  Fletcher, G. J. O., & Fincham, F. D. (1991). Attribution processes in close relationships. In G. J. O. Fletcher & F. D. Fincham (Eds.), *Cognition in close relationships* (pp. 7–36). Hillsdale, NJ: Lawrence Erlbaum Associates, Inc.
10. Taylor, G. J., & Bagby, R. M. (2000). Overview of the alexithymia construct. In R. Bar-On & J. D. Parker (Eds.), *Handbook of emotional intelligence* (pp. 40–67). San Francisco: Jossey-Bass.
11. Epstein, S. (1998). *Constructive thinking: The key to emotional intelligence.* Westport, CT: Praeger.
12. Fitness, J. (2001). Betrayal, rejection, revenge, and forgiveness. In M. Leary (Ed.), *Interpersonal rejection* (pp. 73–103). New York: Oxford University Press.
13. Fitness, J., & Fletcher, G. J. O. (1993). Love, hate, anger, and jealousy in close relationships: A cognitive appraisal and prototype analysis. *Journal of Personality and Social Psychology, 65,* 942–958.
14. Fitness, J. (1996). Emotion knowledge structures in close relationships. In G. J. O. Fletcher & J. Fitness (Eds.), *Knowledge structures in close relationships: A social psychological approach* (pp. 219–245). Mahwah, NJ: Lawrence Erlbaum Associates, Inc.
15. Salovey, P., Mayer, J. D., Goldman, S. L., Turvey, C., & Palfai, T. P. (1995). Emotional attention, clarity, and repair: Exploring emotional intelligence using the Trait Meta-Mood Scale. In J. W. Pennebaker (Ed.), *Emotion, disclosure, and health* (pp. 125–154). Washington, DC: American Psychological Association.
16. Fitness, J. (2000, June). *Emotional intelligence in personal relationships: Cognitive, emotional, and behavioral aspects.* Paper presented at the second joint conference of ISSPR and INPR, Brisbane, Australia.
17. Rusbult, C. E., Bissonnette, V., Arriaga, X. B., & Cox, C. (1998). Accommodation processes during the early years of marriage. In T. Bradbury (Ed.), *The developmental course of marital dysfunction* (pp. 74–113). New York: Cambridge University Press.

18. Gottman, J. (1998). Psychology and the study of marital processes. *Annual Review of Psychology, 49,* 169–197.
19. Feeney, J. (1999). Adult romantic attachment and couple relationships. In J. Cassidy & P. Shaver (Eds.), *Handbook of attachment* (pp. 355–377). New York: Guilford.
20. Huston, T., & Houts, R. (1998). The psychological infrastructure of courtship and marriage: The role of personality and compatibility in romantic relationships. In T. Bradbury (Ed.), *The developmental course of marital dysfunction* (pp. 114–151). New York: Cambridge University Press.
21. Mongrain, M., & Vettese, L. C. (2003). Conflict over emotional expression: Implications for interpersonal communication. *Personality and Social Psychology Bulletin, 29,* 545–555.
22. Richards, J., Butler, E., & Gross, J. (2003). Emotion regulation in romantic relationships: The cognitive consequences of concealing feelings. *Journal of Social and Personal Relationships, 20,* 599–620.
23. Carstensen, L., Gottman, J., & Levenson, R. (1995). Emotional behavior in long-term marriage. *Psychology and Aging, 10,* 140–149.
24. Brackett, M., Warner, R., & Bosco, J. (2005). Emotional intelligence and relationship quality among couples. *Personal Relationships, 12,* 197–212.
25. Mayer, J. D., Salovey, P., & Caruso, D. (2002). *Mayer-Salovey-Caruso Emotional Intelligence Test (MSCEIT), Version 2.0.* Toronto, Canada: Multi-Health Systems.
26. Murray, S., Holmes, J., & Griffin, D. (1996). The benefits of positive illusions: Idealization and the construction of satisfaction in close relationships. *Journal of Personality and Social Psychology, 70,* 79–98.
27. McNulty, J. K., & Karney, B. R. (2004). Positive expectations in the early years of marriage: Should couples expect the best or brace for the worst? *Journal of Personality and Social Psychology, 86,* 729–743.
28. Huston, T. L., Caughlin, J. P., Houts, R. M., Smith, S. E., & George, L. J. (2001). The connubial crucible: Newlywed years as predictors of marital delight, distress, and divorce. *Journal of Personality and Social Psychology, 80,* 237–252.
29. Murray, S. L., Holmes, J. G., & Griffin, D. (2000). Self esteem and the quest for felt security: How perceived regard regulates attachment processes. *Journal of Personality and Social Psychology, 78,* 478–498.
30. Gross, J. J., & John, O. P. (2003). Individual differences in two emotion regulation processes: Implications for affect, relationships, and well being. *Journal of Personality and Social Psychology, 85,* 348–362.

**7**

CHAPTER

Judith Flury
William Ickes

# Emotional Intelligence and Empathic Accuracy in Friendships and Dating Relationships

According to Salovey, Hsee, and Mayer [1], there are three primary domains of emotional intelligence: the accurate appraisal and expression of emotion, the adaptive regulation of emotions, and the use of emotions to plan, create, and motivate action. The present chapter focuses on the first domain as it relates to friends and dating partners, and we expand this focus to include the accurate appraisal of other people's thoughts as well as their feelings. For nearly two decades now, the topic of inferring others' thoughts and feelings has been addressed by a field of study known as *empathic accuracy*. Empathic accuracy involves "reading" people's thoughts and feelings on a moment-to-moment basis; it is, by definition, a measure of the ability to accurately infer the specific content of these successive thoughts and feelings [2–3]. In the sections to follow, we draw on available theory and research to discuss the role of empathic accuracy and emotional intelligence in the relationships of friends and dating partners.

## ☐ The Ability to Infer Other People's Thoughts and Feelings

The ability to infer the attentional and intentional states of others is clearly evident in most normally developing children by the age of 3 or 4 [4–5].

140

The ability to identify others' emotional states takes longer to emerge, and is often not well developed until early or late adolescence [1], [5]. The ability to accurately infer the specific content of other people's thoughts and feelings represents the fullest expression of a perceiver's empathic skills. This level of insight is beyond the capability of most autistic individuals [4], [6], but is clearly evident—though in varying degrees—in most normally developing people by the time they reach adolescence [7].

In fact, the results of a recent study indicate that this ability may play a pivotal role in the social development of adolescents [8]. Gleason found that young adolescents (fifth, sixth, and seventh graders) who have higher empathic accuracy scores are less likely to be victimized by their peers, and that girls with higher empathic accuracy scores tend to have higher quality friendships than girls with lower levels of empathic ability. Gleason also found that children who have low levels of empathic accuracy and who experience low quality friendships are more likely to develop social problems than children who also have low quality friendships but are better at inferring the thoughts and feelings of others.

From a personality standpoint, what are empathically accurate people like? Historically, researchers searched for the attributes of the good judge of others' personality traits, and gave relatively little attention to the more methodologically daunting problem of what might determine perceivers' accuracy in inferring other people's thoughts and feelings. Taft's qualitative review of early trait accuracy research suggested that the best potential correlates of this ability for adult participants were intelligence, good psychological adjustment, and aesthetic interest [9].

Forty-two years later, when Davis and Kraus published their quantitative meta-analysis of the data from 36 "post-Cronbach investigations" (251 effects involving 32 individual difference variables and 30 interpersonal accuracy measures) [10], their list of the best potential correlates of inferential accuracy was only slightly longer than that of Taft. Expanding on Taft's finding that "good judges" tend to be intelligent, Davis and Kraus found that they also tend be cognitively complex, field-independent, and nondogmatic. And qualifying Taft's finding that "good judges" tend to be psychologically well-adjusted, Davis and Kraus found that "good judges" tend to be more mature, trusting, and well-socialized, but not less neurotic and anxious.

A recent attempt to extend this profile of the "good judge" to the empathic accuracy domain produced findings that can only be regarded as tentative and equivocal [7]. Of the four predictor variables that were selected for study on the basis of Davis and Kraus' meta-analytic review [10], only two—verbal intelligence and interpersonal trust—were found to be related to perceivers' empathic accuracy scores. However, verbal intelligence was positively correlated with men's, but not women's, empathic accuracy. And contrary to the findings of Davis and Kraus' meta-analysis [10], interpersonal trust was negatively, rather than positively, correlated with empathic accuracy. Although these relationships clearly warrant further study, the psychological portrait they draw of the empathically accurate perceiver must be regarded as sketchy and tentative.

## ☐ Empathic Accuracy in Friendships and Dating Relationships

Having considered the personality characteristics that have been associated with accuracy in interpersonal perception in general, we now consider research that examines emotional intelligence and empathic accuracy in the context of friendships and dating relationships.

## ☐ Knowing Each Other "From the Inside"

Gesn made the straightforward prediction that the more background information a perceiver has acquired about a friend or acquaintance (e.g., the target person's work schedule, hobbies, career goals, current dating partners), the better the perceiver will be at inferring the specific content of the target person's thoughts and feelings [11]. However, Gesn's findings offered a surprise [11]: empathic accuracy was predicted not by the amount of background knowledge the perceiver had acquired about a target, but by the degree to which the perceiver characterized the relationship with the target as being psychologically close. It appears that simply knowing a lot of objective facts about a target's life is not enough to ensure success in "reading" his or her thoughts and feelings; a perceiver must also acquire extensive information about the target's subjective—and intersubjective—experience. In other words, the perceiver must get to know the target "from the inside" instead of merely "from the outside."

This finding suggests a possible interpretive weakness in a more recent study that compared the empathic accuracy of dating couples versus strangers. In this study, Senecal, Murard, and Hess required the members of dating couples to individually watch a series of videotaped vignettes that were designed to elicit a variety of emotional reactions (happiness, fear, anger, sadness, shame, and guilt) [12]. The participants were instructed to imagine their partner sitting in a chair in front of them while they were watching the vignettes, and at the same time "react as naturally as possible by saying or doing whatever you would naturally say or do in such a situation." The participants were videotaped during this role play. Several weeks later, the participants returned and were asked to individually view a copy of their role-play session, and to rate the intensity of each of their emotional reactions. Participants then viewed the tape of their dating partner's role-play session, as well as those of other participants in the study (strangers), and were asked to rate the intensity of each of the displayed emotions. The results showed that strangers were just as accurate at judging the intensity of an actor's emotion as was the actor's own dating partner.

From this finding the authors concluded that "the level of knowledge and degree of intimacy does not seem to play a role when judging the partners' emotional expressions because strangers, partners, and actors all rated the videotaped emotional expressions quite similarly" [12, p. 35]. Although this conclusion is possibly valid, the results of the previously cited study by Gesn [11] suggest what might have been a potential confound in the Senecal et al. study. Whereas Gesn separated "level of knowledge" (number of objective facts known about a person) from "intimacy" (perceived psychological closeness) and found different effects for these two variables, Senecal et al. did not differentiate between the two. Had they done so, we can speculate that they might have found different results.

The results of a study by Stinson and Ickes [13] point to the same conclusion reached in the Gesn [11] study. Stinson and Ickes found that male friends could infer the specific content of each other's thoughts and feelings with a level of accuracy that was about 50% greater than that of male strangers. Through a series of ancillary analyses, Stinson and Ickes demonstrated that this difference in empathic accuracy could not be attributed to the fact that the friends exchanged more information than the strangers (although they did), or to the fact that the friends had more similar personalities than the strangers (although, on the single dimension of sociability, the friends were indeed more similar). Instead, there was evidence that the friends' advantage derived primarily from the large store of *intersubjective* knowledge that they had acquired in their previous interactions with each other—the type of information which, being shared, may be particularly likely to lead to both greater empathic accuracy and to a feeling of psychological closeness with another.

How do individuals acquire this type of knowledge, and thereby get to know each other "from the inside"? Different authors have proposed complementary, but conceptually distinct, answers to this question [14]. For example, Smither has emphasized "empathy via role taking," which occurs when a perceiver actively attempts to understand another person's thoughts or feelings [15]. Accurate knowledge of this target person's inner world is increased to the extent that the target discusses with the perceiver the "concerns, commitments, beliefs, and ideals" surrounding his or her current emotional state. The more a perceiver has observed a target's behavioral and emotional reactions to different situations, and the more the two of them have discussed the psychological meaning of these situations, the better the perceiver will become at "reading" that target person's thoughts and feelings.

A somewhat different perspective is offered by Karniol, who argued that strangers begin by using relevant social stereotypes to infer each others' thoughts and feelings, and then modify their inferences to rely on more individuating information the longer they have been together [16]. For Stinson and Ickes [13], the most important type of individuating information is that which the partners have come to "share" through their intersubjective experience. By doing things together and discussing their present and past experiences, partners are assumed to develop over-lapping (i.e., "shared") knowledge structures that facilitate their infer-ences about each other's thoughts and feelings. Similarly, Kenny has noted that observations of a partner's behavior often lead to opportuni-ties to discuss with the partner the thoughts and feelings associated with those events [17].

All of the activities noted by these authors—discussing with one's part-ner the beliefs, ideals, and concerns surrounding one's current feeling states, dealing with the partner in an individualized rather than a stereo-typed way, sharing with the partner many life experiences and the sub-jective and intersubjective reactions to these experiences, and discussing with the partner the thoughts and feelings that surround certain behav-iors, reactions, and emotional expressions—should lead to a greater knowledge of the partner's inner world. Collectively, these activities com-prise the process of getting to know the other person "from the inside."

Friends and dating partners should have an advantage, then, when it comes to reading each other's thoughts and feelings, because their inter-actions typically result in shared experiences and corresponding discus-sions of those experiences. However, acquiring and making use of this "inside knowledge" is not guaranteed. It depends upon many factors, including characteristics of the perceiver, characteristics of the target, and characteristics of their relationship. Some relevant factors in each of these categories are reviewed below.

# ☐ Characteristics of the Perceiver

## Empathic Ability

Perceivers not only differ in their overall levels of empathic ability but also tend to maintain similar rank orders when they infer the thoughts and feelings of different target persons (the best, average, and worst per-ceivers tend to maintain their respective ranks *vis-à-vis* each other no matter who the target person is; cf. [18–19]). Although ability differences account for an important source of the variance in empathic accuracy scores, self-report measures of empathically relevant traits and dispositions have typically proved to be rather poor and unreliable predictors of these differences in empathic performance [7], [10]. One interpretation of these null results is that perceivers lack the requisite meta-knowledge of their own empathic ability [7], [20–21].

## Attentiveness

According to both theory and research, how much the perceiver attends to the target is an important determinant of empathic accuracy. Attending to the target person's behavior is the first stage in Funder's realistic accuracy model [22]—the stage upon which the success of all subsequent stages of the perceiver's inference making ultimately depends. Consistent with this reasoning, Ickes, Stinson, Bissonnette, and Garcia found that empathic accuracy in mixed-sex dyads was significantly correlated with the degree to which perceivers looked at their partners (behavioral attentiveness) and the percentage of partner-relevant thoughts and feelings they reported (cognitive attentiveness) [23]. Similarly, Gesn and Ickes found that perceivers' ratings of their attention to and interest in an empathic accuracy task were significantly correlated with their performance on the task [19]. Finally, Trommsdorf and John found that a manipulation that encouraged the members of heterosexual couples to focus on their partner's, rather than their own, feelings during a videotaped discussion caused the couples in the former condition to more accurately decode each others' emotional states from the videotape [24].

## Motivation

There is increasing evidence that perceivers' motivation to be accurate also affects their performance on empathic accuracy tasks. In the first study hinting at the importance of motivation, Ickes et al. found that opposite-sex strangers better inferred their target partners' thoughts and feelings to the extent that these partners were judged to be physically attractive. In a recent meta-analytic study [23], Ickes, Gesn, and Graham reviewed evidence suggesting that significant gender differences favoring female over male perceivers should be attributed more to differential motivation than to differential ability [25]. Klein and Hodges reached essentially the same conclusion, and further demonstrated that men and women achieve similar levels of empathic accuracy when they are motivated by the same financial reward [26].

## Attachment Orientations

Simpson, Ickes, and Grich found that perceivers' attachment orientations can affect their level of empathic accuracy in relationship-threatening situations [27]. Anxious-ambivalent perceivers appear to react to relationship threat by becoming hypervigilant (exceptionally accurate) with regard to their partners' potentially threatening thoughts and feelings. In contrast, avoidant perceivers tend to avoid inferring partners' thoughts and feelings in relationship-threatening situations, resulting in generally lower levels of empathic accuracy.

## Communal Orientation

According to Rothbaum, Weisz, and Snyder, people differ in their relationship to the environment [28]. Those with a "primary" control orientation tend to work on changing the environment to fit their own needs and goals, whereas those with a "secondary" control orientation tend to work towards accommodation—restructuring their own needs and goals according to the perceived realities of the social and physical environment. Trommsdorf and John examined the control orientation of relationship partners in their study of emotion decoding in intimate relationships [24]. They found that individuals with a "secondary" (i.e., accommodative and communal) control orientation were more accurate at decoding their partner's emotions. They also found, however, that the correlation between accurate emotional decoding and secondary control orientation fell from .25 ($p < .05$), to .09 when self-rated femininity was partialled out. Thus, the effect of secondary control orientation appeared to be due primarily to having a feminine gender-role orientation.

In a more recent study, Vogt and Colvin reported evidence for a positive correlation between self-reported communality and accuracy in trait judgment [29]. Unfortunately, however, neither self-rated communality nor self-rated femininity has reliably predicted individuals' performance in the empathic accuracy studies conducted to date [7], [26], [30].

## Empathy for the Target

In an intriguing study, Shearn, Spellman, Straley, Meirick, and Stryker found that friends experienced more empathic blushing for each other than they did for strangers when watching the friend or stranger perform an "embarrassing" act [31]. The participants in this study were asked to sing while being videotaped. In sets of threes, the performer, a friend of the performer, and a stranger to the performer watched the videotaped singing sessions, and cheek sensors monitored the amount of blushing by all three. It was found that friends of the performer blushed just as much as the performer did while watching the tape, whereas the strangers did not show this "empathic blushing."

This finding suggests that friends have more empathy for each other's emotional states than they do for the emotional states of strangers. We may further speculate that this type of emotional empathy could conceivably play a role in the greater empathic accuracy achieved for a friend's, as opposed to a stranger's, thoughts and feelings. Some suggestive evidence in this regard has been obtained by Schweinle and Ickes, who found that feelings of sympathy for a video target were associated with greater empathic accuracy, whereas feelings of contempt and uncaring were associated with poorer empathic accuracy [32]. Much more research will need to be done, however, before we can conclude that empathy for a target's emotional state enhances one's accuracy in inferring the specific content of that target's actual thoughts and feelings.

# ☐ Characteristics of the Target

Individual differences in target "readability" constitute an important source of variance in empathic accuracy scores, accounting on average for about 25% of the variance in the studies reviewed by Ickes et al. [7]. At this point, relatively little is known about the personal characteristics that distinguish more "readable" targets from less "readable" ones. However, characteristics such as self-directedness, consistency, and coherence appear to be the best-candidate predictor variables identified so far.

## Self-Directedness

Hancock and Ickes reported [33] that interaction partners who were more self-directed in terms of the relevant items on Snyder's 18-item self-monitoring scale [34] had thoughts and feelings that were generally easier to "read" than those of their more other-directed partners. Hancock and Ickes speculated that other-directed targets are more difficult to "read" because (1) they allow their interaction partners to take the initiative in conversations and therefore don't disclose much themselves, and/or (2) they mask or suppress the expression of their actual thoughts and feelings in an attempt to behave in what they perceive to be a socially desirable manner [33].

## Consistency and Coherence

The idea that people who are self-directed are easier for their partners to "read" may be analogous to Colvin's argument [35] that people who have a coherent personality structure and who manifest consistent and non-erratic behavior are more "judgable" in terms of their personality traits [14]. The importance of consistency and coherence on target "readability" is also evident in the study reported by Marangoni et al. [18]. In this study, 80 perceivers inferred the thoughts and feelings of three female clients who were videotaped during individual sessions with the same male, client-centered therapist. Marangoni and her colleagues found that the thoughts and feelings of one client were considerably more difficult to infer than the thoughts and feelings of the other two clients [18]. A review of the respective videotapes revealed why: the difficult-to-"read" client was inconsistent in the presentation of her problem, her mood was labile, and she gave conflicting accounts of her feelings toward the same situation at different times.

## ☐ Characteristics of the Perceiver–Target Relationship

### Acquaintanceship and Intimacy

A number of studies have shown that well-acquainted partners can "read" each other's thoughts and feelings better than strangers can [11], [13], [36]. When the data from these studies were combined, the results suggested that most of the gain in partners' ability to "read" each other occurs within the first few weeks of their relationship, with only minor gains occurring after the second month [37]. As Gesn's findings [11] indicate, however, empathic accuracy may be more closely related to the degree of intimacy and closeness in the relationship than to the length of acquaintanceship *per se*.

### Relationship Discord

Researchers have shown that relationship discord can reduce empathic accuracy, and that reduced accuracy can in turn lead to even more discord. For example, Kirchler had spouses rate their own affect and their partner's affect at randomly selected times throughout each day, for several weeks [38–39]. He found that participants were more accurate in identifying their partner's current mood during times of agreement than during times of conflict. In a similar vein, Noller and Ruzzene reported that distressed couples had a particular problem in identifying the specific emotions experienced by their partner during times of conflict [40].

A possible reason for this effect is suggested by the results of a study by Gaelick, Bodenhausen, and Wyer [41]. They found that spouses were not as accurate at decoding their partner's expressions of love as they were at decoding their expressions of hostility during conflict. This finding suggests that the decoding of a partner's positive, rather than negative, emotions may suffer the most in conflict situations. In addition, the Gaelick et al. study showed that spouses tend to reciprocate whatever emotion they *thought* their partner was expressing.

What implications do these findings have for friendships and dating relationships? It depends, of course, on their generality. If such findings prove to be the rule, rather than the exception, we can expect that, during times of conflict, friends and dating partners—particularly those with an anxious attachment style—will be more accurate at reading each other's negative or hostile thoughts or feelings than their positive feelings or expressions of love. If this is indeed the case, then the affect that they are, by inference, "receiving" from their partner during episodes of conflict should be experienced as being mainly negative or hostile. Furthermore, because couples tend to reciprocate whatever emotion they *think* their partner is conveying, and because they are mainly decoding hostility or negativity, they are likely to convey hostility back to the partner. It is therefore easy to see how, despite their initial expressions of both love and hostility, the partners might increasingly respond to each other's hostility and therefore escalate the levels of hostility that they reciprocate.

## Relationship Vulnerability

On the other hand, couples who feel that their relationship is especially vulnerable may display a contrasting effect—a tendency to avoid accurately "reading" each other's relationship-threatening thoughts and feelings. Simpson, Ickes, and Blackstone documented this tendency in a study of over 80 dating couples [42]. They predicted that couples in vulnerable relationships would be especially likely to display empathic *in*accuracy in situations in which the partners were experiencing relationship-threatening thoughts and feelings. For the purposes of their study, vulnerable couples were defined as those who were highly dependent on each other but were also highly insecure about the future of their relationship.

When the vulnerable couples were asked to infer each other's thoughts and feelings in a relationship-threatening situation, they displayed unusually low levels of empathic accuracy. In fact, their average empathic accuracy scores were not significantly different from a chance baseline, and were significantly lower than the average empathic accuracy scores obtained by opposite-sex strangers in an earlier study. Simpson et al. argued that the "motivated inaccuracy" displayed by these couples could actually help to preserve their vulnerable relationships in the face of a strong situational threat [42]. Their argument was supported by the fact that the vulnerable couples, who were unusually inaccurate, were all still dating at a 5-month follow-up, whereas nearly 30% of the other couples in the study had broken up by this point.

A related finding comes from a study by Buysse and Ickes [43], in which both dating couples and opposite-sex strangers discussed the merits of practicing safe sex in order to guard one's partner against the possible health consequences of extradyadic affairs. Buysse and Ickes found that, during these discussions, the dating couples tended to use an avoidant communication style [43]. Although relationship researchers generally regard avoidance as damaging to a relationship [44], the Simpson et al. study [42] suggests that, when couples are confronted by relationship threat, avoiding the issue may actually enhance relationship stability. Indeed, in the Buysse and Ickes study, the couples who used an avoidant communication style in the safe sex/extradyadic affair discussions generally rated themselves as being very satisfied with their dating relationships [43].

A more recent series of studies by Ickes, Dugosh, Simpson, and Wilson has focused specifically on individual differences in the motivation to acquire relationship-threatening information [45]. Ickes and his colleagues developed a self-report measure of motivation to acquire relationship-threatening information (MARTI) and found that dating partners with high MARTI scores were lower in relational trust and reported engaging in more "suspicion behaviors" such as eavesdropping on a partner's private phone conversation or calling to see if a partner was where he or she was supposed to be. Moreover, dating partners with high MARTI scores were more likely to break up within 5 months of being tested in the lab [45].

## ☐ How Can Empathic Accuracy Be Improved in Casual and Close Relationships?

Theory and research have already begun to address the question of how empathic accuracy can be improved in casual and close relationships [11], [13–14], [18], [36]. Ironically, the preliminary answer to this question appears to be that strangers should in some respects act more like intimates, whereas intimates should in some respects act more like strangers.

## Improving the Empathic Accuracy of Strangers

For strangers, the evidence clearly suggests that empathic accuracy can be improved in at least two ways—by increasing their acquaintanceship with the target and by obtaining immediate feedback about the target's actual thoughts and feelings.

### The Effect of Exposure and Acquaintanceship

Stinson and Ickes found that the male friends were, on average, about 50% more accurate than male strangers in inferring each other's thoughts and feelings [13]. This effect (both the friends' advantage and its magnitude) was later replicated in a follow-up study by Graham [36], who found that it extended to the comparison of female friends with female strangers as well. Evidence for a more passive "acquaintanceship" effect was reported in a study by Marangoni et al. [18]. The perceiver-observers in this study were asked to infer from standardized videotapes the thoughts and feelings of three female clients who discussed their personal problems with a male, client-centered therapist. The results indicated that the observers' empathic accuracy improved substantially from the beginning to the end of the tapes. However, this effect was limited to the two clients whose accounts were relatively coherent and straightforward, and whose thoughts and feelings were therefore relatively easy to "read."

### Limitations of the Acquaintanceship Effect

Although increased exposure to and acquaintanceship with a target does generally lead to an increase in the perceiver's empathic accuracy, there are limits to this effect. First, some people are particularly bad judges—even when trying to infer the thoughts and feelings of a friend [33]. Second, some targets are extremely difficult to read—even by perceivers who have been acquainted with them for a very long time (see, for example, Colvin's research on target "judgability" [35] and Hancock & Ickes's research on target "readability" [33]). Third, there may be circumstances when an individual is motivated to make *in*accurate inferences in order to preserve a close relationship. We talk more about the topic of motivated inaccuracy later in this chapter.

## *Obtaining Feedback About the Target's Thoughts and Feelings*

Marangoni et al. further demonstrated that providing a perceiver with immediate, veridical feedback about a target's actual thoughts and feelings served to increase the empathic accuracy of the perceiver's subsequent inferences [18]. Specifically, they reported that perceivers who received such feedback during the middle portion of each therapy tape were generally more accurate during the final portion of the tape than were control subjects who had received no feedback. This feedback effect was not significant, however, for the highly ambivalent client whose thoughts and feelings were particularly difficult to read.

## *Summary*

These findings suggest that strangers can improve their empathic accuracy by acting more like friends—by becoming better acquainted with each other and by seeking a lot of feedback about each other's actual thoughts and feelings. The success of these strategies will be limited, however, by the overall empathic ability of the perceiver and by the overall "readability" of the target person.

## Improving the Empathic Accuracy of Intimates

Surprisingly, there is evidence that the empathic accuracy of spouses actually declines following the first few years of their marriage [46]. This finding not only suggests a curvilinear relationship between length of acquaintanceship and empathic accuracy, but it also raises the important questions of why such decline occurs and how it can be reversed. Thomas et al. found that this decline was mediated by the extent to which the content of the individual partners' thoughts and feelings was divergent [46]. In other words, couples who had been married for longer periods of time tended to have fewer shared thoughts and feelings (and, by implication, more idiosyncratic ones) during their interactions than did more recently married couples; and it was this difference in the level of "shared cognitive focus" that accounted for the lower levels of empathic accuracy attained by couples married for longer periods of time.

Thomas et al. interpreted this finding as evidence that "partners in long-standing relationships become complacent and overly familiar with each other" [46, p. 840]. They therefore lack the motivation to actively monitor each other's words and actions and to attain the kind of common, intersubjective focus in their thoughts and feelings that facilitates empathic accuracy. If this explanation is correct, it suggests that intimates can enhance their empathic accuracy by in some respects acting more like strangers. Specifically, they can attend more closely to each other's words and actions and work harder to maintain a "shared cognitive focus" in their daily interactions.

## ☐ What Factors Can Impair Empathic Accuracy in Close Relationships?

What factors can *impair* empathic accuracy in friendships and love relationships? On the basis of existing theory and research, Ickes and Simpson have proposed a number of likely factors [47].

1. The target person's inability or unwillingness to *express* the content of his or her thoughts and feelings through verbal and nonverbal channels should impair the perceiver's empathic accuracy.
2. Empathic accuracy should also be impaired by the perceiver's inability or unwillingness to correctly *interpret* the target's behavioral cues. The perceiver's impairment may in some cases be attributable to a simple lack of empathic ability. In other cases, however, it may be attributable to either a chronic or temporary lack of empathic motivation or to a phenomenon called "motivated inaccuracy." This "motivated inaccuracy" phenomenon will be discussed in greater detail below.
3. Failure to be "on the same page with" the target person, often because the perceiver and target are preoccupied with their own independent concerns, can also impair the perceiver's empathic accuracy. Indeed, Thomas et al. have argued that it is the diverging tasks and concerns that send husbands and wives down different "tracks" following their honeymoon years that are also responsible for the decline in their average empathic accuracy over time [46].
4. In a similar vein, stress—both acute and chronic—should also impair the perceiver's empathic accuracy. Worries and concerns that arise in the context of both short- and long-term life stressors (e.g., problems related to health, work, finances, or the relationship itself) should draw a perceiver's attention and cognitive effort away from deciphering those behavioral cues in everyday interaction that help to convey the true content of a partner's thoughts and feelings [48].
5. Despite the fact that increased acquaintanceship generally leads to increased empathic accuracy, the advantages conferred by greater knowledge of one's partner may at times be offset by perceptual biases that originate from knowing the partner *too* well. Sillars has proposed that three features of close relationships can short-circuit accurate empathic understanding: excessive familiarity with the partner, high

levels of behavioral interdependence, and strong emotional involvement [49]. *Familiarity* frequently breeds overconfidence in inferential tasks [50], and if overconfidence extends into domains in which partners know little about one another, greater familiarity can result in less understanding. As *interdependence* increases, the actions of each partner must be interpreted within an increasingly complicated interpersonal context. By creating greater attributional ambiguity (i.e., "*Which* of these many contextual factors is/are relevant now?"), these numerous "background" variables should lower the perceived correspondence between the partner's overt behavior and his or her underlying dispositions, and thus impair empathic accuracy. Finally, *strong emotional involvement* should—in some circumstances—also attenuate empathic accuracy in close relationships, either by activating self-serving biases [51] or by restricting the acquisition of new information and the retrieval of old information.

6. Certain situational factors should also impair the perceiver's empathic accuracy. As likely candidates, Ickes and Simpson have targeted situational factors that either (a) draw the perceiver's attention away from their partner's behavioral cues that are relevant to the inferential task (such as being absorbed in one's own thoughts about what to say next), or (b) require difficult, novel, or unfamiliar inferences to be made [47].

## ☐ Empathic Accuracy: Is It Good or Bad for Relationships?

Is empathic accuracy good or bad for relationships? To the casual observer who relies on conventional wisdom, the apparent answer is, "Of course empathic accuracy is good for relationships; if everyone just understood each other better, the world would be a wonderful place."

Upon reflection, however, there may be circumstances in which an accurate understanding of the thoughts and feelings of one's relationship partner could actually harm or destabilize the relationship. Thus, while accurate understanding should be good for relationships as a general rule, too much understanding in certain contexts may have deleterious consequences. In the following sections, we briefly review some theory and research that will help to disentangle the general rule from its important exceptions.

### The Rule: Empathic Accuracy is Good for Relationships

Many studies in the *marital adjustment literature* have documented a positive association between marital adjustment and understanding of the attitudes, role expectations, and self-perceptions of one's spouse (see [52] for a review).

Similarly, the *empathic accuracy literature* also provides some evidence that partners' accuracy in inferring each other's thoughts and feelings is associated with positive relationship outcomes. For example, Simpson, Ickes, and Oriña reported evidence that accurately "reading" one's partner in order to anticipate a need, avert a conflict, or keep a small problem from escalating into a larger one is likely to be healthy and adaptive for dating as well as marriage relationships [53]. This conclusion is consistent with Kilpatrick, Bissonnette, and Rusbult's finding that, in a large sample of newlywed couples, empathic accuracy was positively correlated (*r*s in the range of .4–.6) with such variables as commitment to the relationship, willingness to accommodate the partner's bad behavior, and dyadic adjustment [54]. These effects, which were found when the couples were in the first 12–18 months of their marriages, generally declined in strength across time, so that only the couple-level correlation between empathic accuracy and dyadic adjustment was still significant (.35) 2 years later. Kilpatrick et al. speculated that the positive effects of empathic accuracy on relational outcomes may decrease over time for couples who, having learned each other's idiosyncratic cognitive, emotional, and behavioral predilections, have developed habits that automatically accommodate them [54].

If the link between empathic accuracy and positive relationship outcomes is likely to be most evident in the earlier stages of a relationship, it makes sense that empathic accuracy was significantly related to marital adjustment in Kilpatrick et al.'s newlywed sample [54] but was not significantly related to marital satisfaction in Thomas et al.'s sample of longer married couples [46]. From this standpoint, it also makes sense that Ickes et al. found that opposite-sex strangers were more accurate in inferring each other's thoughts and feelings to the extent they found each other physically attractive, because—like the recently married couples in the Kilpatrick et al. study [54]—they were presumably highly motivated to monitor each other closely and try to achieve a "shared cognitive focus" [23]. Their studies offer additional evidence that empathic accuracy contributes to positive relationship outcomes, particularly during the formative stages of close relationships.

Collectively, these studies support the view that, as a rule, more understanding (i.e., greater empathic accuracy) is good for relationships. The generality of this rule has been questioned, however, by writers such as Noller [55] and Sillars [49]. These authors have argued that the association between understanding and marital adjustment is more complicated than earlier theorists and researchers supposed. In addition, recent empirical and theoretical work indicates that circumstances may exist in which greater empathic understanding might actually *reduce* partner's satisfaction with their relationships.

## The Exceptions: When Empathic Accuracy is Bad for Relationships

To date, the most integrative theoretical work on the question of when empathic accuracy might be bad for relationships has been done by Sillars and his colleagues (e.g., [56–57]). In an early review of the literature [49], Sillars suggested three such conditions:

1. *Irreconcilable differences*. When the partners' thoughts and feelings involve irreconcilable differences that cannot be resolved through greater clarification of each others' respective views about an issue, greater empathic accuracy should increase the level of conflict and dissatisfaction in the relationship [58–59].
2. *Benevolent misconceptions*. When benevolent misconceptions facilitate the stability and satisfaction that partners experience in their relationship, enhanced understanding that alters or destroys these misconceptions should destabilize the relationship through the decreased satisfaction of one or both partners [60].
3. *Blunt, unpleasant truths*. When the partner's words and actions cause the perceiver to experience pain and distress because they appear to express blunt, unpleasant "truths" rather than tactful and benign interpretations of the perceiver's character, motives, or behavior, increased understanding of the partner's thoughts and feelings should impair relationship stability and satisfaction [58], [61–62].

What do these three conditions have in common? They all represent cases in which greater empathic accuracy leads to insights that are not only painful and distressing to one or both partners, but also raise doubts about the strength and permanence of their relationship.

## ☐ A Theoretical Model of How Empathic Accuracy Is "Managed" in Close Relationships

Ickes and Simpson have proposed a theoretical model of how empathic accuracy is "managed" by relationship members [47], [63]. This model starts by assuming that the range of empathic accuracy (the upper and lower boundaries) that can be attained in a given interaction is set by (a) the partners' respective levels of "readability" (the degree to which each partner displays cues that reflect his or her true internal states), and (b) the partners' respective levels of empathic ability (the degree to which each partner can accurately decipher the other's valid behavioral cues). Within these broad constraints, however, the model presumes that empathic accuracy should be "managed" very differently depending on several factors. The most fundamental elements are represented in Figure 7.1.

Figure 7.1 characterizes behavior at the individual, rather than the dyadic, level of analysis. According to the model, each partner makes a preliminary assessment of whether or not the current situation is likely to evoke a *danger zone* topic or issue in the relationship. The term "danger zone" denotes having to confront a topic or issue that could threaten the relationship by revealing thoughts or feelings harbored by one's partner that the individual perceiver might find personally distressing or upsetting.

Of course, individual perceivers might differ in what they find distressing and upsetting in their partners' thoughts and feelings. Male partners, for example, might find their female partner's thoughts about her actual or potential sexual infidelity more threatening than her thoughts about her actual or potential emotional infidelity, whereas the reverse might be true for female partners [64]. Thus, the model begins by acknowledging that relationship partners can follow different "paths" or trajectories if one partner anticipates a danger zone emerging in the current situation whereas the other partner does not. Although developing the theoretical implications of this more complex "dyadic" model is beyond the scope of the present chapter, we consider a few of these implications below.

At the first branching point in the model, each partner infers whether the current situation is or is not likely to evoke a danger-zone issue. Let us first consider the part of the model that applies when an individual perceives that a situation is nonthreatening in the sense that no danger-zone issue is likely to emerge that might force the partners to confront each other's relationship-threatening thoughts and feelings.

## Empathic Accuracy in Nonthreatening Contexts

When perceivers expect to discuss issues that should not have threatening implications for their relationship (see the right-hand portion of Figure 7.1), the model predicts that they should be at least somewhat motivated to accurately infer their partners' thoughts and feelings. Because experience should have taught the partners that mutual understanding usually facilitates their ability to coordinate their actions in the pursuit of individual and dyadic goals, and because the behaviors needed to achieve such understanding typically become habitual through repeated reinforcement

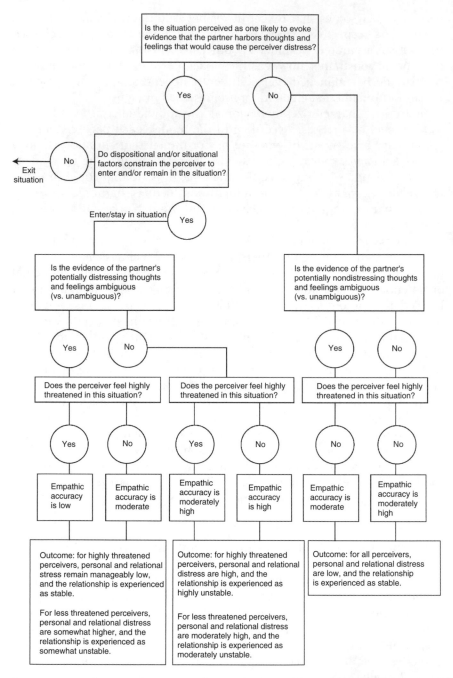

**FIGURE 7.1.** The empathic accuracy model (adapted from [47], [63]).

[65], perceivers should be motivated to attain at least moderate levels of accuracy when inferring their partners' thoughts and feelings in non-threatening contexts.

Accordingly, in nonthreatening situations in which no danger zones are perceived (e.g., everyday conversations about trivial or mundane issues), perceivers should display a habit-based "accuracy orientation." This orientation should help them to clear up misunderstandings about nonthreatening issues, keep minor conflicts from escalating into major ones, and gain a deeper understanding of their partners, all of which should enhance feelings of satisfaction and closeness in the relationship. Thus, as long as situations do not lead perceivers to anticipate the emergence of issues that could evoke and reveal their partners' relationship-threatening thoughts and feelings, perceivers should be motivated to attain at least a moderate level of empathic accuracy.

On the other hand, the motivation of perceivers to be accurate should be attenuated to some degree by the routine, taken-for-granted nature of most mundane, nonthreatening interactions (cf. [46], [66]). The level of empathic accuracy displayed by perceivers in nonthreatening interactions should, therefore, be moderate to moderately high rather than high (see the lower right portion of Figure 7.1). Finally, levels of relationship satisfaction and stability should correlate positively with empathic accuracy in nonthreatening situations, consistent with the premise that higher levels of empathic accuracy are generally good for relationships. These effects may be small, however, because they are likely to be attenuated by the restricted ranges of both the empathic accuracy and the relationship-outcome variables in most nonthreatening interactions.

## Empathic Accuracy in Relationship-Threatening Contexts

Inevitably, perceivers will encounter situations in which "danger zones" are anticipated—situations that have the potential to destabilize their relationships (see the left-hand portion of Figure 7.1). When these situations arise, the model predicts that the first impulse of most perceivers should be to avoid or escape from them, if possible. In other words, the tactic of avoiding or escaping from danger-zone situations should be the first "line of defense" that perceivers can use to keep themselves from having to confront their partners' relationship-threatening thoughts and feelings.

The use of this tactic presumes, of course, that perceivers can recognize—and even anticipate—potential "danger zone" areas in their relationships (e.g., positive feelings about old flames or lustful thoughts about other attractive people). Over time, perceivers in most (but not all) relationships should learn to identify and avoid such danger-zone areas in order to protect their own self-esteem, their partners' self-esteem, and their cherished views of the relationship (cf. [67]). In doing so, perceivers can avoid dealing with danger-zone topics directly, based on the presumption that it is better (and easier) to avoid confronting one's worst fears than it is to have one's worst fears confirmed and then be forced to deal with them.

Avoiding or escaping danger-zone issues is not always possible, however, and the section of the model that is relevant to these cases is depicted in the left and middle portions of Figure 7.1. When perceivers feel obliged to remain in a relationship-threatening situation, the model predicts that their second "line of defense" should be motivated inaccuracy—a conscious or unconscious failure to accurately infer the specific content of their partner's potentially hurtful thoughts and feelings. The success of this strategy should vary, however, depending on the degree to which the inferred content of the partner's distressing thoughts/feelings is perceived as ambiguous versus unambiguous.

If the content of the partners' potentially threatening thoughts and feelings is perceived as ambiguous (see the left-hand portion of Figure 7.1), perceivers should be able to use motivated inaccuracy as a defense. By using subception or other defense mechanisms (e.g., denial, repression, rationalization) to avoid having to deal with the most threatening implications of their partners' potentially destructive thoughts and feelings, perceivers should *mis*infer such thoughts and feelings and therefore display low levels of empathic accuracy. Their defensiveness should provide them with an important payoff, however, by decreasing their distress and by helping to keep their relationship more stable.

Simpson et al. reported some intriguing evidence that romantic partners may indeed use motivated inaccuracy to ward off impending threats to their relationships [42]. Eighty-two dating couples took turns rating and then discussing with each other the desirability of several opposite-sex persons as "potential dating partners." Immediately afterwards, the members of each couple independently viewed a videotape of the rating-and-discussion task. On the first pass through the tape, each partner listed all of the thoughts and feelings that he or she had had during the task. Then, on the second pass through the tape, each partner was asked to infer each of his or her *partner's* thoughts and feelings at the exact points on the tape at which they had been reported.

As predicted by Ickes and Simpson's model [47], [63], partners who reported the greatest perceived threat to their relationships displayed the least empathic accuracy. Of even greater interest, all of the highly threatened/low accuracy couples were still dating at 4-month follow-up, whereas 28% of the remaining couples in the study had broken up. That is, couples who displayed the least accuracy in this relationship-threatening situation were the most stable at follow-up, suggesting that motivated inaccuracy might indeed function as a preemptive relationship maintenance strategy.

A more recent study involving 96 married couples provides further evidence in support of Ickes and Simpson's empathic accuracy model [47], [63], [68]. In this study, married couples were videotaped as they attempted to resolve a problem in their marriage. They then completed the same thought/feeling inference task as the dating couples in the Simpson et al. study [42]. The results showed that spouses who displayed greater empathic accuracy for their partner's relationship-threatening thoughts and feelings experienced a decline in feelings of subjective closeness with their partner over the course of the experiment. In contrast, greater empathic accuracy for non-threatening thoughts and feelings was associated with increased feelings of subjective closeness with one's partner.

Just as the empathic accuracy model predicts, there appear to be circumstances in which motivated inaccuracy can actually help to stabilize and sustain relationships in the face of serious perceived threats. There are other circumstances, however, in which motivated inaccuracy is simply not an option. What happens, for example, when perceivers feel obliged to remain in a relationship-threatening situation but cannot use motivated inaccuracy as a secondary strategy for dealing with the threat? The middle portion of Figure 7.1 depicts one case of this type, in which the relationship-threatening content of the partner's thoughts and feelings is perceived to be clear and unambiguous (e.g., the partner openly admits that s/he loves someone else). The sheer clarity of this information should force the perceiver to achieve at least moderately high levels of empathic accuracy, accompanied by very low relationship satisfaction and instability.

Obviously, this case is one in which increased empathic accuracy can actually harm relationships. However, because the perceiver is forced to be accurate by virtue of the sheer clarity of the available information, it does not illustrate a case in which *motivated* accuracy hurts relationships. Such a case should occur, however, if the perceiver has a strong personal need to confront the truth about the partner's relationship-relevant thoughts and feelings. For example, Simpson et al. have demonstrated that more anxiously attached (preoccupied) dating partners tend to display motivated accuracy (rather than motivated inaccuracy) in response to at least one type of relationship threat—the possibility of relationship loss [27]. This finding suggests that a strong, dispositionally based accuracy motive can override such tendencies as avoiding danger-zone situations or using motivated inaccuracy to stave off relationship-threatening information.

## ☐ Conclusions

In this chapter, we have examined several aspects of emotional intelligence and empathic accuracy as they relate to friendships and dating relationships. Knowing one's partner "from the inside," as friends and dating partners typically come to do, can facilitate empathic accuracy for the partner's thoughts and feelings. Making effective use of this inside information is not guaranteed, however. It depends on a variety of factors that include characteristics of the perceiver (empathic ability, attentiveness, motivation, attachment orientation), characteristics of the target (self-directedness, consistency, coherence), and characteristics of their relationship (e.g., intimacy and relationship discord).

We have also pointed out factors that may impair empathic accuracy in close relationships. These factors include the target's inability or unwillingness to express thoughts and feelings, the perceiver's inability or unwillingness to interpret the target's behavioral cues, and the perceiver's current level of stress. And, paradoxically, there are at least three reasons (overconfidence, interdependence, strong emotional involvement) why knowing one's partner *too* well can also impair empathic accuracy.

Perhaps the most interesting aspect of empathic accuracy is its capacity to generally help, but sometimes hurt, close relationships. One aim of Ickes and Simpson's theoretical model [47], [63] is to specify the conditions in which empathic accuracy will either benefit or hurt a close relationship. In situations where improved empathic accuracy is desirable, we know that this can generally be accomplished by increased acquaintanceship with the target (although there are limits to the acquaintanceship effect), and by obtaining feedback about the target's thoughts and feelings. On the other hand, to reduce the tendency for longtime partners to lose empathic accuracy for each other's thoughts and feelings, couples would do well to act a little more like strangers in some respects—closely attending to each other's behavior during interactions and attempting to maintain a shared cognitive focus.

## ☐ References

1. Salovey, P., Hsee, C. K., & Mayer, J. D. (1993). Emotional intelligence and the self-regulation of affect. In D. M. Wegner (Ed.), *Handbook of mental control* (pp. 58–277). Englewood Cliffs, NJ: Prentice Hall.
2. Ickes, W. (Ed.). (1997). *Empathic accuracy*. New York: Guilford Press.
3. Ickes, W. (2003). *Everyday mind reading: Understanding what other people think and feel*. Amherst, NY: Prometheus Books.

4. Baron-Cohen, S. (1995). *Mindblindness: An essay on autism and theory of mind* Cambridge, MA: MIT Press.

5. Eisenberg, N., Murphy, B. C., & Shepard, S. (1997). The development of empathic accuracy. In W. Ickes (Ed.), *Empathic accuracy* (pp. 73–116). New York: Guilford Press.

6. Roeyers, H., Buysse, A., Ponnet, K., & Pichal, B. (2001). Advancing advanced mind-reading tests: Empathic accuracy in adults with a pervasive developmental disorder. *Journal of Child Psychology and Psychiatry and Allied Disciplines, 42*(2), 271–278.

7. Ickes, W., Buysse, A., Pham, H., Rivers, K., Erickson, J. R., Hancock, M., et al. (2000). On the difficulty of distinguishing "good" and "poor" perceivers: A social relations analysis of empathic accuracy data. *Personal Relationships, 7,* 219–234.

8. Gleason, K. (2004). *The effects of empathic accuracy on childhood relationships.* Unpublished doctoral dissertation, University of Texas at Arlington.

9. Taft, R. (1955). The ability to judge people. *Psychological Bulletin, 52,* 1–23.

10. Davis, M. H., & Kraus, L. A. (1997). Personality and empathic accuracy. In W. Ickes (Ed.), *Empathic accuracy* (pp. 144–168). New York: Guilford Press.

11. Gesn, P. R. (1995). *Shared knowledge between same-sex friends: Measurement and validation.* Unpublished master's thesis, University of Texas at Arlington.

12. Senecal, S., Murard, N., & Hess, U. (2003). Do you know what I feel? Partners' predictions and judgments of each other's emotional reactions to emotion-eliciting situations. *Sex Roles, 48,* 21–37.

13. Stinson, L., & Ickes, W. (1992). Empathic accuracy in the interactions of male friends versus male strangers. *Journal of Personality and Social Psychology, 62,* 787–797.

14. Colvin, C. R., Vogt, D., & Ickes, W. (1997). Why do friends understand each other better than strangers do? In W. Ickes (Ed.), *Empathic accuracy* (pp. 169–193). New York: Guilford Press.

15. Smither, S. (1977). A reconsideration of the developmental study of empathy. *Human Development, 20,* 253–276.

16. Karniol, R. (1990). Reading people's minds: A transformation rule model for predicting others' thoughts and feelings. *Advances in Experimental Social Psychology, 23,* 211–247.

17. Kenny, D. A. (1994). *Interpersonal perception: A social relations analysis.* New York: Guilford Press.

18. Marangoni, C., Garcia, S., Ickes, W., & Teng, G. (1995). Empathic accuracy in a clinically-relevant setting. *Journal of Personality and Social Psychology, 39,* 1135–1148.

19. Gesn, P. R., & Ickes, W. (1999). The development of meaning contexts for empathic accuracy: Channel and sequence effects. *Journal of Personality and Social Psychology, 77,* 746–761.

20. Ickes, W. (1993). Empathic accuracy. *Journal of Personality, 61,* 587–609.

21. Ickes, W., Marangoni, C., & Garcia, S. (1997). Studying empathic accuracy in a clinically relevant context. In W. Ickes (Ed.), *Empathic accuracy* (pp. 282–310). New York: Guilford Press.

22. Funder, D. C. (1995). On the accuracy of personality judgment: A realistic approach. *Psychological Review, 102*(4), 652–670.

23. Ickes, W., Stinson, L., Bissonnette, V., & Garcia, S. (1990). Naturalistic social cognition: Empathic accuracy in mixed-sex dyads. *Journal of Personality and Social Psychology, 59,* 730–742.

24. Trommsdorff, G., & John, H. (1992). Decoding affective communication in intimate relationships. *European Journal of Social Psychology, 22,* 41–54.

25. Ickes, W., Gesn, P. R., & Graham, T. (2000). Gender differences in empathic accuracy: Differential ability or differential motivation? *Personal Relationships, 7*(1), 95–109.

26. Klein, K. J. K., & Hodges, S. (2001). Gender differences, motivation, and empathic accuracy: When it pays to understand. *Personality and Social Psychology Bulletin, 27*(6), 720–730.

27. Simpson, J. A., Ickes, W., & Grich, J. (1999). When accuracy hurts: Reactions of anxious-uncertain individuals to a relationship-threatening situation. *Journal of Personality and Social Psychology, 76*, 754–769.

28. Rothbaum, F., Weisz, J. R., & Snyder, S. S. (1982). Changing the world and changing the self: A two-process model of perceived control. *Journal of Personality and Social Psychology, 42*, 5–37.

29. Vogt, D. S., & Colvin, C. R. (2000). *The good judge of personality: Theory, correlates, and Cronbachian "artifacts".* Unpublished manuscript.

30. Ickes, W., Hancock, M., Graham, T., Gesn, P. R., & Mortimer, D. C. (1994). *(Nonsignificant) individual difference correlates of perceivers' empathic accuracy scores.* Unpublished data, University of Texas at Arlington.

31. Shearn, D., Spellman, L., Straley, B. Meirick, J., & Stryker, K. (1999). Empathic blushing in friends and strangers. *Motivation and Emotion, 23*(4), 307–316.

32. Schweinle, W. E., & Ickes, W. (2005). *The role of men's critical/rejecting overattribution bias, affect, and attentional disengagement in marital aggression.* Manuscript under review.

33. Hancock, M., & Ickes, W. (1996). Empathic accuracy: When does the perceiver–target relationship make a difference? *Journal of Social and Personal Relationships, 13*, 179–199.

34. Snyder, M. (1987). *Private appearances/public realities: The psychology of self-monitoring.* New York: W. H. Freeman.

35. Colvin, C. R. (1993). Judgable people: Personality, behavior, and competing explanations. *Journal of Personality and Social Psychology, 64*, 861–873.

36. Graham, T. (1994). *Gender, relationships, and target differences in empathic accuracy.* Unpublished master's thesis, University of Texas at Arlington.

37. Hutchison, J., & Ickes, W. (2000). *Empathic accuracy in same-sex dyads as a function of the length of the relationship.* Unpublished data, University of Texas at Arlington.

38. Kirchler, E. (1988). Marital happiness and interaction in everyday surroundings: A time-sample diary approach for couples. *Journal of Social and Personal Relationships, 5*, 375–382.

39. Kirchler, E. (1989). Everyday life experiences at home: An interaction diary approach to assess marital relationships. *Journal of Family Psychology, 2*, 311–336.

40. Noller, P. & Ruzzene, M. (1991). Communication in marriage: The influence of affect and cognition. In G. J. O. Fletcher & F. D. Fincham (Eds.), *Cognition in close relationships* (pp. 203–233). Hillsdale, NJ: Lawrence Erlbaum Associates, Inc.

41. Gaelick, L., Bodenhausen, G., & Wyer, R. S. (1985). Emotional communication in close relationships. *Journal of Personality and Social Psychology, 49*, 1246–1265.

42. Simpson, J. A., Ickes, W., & Blackstone, T. (1995). When the head protects the heart: Empathic accuracy in dating relationships. *Journal of Personality and Social Psychology, 69*, 629–641.

43. Buysse, A., & Ickes, W. (1999). Communication patterns in laboratory discussions of safer sex between dating versus nondating partners. *Journal of Sex Research, 36*(2), 121–134.

44. Gottman, J. M. (1993). The roles of conflict engagement, escalation, and avoidance in marital interaction: A longitudinal view of five types of couples. *Journal of Consulting and Clinical Psychology, 61*, 6–15.

45. Ickes, W., Dugosh, J. W., Simpson, J. A., & Wilson, C. L. (2003). Suspicious minds: The motive to acquire relationship-threatening information. *Personal Relationships, 10*, 131–148.

46. Thomas, G., Fletcher, G. J. O., & Lange, C. (1997). On-line empathic accuracy in marital interaction. *Journal of Personality and Social Psychology, 72*(4), 839–850.

47. Ickes, W., & Simpson, J. A. (1997). Managing empathic accuracy in close relationships. In W. Ickes (Ed.), *Empathic accuracy* (pp. 218–250). New York: Guilford Press.

48. Schroder, H. M., Driver, M. J., & Streufert, S. (1967). *Human information processing.* New York: Holt, Rinehart, & Winston.

49. Sillars, A. L. (1985). Interpersonal perception in relationships. In W. Ickes (Ed.), *Compatible and incompatible relationships* (pp. 277–305). New York: Springer-Verlag.
50. Shapiro, A., & Swensen, C. (1969). Patterns of self-disclosure among married couples. *Journal of Counseling Psychology, 16*, 179–180.
51. Weary-Bradley, G. (1978). Self-serving biases in the attribution process: A re-examination of the fact or fiction question. *Journal of Personality and Social Psychology, 36*, 56–71.
52. Sillars, A. L., & Scott, M. D. (1983). Interpersonal perception between intimates: An integrative review. *Human Communication Research, 10*, 153–176.
53. Simpson, J. A., Ickes, W., & Oriña, M. (2001). Empathic accuracy and preemptive relationship maintenance. In J. H. Harvey & A. Wenzel (Eds.), *Close romantic relationships: Maintenance and enhancement* (pp. 27–46). Mahwah, NJ: Lawrence Erlbaum Associates, Inc.
54. Kilpatrick, S. D., Bissonnette, V. L., & Rusbult, C. E. (2002). Empathic accuracy and accommodative behavior among newly married couples. *Personal Relationships, 9*(4), 369–393.
55. Noller, P. (1984). *Nonverbal communication and marital interaction*. Oxford, UK: Pergamon.
56. Sillars, A. L. (1981). Attributions and interpersonal conflict resolution. In J. H. Harvey, W. J. Ickes, & R. F. Kidd (Eds.), *New directions in attribution research* (Vol. 3). Hillsdale, NJ: Lawrence Erlbaum Associates, Inc.
57. Sillars, A. L., & Parry, D. (1982). Stress, cognition, and communication in interpersonal conflicts. *Communication Research, 9*, 201–226.
58. Aldous, J. (1977). Family interaction patterns. *Annual Review of Sociology, 3*, 105–135.
59. Kursh, C. O. (1971). The benefits of poor communication. *Psychoanalytic Review, 58*, 189–208.
60. Levinger, G., & Breedlove, J. (1966). Interpersonal attraction and agreement. *Journal of Personality and Social Psychology, 3*, 367–372.
61. Rausch, H. L., Barry, W. A., Hertel, R. K., & Swain, M. A. (1974). *Communication conflict and marriage*. San Francisco: Jossey-Bass.
62. Watzlawick, P., Weakland, J., & Fisch, R. (1974). *Principles of problem formation and problem resolution*. New York: Norton.
63. Ickes, W., & Simpson, J. A. (2001). Motivational aspects of empathic accuracy. In G. J. O. Fletcher & M. S. Clark (Eds.), *Interpersonal processes: Blackwell handbook in social psychology* (pp. 229–249). Oxford, UK: Blackwell.
64. Buss, D. M., Shackelford, T. K., Kirkpatrick, L. A., Choe, J. C., Lim, H. K., Hasegawa, M., et al. (1999). Jealousy and the nature of beliefs about infidelity: Tests of competing hypotheses about sex differences in the United States, Korea, and Japan. *Personal Relationships, 6*, 125–150.
65. Bissonnette, V. L., Rusbult, C. E., & Kilpatrick, S. D. (1997). Empathic accuracy and marital conflict resolution. In W. Ickes (Ed.), *Empathic accuracy* (pp. 251–281). New York: Guilford Press.
66. Thomas, G., & Fletcher, G. J. O. (1997). Empathic accuracy in close relationships. In W. Ickes (Ed.), *Empathic accuracy* (pp. 194–217). New York: Guilford Press.
67. Murray, S. L. & Holmes, J. G. (1996). The construction of relationship realities. In G. J. O. Fletcher & J. Fitness (Eds.), *Knowledge structures in close relationships: A social psychological approach* (pp. 91–120). Mahwah, NJ: Lawrence Erlbaum Associates, Inc.
68. Simpson, J. A., Oriña, M. M., & Ickes, W. (2003). When accuracy hurts, and when it helps: A test of the empathic accuracy model in marital interactions. *Journal of Personality and Social Psychology, 85*, 881–893.

## 8
CHAPTER

Maurice J. Elias
Jeffrey S. Kress
Lisa Hunter

# Emotional Intelligence and the Crisis in Schools

Leaders in Western society have long articulated the close tie between a strong public education system and democracy itself. Schools are clearly for the common good, and they serve as the gateway to, and potential equalizer for, economic and life success for millions of underserved children . . . Yet, we have seen countless threats to public schools in recent years. Moreover, it often appears that public policy itself is harmful to public education. Although public officials call for "leaving no child behind," they rarely accompany that call with adequate resources to meet the challenge . . . Standing up for why we are in this field is essential to our personal and professional well-being. Equally important, it imperative for our very future—and that of our children. In this, failure is indeed not an option.[1, pp. 3–4]

Students, professionals, employers, indeed, every citizen should care deeply about that state of our schools. Eli Bower referred to schools as society's "humanizing" agents, the way in which the older generation showed youth the path to follow into adulthood [2]. But this role seems to be increasingly taken up by mass media and mass culture, in part because schools have narrowed their focus on children's academic skills and parents are distracted by economic and personal agendas [3]. Doctrinaire approaches have replaced a genuine focus on the courageous leadership needed for success in school and life [1].

Schools are being beset by an epidemic of bullying, peer harassment, violence, and other forms of victimization [4]. International research confirms the high prevalence of these problems in schools—as much as 60% in middle schools and substantial rates in elementary and high schools. A climate of fear inhibits academic risk taking, expression, and curiosity. Increasingly, such problems are viewed not as the failings of individual children but rather as products of the organization, climate, and values of the schools [5]. The pressures of No Child Left Behind legislation and policies focused around high-stakes academic testing create a "me first" climate that is highly competitive and anxiety provoking, beyond that which is beneficial for motivation; further, children who are most behind see themselves as least able to catch up [6]. They perceive that the school is not much interested in what they most have to offer. As one might expect, these difficulties are exacerbated under conditions of poverty, urban dangers, parental discord and employment difficulties, language and acculturation challenges, and histories of poor home–school connections.

## ☐ The Need to Address Children's Social-Emotional Intelligence

The crisis in schools has come from a failure to recognize that schools must address the whole child. Academic knowledge not tempered by social-emotional intelligence and ethical guidance can be a danger to society, not a boon. Being educated involves being knowledgeable, responsible, and caring, and, many would add, nonviolent and drug-free [7]. It means that the traditional focus on intellectual skills—IQ—must be supplemented by a strong concern with social and emotional skills—"EQ," the skills of emotional intelligence. The reasons for this are numerous, but none more compelling than what we have learned about brain function, human memory, and the difference between learning for test performance and learning for the purpose of living one's everyday life. For the latter, social and emotional factors are paramount [8].

A primary principle of emotional intelligence is that caring relationships form the foundation of all genuine and enduring learning [9]. A moment's reflections on one's own educational experiences will reveal the fundamental truth of this view. Most people can recall an experience with a supportive, caring teacher and the dramatic impact this had upon them (and, unfortunately, many can remember the harm done by a teacher perceived as unkind and uncaring). We all have learned under adverse conditions; but it is not the best way to produce regular and lasting learning, and we need to bring our educational systems into alignment with this reality.

Elias, Hunter, and Kress review the history of how emotional intelligence has been applied to education—from the emerging recognition of the importance of skills in the social and emotional realms, through the creation of social and emotional learning (SEL) curricula, and to the creation of guidelines for best practices [10]. Virtually everyone remembers the "other side" of their report cards, the side that listed such things as "comes prepared to class" and "works well with others." Over the past century of public education, it has become clear that life success is strongly influenced by one's accomplishments on that "other side"; yet, educators have failed to examine those attributes systematically [11].

Most recently, the Collaborative for Academic, Social, and Emotional Learning (CASEL; www.CASEL.org) has become the pre-eminent organization focusing on emotional intelligence in schools. CASEL was founded in 1994 by Dan Goleman and Eileen Rockefeller Growald to establish SEL as an essential part of education from preschool through high schools. Since then, CASEL has accomplished its work by advancing the science of SEL, translating our best knowledge into effective school practices, enhancing preparation and training of educators to carry out SEL, and creating networks of scientists, educators, advocates, policy makers, and interested citizens. CASEL has emerged not only as the national voice of SEL in the schools, but as an international force [12].

Part of the mission of schools in "humanizing" children involves building "EQ" since social-emotional intelligence is comprised of a set of skills and most skills can be improved through education [13]. The listing of specific skills identified by CASEL as the focus for educational efforts can be found in Table 8.1. Schools are beginning to find ways to address students' development in these areas on their report cards and through other means. However, while schools are "the one place communities can turn to for correctives to children's deficiencies in emotional and social competence" [14, p. 279], it is also recognized that the learning of emotional skills begins at home. Given that children enter school at different "emotional starting places" [13], schools are reluctant to be held accountable for students' social-emotional development. Yet, as Blankstein has noted [1], failure is not an option and genuine success in school and life cannot take place without the development of the relevant SEL skills. Fortunately, much is known about how schools can meet the challenge of building students' emotional intelligence and, in so doing, address the educational crisis.

## How Social-Emotional Intelligence Can be a Solution to the Education Crisis

Schools face the challenge of teaching children that are distracted from learning by a variety of pulls on their emotions and attention. This challenge can be met by infusing emotional literacy into the standard

**TABLE 8.1. CASEL's list of skills of social-emotional intelligence**

| | |
|---|---|
| Self-awareness | Identifying and recognizing emotions<br>Accurate self-perception<br>Recognizing strengths, needs, and values<br>Self-efficacy<br>Spirituality |
| Social awareness | Perspective taking<br>Empathy<br>Appreciating diversity<br>Respect for others |
| Responsible decision making | Problem identification and situation analysis<br>Problem solving<br>Evaluation and reflection<br>Personal, moral, and ethical responsibility |
| Self-management | Impulse control and stress management<br>Self-motivation and discipline<br>Goal setting and organizational skills |
| Relationship management | Communication, social approach and engagement, and building relationships<br>Working cooperatively<br>Negotiation, refusal, and conflict management<br>Help seeking and providing help to others |

curriculum as well as creating school climates that foster the development and application of social-emotional skills. Current research suggests that comprehensive approaches to building skills and creating school climates that foster their use will be more effective than piecemeal efforts [15]. Schools must organize themselves toward the goal of helping students see themselves and their learning as positive resources for their families, schools, workplaces, and communities. Skills must be imparted in contexts that are supportive of and consistent with the use of those skills if students are to internalize them and put them to use in all facets of school and extracurricular activities.

Schools programs that effectively engage in social-emotional intelligence and character education share five main characteristics [7]:

1. A school climate articulating specific themes, character elements, and/or values.
2. Explicit instruction in social-emotional intelligence skills.

3. Developmentally appropriate instruction in health-promotion and problem-prevention skills.
4. Services and systems to enhance coping skills and social support for transitions, crises, and resolving conflicts.
5. Widespread, systematic opportunities for positive, contributory service.

Schools with these features send messages about how students should conduct themselves as learners in all parts of the school building and respectful ways that staff should conduct themselves as educators and when interacting with students, colleagues, and parents [16]. Social-emotional skills, whether by that name or related terms, are integral to the mission of such schools. These schools are characterized by coordinated, high-quality, empirically supported programs for teaching life skills and infusing character into various aspects of the school routine and environment. Time is also devoted to preventing problems such as bullying and other forms of violence, alcohol, tobacco, and other drug use, and pregnancy.

The most forward-looking of these schools organize guidance and related services to be anticipatory, rather than reactive. They proactively provide support for children as they and their families face life crises, conflicts, and challenges, realizing that by the time academic or behavioral deterioration becomes manifest, issues are far more difficult to deal with. Finally, high quality service learning experiences are central to these schools' view of their purpose.

In short, what we are seeing is that schools of excellence integrate social-emotional intelligence into every aspect of school life. Unfortunately, such schools are still not the norm. In the following section, we discuss the promising new areas—we refer to them as frontiers—through which schools are bringing social-emotional intelligence into their core functions. We then describe the procedures schools follow to implement these and related approaches successfully.

# ☐ Emotional Intelligence Frontiers in the Schools

## Emotional Intelligence and Academic Success

A common question that has been asked when ideas about emotional intelligence are introduced in schools is, "If schools are to focus on social and emotional issues, and to promote EI, might this detract from the role of the schools in conveying academic content areas?" In the current high-stakes testing environment in place in many schools, anything that takes away from time devoted to mathematics and literacy skills is seen as "off mission" [6], [17]. This is due in large part to an accountability structure that focuses on math and literacy test scores. When tests are given in science and history areas, these, too, become added to the list of focal concerns. In addition to the argument that SEL may take away from traditional academics, some raise philosophical objections to SEL: schools are the place to learn academics, social-emotional matters skills should be learned elsewhere (e.g., the home, faith communities).

While we do not dispute that the promotion of EI skills involves coordinated effort with parents and communities, we do take issue with the idea that EI and "academics" are in some way incongruent with one another. Rather, we see a convergence in efforts to build academics and EI.

A growing amount of recent research shows the connection between social-emotional intelligence and academic success, as well as the positive impact of social-emotional programs on academic skill development [3]. For example, in experimental/control studies, the Responsive Classroom Program has been found to lead to a linear increase in students' math achievement scores over a 5 year period of time; the Seattle Social Development Program showed significant positive impact on grade retention and school dropout; the Social Decision Making/Social Problem Solving Program showed positive increases in language arts report card grades; and the PATHS curriculum led to growth on cognitive processing indicators, including intelligence test score subscales [3] (see www.CASEL.org to monitor the continued progress of this research).

We could go one step further than saying SEL benefits academic performance. Perhaps, SEL and academics are inseparable [12]. Closer examination of what we call "academics" points out similarities of curriculum content areas and EI, and shows that EI skills rest clearly within the central mission of the schools. For example, recently, each state has developed standards outlining expectations for student attainment for all content areas. States have codified, for example, the "social studies" skills students should have upon completion of eighth grade. An analysis of curriculum standards reveals that expectations for curriculum attainment contain many essential EI skills [17]. For example, in analyzing literature, students are expected to be able to understand the feelings and motivations of characters. In social studies, students are expected to understand consequences of historical events. A literature lesson that does not touch on the goals of characters or the emotions that a poem stir in a student misses an EI "teachable moment" *and* overlooks an important aspect of the academic content area. Similarly, the dispassionate study of historical events may well contribute to past errors being replicated in the future.

## Advances in SEL Curricula

CASEL has undertaken extensive analysis of school-based programs to enhance emotional intelligence. In a landmark publication, "Safe and Sound" [15], over 80 programs were subjected to exhaustive study and 22 were designated as SELect programs, indicating that they were comprehensive, met existing criteria for sound implementation elements, and also had demonstrable evidence that they successfully met their goals. In the course of this work, CASEL advanced our understanding of successful school-based curricula by articulating two complementary strategies that are increasingly being used in concert: school-level strategies and social-competence enhancement programs.

*School-level strategies* aim to facilitate collaborative and productive relationships among the key stakeholders in a school community (i.e., administrators, teachers, parents, and students). Such relationships can help a school coordinate its prevention efforts and create a climate conducive to learning and the promotion of mental health. This is especially important when addressing such areas as smoking and other substance use. James Comer's School Development Program [18] and the Positive Action through Holistic Education (PATHE) Project [19] are examples of promising coordinated school-level organizational development and planning strategies.

School-level programs also focus on the climate of the building and the classrooms within them. These programs attempt to achieve this goal by increasing school-wide and classroom opportunities for active participation in learning and the development of supportive relationships with adults and peers. The Child Development Project (now called the Caring School Community Program) [20], the Seattle Social Development Project [21–22], and the School Transitional Environment Project [23] offer examples of successful approaches at the school–organizational level.

Among the most effective *social-competence enhancement programs* identified by CASEL [7], [15] are the New Jersey-based Social Decision Making/Social Problem Solving Program, the Promoting Alternative Thinking Strategies (PATHS) Curriculum, based at Penn State University, the Massachusetts-based Responsive Classroom and Open Circle programs, the Lions Club-Quest International program based in Ohio, the spiritually focused Passages program of Rachael Kessler in Colorado, and, on the West Coast, the Raising Healthy Children and Second Step programs. All these programs share a common focus on developing and improving children's self-control, stress management, problem-solving, and decision-making skills, as well as building their affective awareness and reflective capacities.

In a climate focused on standards and evidence-based programs, schools are now able to choose from a number of tested, sophisticated, systemic, curriculum-based approaches to use as vehicles for bring social-emotional intelligence into their structures. Not surprisingly, schools are looking for integrative frameworks within which to bring in the range of social-emotional intelligence approaches just noted. One of the most promising of these frameworks is that of school mental health.

## School Mental Health

In recent years, there has been tremendous interest in school mental health. An increasing awareness of the gap between children who need mental health services and those who actually receive these services and advances in the science of child and adolescent mental health are just some of the reasons for this interest [24]. Schools, however, are not "in the mental health business" [25, p. 138], and getting them to address mental health and social-emotional competence can be challenging. Given this challenge, it is important to define school mental health and match school mental health programs to the specific needs and interests of schools.

For many, the term "school mental health" simply means providing mental health treatment to students with diagnosed emotional or behavioral disorders. We view school mental health more broadly and define it as a range of programs across the prevention spectrum (i.e., universal, selected, indicated) that can be implemented in schools to address the social, emotional, and behavioral needs of students.

Universal interventions are for all students in a school setting and help prevent students from developing serious problem behaviors. Selected interventions are for students who are at risk for developing problem behaviors. These interventions provide more intensive services than universal interventions in an attempt to decrease the chances that a student at risk for the development of a serious problem behavior will actually develop the behavior. Lastly, indicated interventions are for the small percentage of students in a school with intense problem behaviors. These interventions help stabilize and manage children in a way that is conducive to learning.

Ideally, schools should implement school mental health interventions at the universal, selected, and indicated level. Walker et al.'s three-tiered model [26], depicted in Figure 8.1, illustrates the value of such a proactive and comprehensive approach to school mental health.

Although a complete review of effective school mental health programs across the prevention spectrum is beyond the scope of this chapter, some

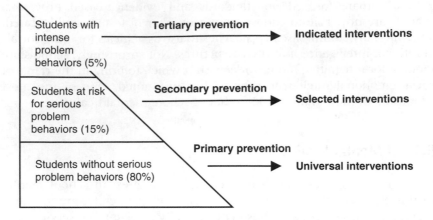

**FIGURE 8.1.** Walker et al.'s three-tiered model [26].

examples will be presented here to provide a sense of the types of available programs. These clearly map well into the range of services presented earlier as essential for building emotionally intelligent schools, as defined by CASEL [15].

*Universal programs* target all students in a school regardless of their risk status. These programs typically aim to enhance the social-emotional competence of students. The most effective programs in this category include those listed previously as "social competency enhancement programs which target skills in affective awareness, self-control, stress management, problem solving, and decision making."

*Selected* school mental health programs are for students at risk for the development of problem behaviors such as substance abuse, high-risk sexual behavior, or violence. The FAST Track program developed by the Conduct Problems Prevention Research Group and the First Steps Program by Walker et al. are examples of effective selected school mental health programs. Both of these programs focus on the prevention of conduct disorder in youth [27].

Students with serious problem behaviors or a diagnosed psychological disorder require an *indicated school mental health program*. A growing number of schools have school-based health or mental health centers that can provide direct clinical services to such students. According to the 2002 State Survey of School-Based Health Center Initiatives [28], there are 1498 school-based health centers (SBHCs) across the country. This number represents a significant increase in the number of SBHCs nationwide (in 1993 there were only 500), and shows that for many schools the SMH model is a viable and organized way to bring comprehensive emotional intelligence-enhancing efforts into schools.

Schools are also finding themselves asked, to an increasing extent, to assist students in developing a sense of civic engagement. That voting takes place in schools seems to regularly spur the recognition that opportunities to better prepare students for their roles as citizens are being squandered. As service learning and civic engagement have been reconsidered in light of emotional intelligence theory and practice, schools are making inroads that in the past turned into dead ends.

## Service Learning and Civic Engagement

John Dewey thought deeply about the nature of classrooms and concluded that they were places where students had to learn about democracy: the skills needed to preserve it, the reflective state of mind needed to advance it, and the social and emotional climate needed to convey it. To Dewey, there was a seamless relationship between the material to be learned, the context in which it was learned, and the arenas to which that learning needed to be applied [29]. In his book, *How We Think*, Dewey outlined many of the skills that we view as necessary for citizens in a democracy—not only analytic skills, but skills for perspective taking, social debate and exchange, and interpersonal commerce [30]. Service learning is the context in which all of Dewey's concerns converge.

Service learning also turns out to be an effective way to build a central social-emotional intelligence skill: empathy. CASEL concluded that there was no more powerful way to build empathy and enable the perspective taking essential for civic engagement than an orientation toward positive, contributory service [7]. Examples begin as early as preschool, in Head Start programs, and should not wait until high school to begin, as is typically the case. In the early grades, all children need to learn that they are valued contributors to their classrooms and their schools. Getting to know and appreciate the diversity of students in their classroom and school communities helps build both empathy and perspective taking. Beginning in middle school, there are programs that help prepare children for service outside the classroom and a broadening of their perspectives.

The Giraffe Heroes Program teaches kids to "stick their necks out" and make a difference in their communities. It does so in part through understanding historical and local examples of heroes and what they did that made them special. Then, they follow this with planning ways to address issues in their local communities (www.giraffe.org). Lions-Quest International's Skills for Action Program (www.quest.edu) is based around an empirically supported process of organizing service learning experiences:

1. Preparation (acquire background related to the recipients of the service).
2. Action (provide meaningful service with real consequences, based on appropriate social-emotional and academic skills).
3. Reflection (keep records of the experience, discuss thoughts and feelings, look at broader perspective).
4. Demonstration (show others what one has done, learned, accomplished through service, perhaps including carrying out projects in the community).

As service learning programs become more prominent, their presence casts a new light on an old problem. Bullying is now recognized as a major barrier to student participation and learning. Once again, reconceptualizing bullying and related phenomena in emotional intelligence terms has made them more amenable to systematic interventions, as well as better integration with progress in the other frontiers already covered.

## Bullying Prevention

Unfortunately, for increasingly large numbers of students, schools are no longer the bastion of safety that they should be. Although large-scale acts of school violence such as the Columbine High School shootings receive a lot of media attention, they are relatively rare. Bullying, however, is a more common threat to school safety that can result in immediate physical and psychological harm as well as long-term adjustment problems [31]. Further, it promotes a climate of fear that shortcircuits learning and disrupts positive school relationships [4].

Bullying is "a form of aggression in which one or more students physically and/or psychologically harass another student repeatedly over time" [32, p. 165]. It is characterized by an imbalance of power or strength. Approximately 27% of students experience some form of bullying in school [33]. A smaller percentage (10%) are victims of persistent bullying [34].

The *Bullying Prevention Program* [5] is particularly successful at reducing and preventing bullying through various school-wide core components [5]:

• Adult awareness of bullying in the school.
• Assessment of the level of school bullying through student questionnaires.

- School conference day on bullying.
- Enhanced supervision during recess.
- Class rules against bullying.
- Class meetings.
- Serious talks with bullies and victims.
- Serious talks with parents of involved students.

Although the success of the *Bullying Prevention Program* has yet to be replicated in any US schools, the US Department of Education has identified some model anti-bullying programs. Bully Proofing Your School and the Bullying Prevention Project are among these programs.

*Bully Proofing Your School* [35] is an anti-bullying program for elementary school students that advocates a comprehensive, school-wide approach towards bullying similar to that of [5]. The program emphasizes heightening awareness of bullying, teaching students skills to deal with bullying, and promoting a positive school climate or "caring majority" [36, p. 17].

A seven-session, classroom-based curriculum is the foundation of the program. Members of a school's mental health team or teachers can deliver the curriculum, which can easily be integrated with a school's overall social-emotional skill-building curriculum. Once students are exposed to the curriculum, the program shifts to building and maintaining a "caring majority." This is accomplished by rewarding children for demonstrating caring behaviors (e.g., asking an excluded child to play, standing up for a child who is being bullied) in the classroom, school-wide acknowledgement of caring behaviors, and classroom meetings to discuss and acknowledge caring behavior [36]. Such activities are similar to procedures that are part of many comprehensive social-emotional curricula and climate-building approaches, but allow for more explicit connections to the prevention of bullying.

The *Bullying Prevention Project* is based on the Bullying Prevention Program developed by Olweus [5]. It emphasizes school-wide interventions (e.g., school rules against bullying, reinforcement for positive behaviors, and sanctions for bullying), classroom interventions, and staff and parental involvement. The program has been implemented in South Carolina elementary and middle schools with "promising" preliminary results [37].

*Steps to Respect* [38] is an off-shoot of and complement to the acclaimed Second Step social-emotional intelligence program and uses the techniques and pedagogy of that program to focus on bullying prevention. It has been implemented in US schools with promising results. A classroom-based curriculum and school-wide components similar to those proposed by Olweus [5] are the foundation of the program. The three-level curriculum, designed for children in grades third through sixth, focuses on developing general social competence skills, building friendship skills, and teaching students how to respond to bullying. Each curriculum level is composed of ten 45-minute skill lessons delivered by teachers. These lessons are reinforced by weekly, 15–20 minute booster sessions. Together, these components and the classroom-based curriculum are designed to prevent bullying and promote a positive school climate.

There is widespread agreement that bullying prevention programs must address the entire school climate, not just victims or perpetrators of bullying [5], [31], [39–40]. "Bullying and victimization do not occur in isolation. Therefore, interventions with the bully and/or victim are necessary but not sufficient" [41, p. 12]. Pepler and Craig emphasize the importance of systemic approaches to bullying that implement interventions "not only with the bully and victim, but also within the school, within the peer group (classroom and playground), and with parents" [41, p. 12].

Because of this systemic emphasis, many schools are able to initiate comprehensive social-emotional intelligence efforts by starting with a focus on bullying prevention. Regardless of the starting point, however, many schools are finding that there is a common implementation process on the road to successfully bringing emotional intelligence programs to their students. In the following section, we summarize some of the elements in that journey.

## ☐ How to Bring Social-Emotional Intelligence into Schools

Schools have been slow to incorporate social-emotional intelligence into their structure. They continue to be test-driven and focused on a narrow range of academic outcomes, in part because they lack clear guidance as to how to proceed differently. Fortunately, work has been done to help schools operationalize new realizations about what it means for our children to be "educated."

What is needed is not "either/or" thinking, but rather, a "both/and" point of view. Children need to be knowledgeable, responsible, *and* able to deal effectively with their emotions. Our education system must work for the integration of all these. For this to happen, schools must be reconceptualized as emotionally intelligent learning communities. For too long and for too often, our schools have suffered from a program-of-the-month approach, as a revolving door of disconnected, narrow, problem-specific programs have been invoked in schools, typically in response to crisis. The response to tragic shootings such as occurred in Columbine

High School, or when there is a suicide in a school, are clear examples. The result, even when the specific programs that are put in place have been individually acclaimed, is educational chaos. This is represented by the jumble of puzzle pieces in the schoolhouse at the top of Figure 8.2 [7].

In Figure 8.2, the bottom schoolhouse represents what is needed. Here, social-emotional learning (SEL) provides synergy. Under this conceptual umbrella, an array of life skill promotion and problem behavior prevention efforts can be organized and unified in a proactive manner. There is continuity and coordination. With SEL firmly in place as a facet of schooling, there is a vehicle for addressing troubling issues that we know children bring to schools. As children see schools as places where their social and emotional needs are addressed in a focused and concerned way, they are likely to open themselves up to academic learning to a greater degree.

Perhaps even more disconcerting than uncoordinated programming is the fact that many programs are implemented with poor fidelity, if at all [42–44]. Early efforts at building emotional intelligence in schools focused on creating "model" programs that can be implemented and researched in a consistent and replicable manner. However, data have not borne out the idea that model programs can simply be "imported" into a setting. Gager and Elias showed that these "model" programs, when

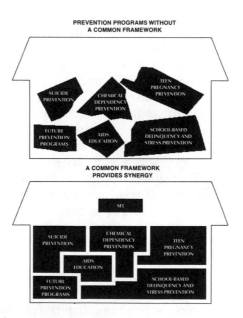

**FIGURE 8.2.** Social-emotional learning can provide synergy for programmatic efforts.

implemented in different settings, resulted in inconsistent levels of success [45]. The strongest impact on outcome was how the program was implemented in the particular setting. Other evidence supports the idea that program implementation cannot be assumed even in a setting that is reportedly "using" a program. In a survey of educators in public and private schools, only 14% of respondents reported that their efforts in substance abuse prevention programming employed the most effective teaching strategies and content [42]. Likewise, a survey of 81 Safe and Drug-Free School district coordinators across 11 states points out the disparity between good intentions and actual implementation [44]. Although 59% of respondents had selected a research-based curriculum for use in setting, fidelity of implementation was reported by only 19% [44].

For these reasons, there has been a renewed focus on the process of EI/SEL program implementation. The issue of implementation can be understood through a metaphor of an iceberg at sea. Jutting above the water are such things as the curricular materials associated with the program and new skills and modes of interactions learned by teachers and students. One can expect to see teachers leading the program and students demonstrating new skills in self-control and communication. These are the parts of the program that would be visible to a visitor at a school implementing a social-emotional intelligence program. However, the largest part of an iceberg—and of an innovation—exists "underwater." The submerged segment is crucial in providing stability, but also can be disastrous if ignored. For program implementation, these hidden aspects include "behind the scenes" work in planning for implementation both before and during the launch of a program.

In their work on how best to map the undercurrents of implementation, Novick et al. [16] draw parallels between the pedagogy of programs and the creation of caring learning communities. The core skills of most social-emotional intelligence programs—communication skills, proactive, productive, collaborative problem solving, self-reflectivity, and emotional self-awareness and self-regulation—aim to produce effectively functioning, productive classrooms. These same skills can help in the creation of the type of sustained implementation that is essential for programmatic success. There are two major elements that infuse this approach—planful problem solving and collaborative involvement.

## Planful Problem Solving

Too often, good intentions for programming exceed realistic considerations about how programs will actually be implemented. New programming often requires the creation of new roles—who will have oversight for the program? How will staff be trained? How will new teachers be oriented in future years? Also, programs are implemented "into" environments with ever-changing mandates and priorities, but are often treated as if they were "static" and immutable. A flexible approach is needed to work in such shifting contexts. Novick et al. recommend an implementation process based on a strategy for problem solving. The steps in this process are [16]:

1. Readiness: Assess your school's readiness for change.
2. Recognize feelings: Know when to start problem solving.
3. Identify problems: Look at the current situation.
4. Set goals: Focus the change efforts.
5. Generate options: Think of many things to do.
6. Envision outcomes: Consider all the consequences.
7. Choose carefully: Select a goal-oriented or goal-driven solution.
8. Plan prescriptively: Anticipate all details and roadblocks.
9. Learn constantly: Obtain feedback and modify accordingly.

A problem-solving approach leads to questions such as: how does the program fit within new mandates? How does programming at different levels interrelate? How do we know if the program is working? What modifications may need to be made to the program once it is in progress? Whose task is it to make these changes, and how will they be communicated to the staff?

Community-enhancing implementation involves planful consideration of the context within which the program is being implemented (e.g., the strengths and constraints of the school and its staff) as well as the impact implementation will have on the existing system (e.g., the shifting of class schedules to accommodate time for the program). If such matters are not considered, then the implementers will find themselves swimming against the strong current of the status quo. Such an approach to programming acknowledges the real challenges faced by well-intentioned educators in changing their practice. The process is iterative, with the final step of the process—obtaining feedback—included for the sake of continuously improving programmatic efforts. Such an approach leads to programmatic flexibility (especially important in settings in which staff turnover and new mandates are common).

## Collaborative Involvement

In sites that have been able to maintain sustained implementation, leaders have sought the input of various constituents throughout the project. Effective programs are often "managed" by a committee made up of representatives of various school constituencies (e.g., teachers, parents, administration, students, community members). Such a committee can play an active role in any and all of the nine problem-solving steps listed above. Committee members can serve as liaisons to their particular constituencies, helping to foster communication and input about the program. In particular, implementers and recipients have opportunities to voice concerns and give suggestions.

A collaborative approach helps school leadership to anticipate any rough waters, strong currents, or sandbars that might appear in the seas ahead. Including multiple perspectives not only gives voice to those who may not be "on board," but also may provide extra information from those who are better at spotting a dangerous iceberg fragment jutting out below the surface. (Remember the *Titanic*!) Further, a collaborative approach allows the various constituencies to be active members of the process and to be more engaged and involved in the school community's implementation process. Of course, the EI/SEL skills of these collaborators will go a long way toward determining whether a program can be effectively delivered to improve the EI/SEL skills of students, further supporting the need for attending to EI/SEL in the workplace [46].

## Engaging Parents

While many school-based constituencies are important for bringing social-emotional intelligence efforts to the students, parental support also is essential for successful implementation. Parents must be educated about emotional intelligence and the important links between social-emotional skills and academic learning. This can be done through presentations at PTA meetings and articles in school newsletters. Once parents recognize the importance of emotional intelligence for schools, they can serve as powerful advocates for appropriate programming at the classroom and school levels and can be receptive to improving their own social-emotional skills.

Two resources have been developed for parents, based on the work of Dan Goleman and CASEL and consistent with their principles. *Emotionally Intelligent Parenting: How to Raise a Self-Disciplined, Responsible, and Socially Skilled Child* [47] focuses on practical applications of emotional intelligence to all areas of parenting, with particular focus on issues related to schooling: homework, competition from media, after-school activities, peers, time demands on all families, and the various interpersonal stresses and strains of the daily routine. This book has been published in eight international editions at the time of writing this, showing the strong cross-cultural relevance of the issues addressed. *Raising*

*Emotionally Intelligent Teenagers: Guiding the Way for Compassionate, Committed, Courageous Adults* [48] focuses especially on the stressors of school, relationships, career decisions, and family relationships. There also is an emotional intelligence quiz and a clinical corner chapter, to help parents recognize the difference between normal teenage quirks and serious deficiencies in emotional intelligence skills. These tools can help individual and groups of parents work in parallel to school-based efforts to build children's emotional intelligence skills.

# ☐  Final Thoughts

As programs are implemented in coordinated and continuous ways across all domains, there is greater likelihood that the synergy of the SEL-oriented schoolhouse will occur. We are optimistic that advances will continue to be made along the frontiers we have identified and that more and more schools will use systematic and proven methods for building their social-emotional intelligence efforts. However, there are certain conditions that need to be in place in schools to optimize both social-emotional and academic learning. While not exhaustive (cf. [48]), the list below is a set of basic assumptions that underlie what we have presented and that characterize schools that have been able to effectively and enduringly "walk the talk."

- Sound classroom structure and function is based on a foundation of caring relationships. Students must feel welcomed and protected in their schools.
- Students behave more responsibly and respectfully when given opportunities for moral action and community service.
- A challenging academic curriculum that respects all learners motivates and helps them succeed. A culture of "You Can" must predominate over a culture of "You Can't."
- The school staff must believe in the importance of becoming a caring, moral community of learners, and must model as well as teach caring and moral behavior for students.
- The needs and concerns of all students, including those with special education classifications and other needs, must be fully integrated into the mainstream functioning of the school.

When these five statements are seen as the norm in schools, we will know that the crisis in education is receding and social-emotional intelligence has taken its place as a core element in our schools.

# ☐ References

1. Blankstein, A. (2004). *Failure is not an option: Six principles that guide student achievement in high-performing schools.* Thousand Oaks, CA: Corwin Press.
2. Bower, E. (1972). Education as a humanizing process. In S. Golann & C. Eisdorfer (Eds.), *Handbook of community mental health.* New York: Appleton-Century-Crofts.
3. Zins, J. E., Weissberg, R. P., Wang, M. C., & Walberg, H. J. (Eds.). (2004). *Building school success through social and emotional learning.* New York: Teachers College Press.
4. Elias, M. J., & Zins, J. E. (Eds.). (2003). *Bullying, peer harassment, and victimization in the schools: The next generation of prevention.* New York: Haworth.
5. Olweus, D. (1994). Annotation: Bullying at school: Basic facts and effects of a school based intervention program. *Journal of Child Psychology and Psychiatry, 35*(7), 1171–1190.
6. Comer, J. P. (2004). *Leave no child behind: Preparing today's youth for tomorrow's world.* New Haven, CT: Yale University Press.
7. Elias, M. J., Zins, J., Weissberg, K. S., Greenberg, M. T., Haynes, N. M., Kessler, R., et al. (1997). *Promoting social and emotional learning: Guidelines for educators.* Alexandria, VA: Association for Supervision and Curriculum Development.
8. Brandt, R. (2003). How new knowledge about the brain applies to social and emotional learning. In M. J. Elias, H. Arnold, & C. Steiger-Hussey (Eds.). *EQ + IQ: Best practices in leadership for caring and successful schools* (pp. 57–70). Thousand Oaks, CA: Corwin Press.
9. National Center for Innovation and Education. (1999). *Lessons for life: How smart schools boost academic, social, and emotional intelligence* [Videotape]. Bloomington, IN: HOPE Foundation. (Available from www.communitiesofhope.org)
10. Elias, M. J., Hunter, L., & Kress, J. S. (2001). Emotional intelligence and education. In J. Ciarrochi, J. P. Forgas, & J. D. Mayer (Eds.), *Emotional intelligence in everyday life: A scientific inquiry* (pp. 133–149). New York: Psychology Press.
11. Elias, M. J., Wang, M., Weissberg, R., Zins, J., & Walberg, H. (2002). The other side of the report card. *American School Board Journal, 189*(11), 28–31.
12. Elias, M. J. (2003). *Academic and social-emotional learning* (Educational Practices booklet No. 11). Geneva, Switzerland: International Academy of Education and the International Bureau of Education, UNESCO.
13. Mayer, J. D., & Salovey, P. (1997). What is emotional intelligence? In J. D. Mayer & P. Salovey (Eds.), Emotional development and emotional intelligence (pp. 3–31). New York: Basic Books.
14. Goleman, D. (1995). *Emotional intelligence.* New York: Bantam Books.
15. Collaborative for Academic, Social, and Emotional Learning. (2003). *Safe and sound: An education lead-guide.* retrieved from http://www.casel.org/downloads/Safe%20and%20Sound/1A_Safe_&_Sound.pdf
16. Novick, B., Kress, J. S., & Elias, M. J. (2002). *Building learning communities with character: How to integrate academic, social, and emotional learning.* Alexandria, VA: Association for Supervision and Curriculum Development.
17. Kress, J. S., Norris, J. A., Schoenholz, D., Elias, M. J., & Seigle, P. (2004). Bringing together educational standards and social and emotional learning: Making the case for educators. *American Journal of Education, 111*, 68–89.
18. Comer, J. P., Haynes, N. M., Joyner, E. T., & Ben-Avie, M. (1996). *Rallying the whole village: The Comer process for reforming education.* New York: Teachers College Press.
19. Gottfredson, D. C. (1986). An empirical test of school-based environmental and individual interventions to reduce the risk of delinquent behavior. *Criminology, 24*, 705–731.
20. Battistich, V., & Solomon, D. (1995, April). Linking teacher change to student change. In E. Schaps (Chair), *Why restructuring must focus on thinking and caring: A model for deep,*

*long term change through staff development*. Symposium conducted at the meeting of the American Educational Research Association, San Francisco.

21. Hawkins, J. D., & Catalano, R. F. (1992). *Communities that care: Action for drug abuse prevention*. San Francisco: Jossey-Bass.

22. Hawkins, J. D., & Weis, J. G. (1985). The social development model: An integrated approach to delinquency prevention. *Journal of Primary Prevention, 6*, 73–97.

23. Felner, R. D., & Adan, A.M. (1988). The school transitional environment project: An ecological intervention and evaluation. In R. H. Price, E. L. Cowen, R. P. Lorion, & J. Ramos-McKay (Eds.), *14 ounces of prevention: A casebook for practitioners* (pp. 11–122). Washington, DC: American Psychological Association.

24. Weist, M. D., Evans, S. W., & Lever, N. A, (2003). Advancing mental health practice and research in schools. In M. D. Weist, S. W. Evans, & N. A. Lever (Eds.), *Handbook of school mental health advancing practice and research* (pp. 1–7). New York: Kluwer Academic.

25. Adelman, H. S., & Taylor, L. (1999). Mental health in schools and system restructuring. *Community Psychology Review, 19*, 137–163.

26. Walker, H. M., Horner, R. H., Sugai, G., Bullis, M., Sprague, J. R., Bricker, D., & Kaufman, M. J. (1996). Integrated approaches to preventing antisocial behavior patterns among school-age children and youth. *Journal of Emotional and Behavioral Disorders, 4*, 193–256.

27. Walker, H. M., Kavanagh, K., Stiller, B., Golly, A., Steverson, H. H., & Feil, E. G. (1998). First step to success: An early intervention approach for preventing school antisocial behavior. *Journal of Emotional and Behavioral Disorders, 6*, 66–80.

28. Center for Health and Health Care in Schools. (2002). State Survey of School-Based Health Center Initiatives. Available from http://www.healthinschools.org/sbhcs/survey02.htm

29. Dewey, J. (1938). *Experience and education*. New York: Macmillan.

30. Dewey, J. (1933). *How we think*. Lexington, MA: Heath.

31. Hanish, L. D., & Guerra, N. G. (2000). Children who get victimized at school: What is known? What can be done? *Professional School Counseling, 4*(2), 113–119.

32. Batsche, G. M., & Knoff, H. M. (1994). Bullies and their victims: Understanding a pervasive problem in the schools. *School Psychology Review, 23*(2), 165–174.

33. Whitney, I., & Smith, P. K. (1993). A survey of the nature and extent of bullying in junior/middle and secondary schools. *Educational Research, 35*(1), 3–25.

34. Olweus, D. (1978). *Aggression in the schools: Bullies and whipping boys*. Washington, DC: Hemisphere.

35. Garrity, C., Jens, K., Porter, W., Sager, N., & Short-Camilli, C. (1994). *Bully proofing your school*. Longmont, CO: Sopris West.

36. Epstein, L., Plog, A. E., & Porter, W. (2002). *Bully proofing your school: Results of a four-year intervention*. Unpublished manuscript.

37. US Department of Education. (1998). *Annual Report on School Safety*. Washington, DC: Author. Retrieved from http://www.ed.gov/PDFDocs/schoolsafety.pdf

38. Committee for Children. (2001). *Steps to respect: A bullying prevention program guide*. Seattle, CA: Committee for Children.

39. Peterson, R. L., & Skiba, R. (2000). Creating school climates that prevent school violence. *Preventing School Failure, 44*(3), 122–129.

40. Roberts, W. B., & Coursol, D. H. (1996). Strategies for intervention with childhood and adolescent victims of bullying, teasing, and intimidation in school settings. *Elementary School Guidance and Counseling, 30*, 204–212.

41. Pepler, D. J., & Craig, W. (2000). *Making a difference in bullying*. Retrieved September 29, 2004, from http://www.arts.yorku.ca/lamarsh/pdf/Making_a_Difference_in_Bullying.pdf

42. Ennett, S. T., Ringwalt, C. L., Thorne, J., Rohrbach, L. A., Vincus, A., Simons-Rudolph, A., & Jones, S. (2003). A comparison of current practice in school-based substance use prevention programs with meta-analysis findings. *Prevention Science, 4*, 1–14.

43. Gottfredson, G. D., & Gottfredson, D. C. (2001). What schools do to prevent problem behavior and promote safe environments. *Journal of Educational and Psychological Consultation, 12,* 313–344.

44. Hallfors, D., & Godette, D. (2002). Will the "principles of effectiveness" improve prevention practice? Early findings from a diffusion study. *Health Education Review, 17,* 461–470.

45. Gager, P. J., & Elias, M. J. (1997). Implementing prevention programs in high risk environments: Application of the resiliency paradigm. *American Journal of Orthopsychiatry, 67*(3), 363–373.

46. Cherniss, C., & Goleman, D. (Eds.). (2002). *The emotionally intelligent workplace: How to select for, measure, and improve emotional intelligence in individuals, groups, and organizations.* San Francisco: Jossey-Bass.

47. Elias, M. J., Tobias, S., E., & Friedlander, B. S. (2000). *Emotionally intelligent parenting: How to raise a self-disciplined, responsible, and socially skilled child.* New York: Three Rivers Press/Random House.

48. Elias, M. J., Tobias, S., E., & Friedlander, B. S. (2002). *Raising emotionally intelligent teenagers: Guiding the way for compassionate, committed, courageous adults.* New York: Three Rivers Press/Random House.

David R. Caruso
Brian Bienn
Susan A. Kornacki

CHAPTER

# Emotional Intelligence in the Workplace

Our story of emotional intelligence (EI) in the workplace takes place in two phases in this chapter. We begin by telling you a story—a composite of actual clients and research—about Robert, a new hire, his manager Marsha, his team leader Matthew and the organization they work in. But with so much hyperbole surrounding this topic, the second part of our chapter provides you with a synopsis of the research on emotional intelligence. We hope to engage you, the reader, with the story of Robert, Marsha and Matthew, to challenge you to consider the importance of emotional intelligence and to be a discriminating user of the concept and the model of emotional intelligence that we describe.

## ☐ Robert, Marsha and Matthew

Our story begins with Robert's first day in the new job. A significant step up from his previous role, Robert was walking into a program management position within a mission-critical software development team. His role involved significant customer contact, as well as navigating his way through the daily in's and out's of program management. His boss, Marsha, greeted him in her office at the start of the day, welcoming him on board. As she recited a list of challenges ahead, Robert smiled and bobbed his head up and down, seemingly eager to get started. Marsha paused, sensing that Robert was more than a bit nervous. He wasn't nodding in agreement, she thought to herself, he was quivering with fear.

**187**

Maybe, she wondered, her boss was right after all, and she had made a dreadful selection decision.

It was a difficult decision for Marsha to justify. After all, Robert had years less experience than almost all of the other candidates. To make matters worse, the executive vice president had gushed over one of the finalists, Jimmy, a newly minted MBA who had previously been a manager of a competitor's software development operation. But Marsha felt that Robert was a better fit. She felt quite strongly about this, even though she found it difficult to at first express the reasons for her preference. "I don't feel comfortable with Jimmy. He doesn't seem like he would work out in this role. After all, it would be a new environment, a different culture and different expectations than he is used to. Robert doesn't have the exact competencies we are looking for, I admit that. But, I feel that he will thrive here."

The EVP was angry at first, but he acquiesced and bowed to Marsha's judgment in this matter, reasoning that she had a good hiring track record, a knack for reading people. And he was right in this at least: Marsha could size people up with relative ease. As such, she is an anomaly. Even though many people feel that they are excellent judges of others' abilities, it is relatively difficult to accurately gauge the ability of other people, or your own for that matter. When asked to evaluate one's own IQ, for instance, the correlation with measured IQ hovers around .10 to .20 [1]. (Teacher ratings of their students' IQs correlate at around the .5 level, significantly higher.) The situation is made even more difficult in the realm of dispositional personality traits (see, for instance [2]).

Marsha became aware of second-guessing her decision and recognized that continuing to do so would not be productive. She decided to refocus her attention on Robert, in the hope that she could further assess and understand the feelings he was experiencing. She had judged Robert to be a somewhat anxious person when she had interviewed him. And he was certainly living up to that judgment. But that low level, background anxiety she had detected in him earlier was displayed at a much higher level of intensity this first morning on the job. She surprised Robert when she asked, "You seem apprehensive. Perhaps there is something I can help you with?" Robert was taken aback. He felt he had a terrific poker face, and while he did feel anxious, who wouldn't in his position, he was positive that other people only saw his plastered-on smile, not his underlying anxiety. Robert broadened his smile, and was about to laugh off the comment when he caught Marsha's look. It was a perceiving, but unthreatening look. She communicated concern. So Robert took a leap, and said "Well, I am a bit. I ran into an ex-classmate last week who said he had interviewed for this job and had turned it down. He said that the project was hopelessly off-schedule and that he didn't want any part of it." Upon which, poker-faced Robert thought to himself, "Idiot. Why did I ever say that?"

Once more, to Robert's surprise, Marsha did not use his admission against him like a weapon, as might many another boss. Instead, Marsha smiled and chuckled out loud. "This role of yours is a highly visible one. And the program is critical to the organization. But you were my first choice for the job, and in fact the offer went first, and only, to you. You should be concerned: there are lots of unresolved issues. It's a tough job. But I hired you because I believe you are capable of bringing this project to a successful conclusion." Robert relaxed, and smiled, this time a real smile of relief and satisfaction. Sensing his relief, Marsha said that she would introduce Robert to his team.

Marsha's insight into Robert's feelings of discomfort was based on her close observation of his facial expression, the nervous tapping of his fingers and the quavering tone of voice. She readily felt for Robert, sensing his discomfort and putting herself in his position. Marsha realized that Robert was not ready to focus his attention on the immediate proprieties of his new position. With a single, probing question, she gained understanding into the underlying cause of his feelings, and then helped Robert to alleviate his concerns, and to get ready to start his new job feeling confident in his ability to succeed.

## ☐  An Emotional Intelligence Blueprint

Marsha's management style is a blend of certain innate abilities and a conscious focus on a structured approach to managing people. This approach is an emotional blueprint (illustrated in Figure 9.1), a deceptively simple and yet elegant four-phase emotion-focused problem-solving process.

### Step 1: Accurately Identify Emotions—Gather the Available Data

The first step of the process is emotion identification. More than simple emotional awareness, this ability is based upon accurate identification of one's own emotions as well as those of others. It involves picking up emotional cues, both verbal and non-verbal, and discerning the difference between a genuine emotional expression and a forced expression. Robert smiled, but Marsha was too skilled to be fooled by this insincere emotional expression: Robert's mouth was turned upwards in a smile, but he did not display a true smile as reflected in his eyes. He was posing, faking it. Certainly, his tone of voice suggested nervousness as well, and not a sense of contentment or happiness.

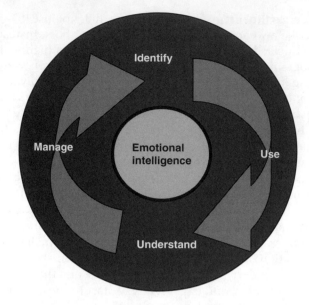

**FIGURE 9.1.** The four-step emotional blueprint.

## Step 2: Use Emotions to Enhance Thinking—Generate a Shared Emotional Perspective

The next step in the four-step emotional blueprint is using emotions to enhance thinking. It is not an ability that many people grasp readily, as most of us are taught that emotions interfere with, and disrupt, thought. We are schooled not to make emotion-based decisions or to be too emotional. Yet, emotions are the foundation of good decision making, as the work of neuroscientist Antonio Damasio demonstrates. Damasio, in fact, goes even further, noting that "Feelings . . . are not a luxury. They serve as internal guides, and they help us communicate to others signals that can also guide them" [3, p. xv]. In addition to the role of emotion in decision making, this emotional ability allows us to take a shared perspective of another, to feel what they feel, to have empathy for another and to view the world through their eyes. Marsha generated a mild feeling of unease in herself, recalling her first day on her first real job more than 20 years previously. And with that feeling, she related to Robert's predicament and her observations of him were almost unnerving in their insight and accuracy. Robert felt that Marsha truly understood him—and that she was someone he could trust.

## Step 3: Understand the Causes and Progression of Emotions—Ask "What If" Questions

Marsha's abilities do not extend to mind reading, so she needed to ask a simple probing question in order to ascertain the underlying cause of Robert's discomfort. She recognized that Robert's baseline feeling was mildly anxious. She reasoned that mild anxiousness, by itself, could actually be useful to Robert, helping him focus on diagnosing potential problems with the complex programs he would be involved in. But this level of discomfort appeared to be well above that background noise of his anxious mood. By asking a question, she could both confirm her hypothesis regarding his current emotional state and, if she received a valid answer, obtain information on the underlying cause of his discomfort. In doing so, Marsha demonstrated her in-depth emotional understanding: her ability to reason about the causes and progressions of emotions.

## Step 4: Manage Emotions to Achieve Intelligent Outcomes—Base Strategic Decisions on Emotions and Reasoning

Marsha's approach to working with Robert that first day on the job was guided by her interest in having Robert start off in the most successful manner possible. The decisions that Marsha made throughout the day were designed to support that outcome. And with each decision point, Marsha recognized the importance of using all of the data available to her. Her decisions combined her logical reasoning with the data available from Robert's expressions of emotion. Slight anxiety or discomfort, if unchecked, can transition into fear. Knowing this and accurately perceiving the emotions data, Marsha made an emotionally intelligent decision that helped promote Robert's likelihood of success that first day. This illustrates the essence of Step 4 of the emotional blueprint. Marsha managed the situation emotionally. Through her forceful support of Robert's qualities she reassured him and altered his feeling from anxiety and concern to one of acceptance. It is difficult, but entirely possible, to intentionally manage our emotions as well as those of others. Many things can put us into a bad mood—such as battling traffic on the daily commute, receiving a negative performance review or having a fight with our partner as we leave the house. If such daily occurrences result in a change in mood, then conscious acts designed to alter our own and other's moods can be equally and even more effective.

The four abilities demonstrated by Marsha represent the ability model of emotional intelligence first proposed by Peter Salovey and John Mayer in 1990 [4], and updated by them and colleague David Caruso (see, for instance [5–6]). The model includes four emotional abilities: (1) accurately *identifying* emotions in self, others and the environment; (2) *using* emotions to enhance thinking and to generate a shared emotional perspective; (3) *understanding* the causes of emotions and how they transition over time; and (4) *managing* the integration of reasoning and the data of emotions to make strategic decisions. The shorthand labels for these abilities are Identifying Emotions, Using Emotions, Understanding Emotions and Managing Emotions. While not originally intended as a sequential processing model, these four abilities have been employed as a form of problem-solving methodology, where a person first identifies an emotion, allows the emotion to direct attention and influence thinking, attempts to understand the emotion's cause and possible emotional "what-if" scenarios and, finally, manages to stay open to information contained in the emotion and to incorporate this into a strategic decision. This ability model of emotional intelligence has been operationalized by the Mayer-Salovey-Caruso Emotional Intelligence Test (MSCEIT [7]) in the form of a set of emotional problem-solving tasks. The MSCEIT is unusual in a number of respects. It is an ability test, which means it is scored objectively. The nature of the items is also somewhat unusual, as some of the MSCEIT tasks request the test taker to match physical sensations to their respective emotions, or to identify emotions in artistic designs. And yet, in spite of the unique and unusual nature of the MSCEIT, it has adequate reliability and is predictive of important outcomes involving interpersonal behaviors, social networks and leadership style.

Perhaps the most important aspect of tests like the MSCEIT is that it does not require people to report their level of ability. As we noted earlier, people are generally not very accurate when reporting their level of intellectual ability. The same is true for self report of emotional abilities. Ask people to estimate their EI, for instance, and then give them an objective, performance measure of EI, and you find the correlation to be low, and usually not statistically significant (see, for instance [8]). Similarly, observer reports of intelligence are only moderately correlated with actual, measured intelligence.

Consider Marsha, for a moment. Most people interacting with her assume that she is not an especially emotionally intelligent manager. She is reserved and unassuming. She does not tend to exhibit cheerleader-type qualities demonstrated by some of her more visibly enthusiastic and charismatic colleagues. Marsha is not an extremely assertive individual, although she speaks up, and stands up, for herself. As a result, Marsha had been passed over for promotion on several occasions. The VP of the division, during the last re-organization, had taken note of Marsha's behavior in several team situations. She demonstrated a unique ability to read team members and to connect with them. Marsha was able to verbalize the team dynamics and bring conflicts to light and then, to resolution. But her skills easily went undetected by the casual observer. To others, it was not the in-your-face style of leadership that was noticed by the crowds. This particular VP wanted Marsha to be promoted to a team leader position, but she didn't have the hard data to convince others of the selection decision. When discussing Marsha with the small executive team assigned to slot individuals into positions in the new organization, the group looked askance at the VP when she mentioned Marsha's name. "We need more than your gut feel to go on," was the majority opinion of the executive committee. "We need some facts to back up your hunch."

Just how do you validate a hunch? Is it possible to quantify a gut feel? These questions danced through the head of the VP, and she assumed that Marsha would have to be passed over, one more time. Apparently, she wore her disappointment on her sleeve, for her HR manager noted her look of disappointment the next day over a cup of coffee. The VP told the short version of her story, complaining that "we have tests for everything, why not a way to measure critical abilities such as insight, gut feel, or whether you can read people?" The HR manager smiled at her, and replied, "Well, it just so happens we can measure those types of skills. And we can do it objectively, so it's not my opinion or your opinion." Clearly, the VP was intrigued. "Tell me more," she eagerly requested. The HR manager told her about a unique assessment that, although unusual, seemed to be able to tap into certain sorts of "people skills" or what he referred to as emotional intelligence. The test he was describing was, of course, the MSCEIT. And so, without delay, Marsha received a call from HR indicating that her VP wanted her to take an assessment. Always interested in learning more about herself, Marsha readily agreed, and later that day she received a call from the organization development professional consulting to her company. The consultant, given a briefing about Marsha, and about the interest the VP had in determining Marsha's promotion potential, readily agreed that the MSCEIT would be a useful tool. And so, by the end of the day, Marsha had logged into the consultant's website and about half an hour later, had completed the MSCEIT.

Most MSCEIT profiles are interesting: this was true for Marsha's as well (see Figure 9.2). Marsha's results indicated that she was superb at identifying emotions. She had the basic emotional awareness necessary for emotional intelligence, but she could also read people with great accuracy. She was able to access a range of emotions, and to feel what others were feeling. Marsha was highly skilled in using emotions to help her think creatively, solve problems, and possibly lead in a charismatic manner by connecting emotionally with others. Marsha's emotional vocabulary was

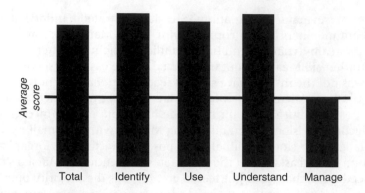

**FIGURE 9.2.** Marsha's MSCEIT results.

rich and quite sophisticated. She generated accurate emotional "what-if" scenarios with ease. While Marsha was masterful at helping other people manage emotions, she was not as skilled in managing her own emotions. It was possible that her advice giving was well received by people in general, but that she tended to put others' needs first, or to get overwhelmed at times.

In any event, Marsha was at the 98th percentile on the MSCEIT, meaning that she scored higher than 98% of people taking the MSCEIT. She clearly had superior emotional skills, something to which her VP had somehow been attuned. When the results were reported back to the VP by the consultant, in accordance with what he had told Marsha, the VP finally had some rational, hard data to support her gut feel. It was all she needed: Marsha received the promotion. The feedback report Marsha received on her MSCEIT results, and the follow-up action planning through the organizational consultant, allowed her to leverage these powerful skills, and to carefully avoid the problems attendant with the lower score on managing her own emotions. Of additional value to Marsha was learning to use the four emotional intelligence abilities as an emotional blueprint to assist her in solving problems and addressing critical issues in her new role.

It was on Robert's second day on the job that he got to see emotional intelligence at work in a team environment. Robert was introduced to his development team early that morning, as part of their weekly update. The team had an agenda to follow, and Robert was surprised to see that his name was listed as the first item on the agenda! Noting Robert's surprise, Matthew, the team leader, told Robert that they found that it was best to integrate a new team member into an existing team as soon as possible. "Won't that take time away from the meeting?" Robert enquired. "Well, sure it will," Matthew replied. "But it is time well spent. The quicker you feel one of the team, feel comfortable with us, and all of us with you, the quicker you'll be contributing to our development effort. Believe me, this works. We never used to do this. It's one of Marsha's ideas, something she mentioned, and that we all agreed to try. It's been great."

Robert did indeed lead the agenda that morning. He told about his background, some of his interests, and his goals for the team and for himself. Each team member introduced themselves to Robert and shared a short story about their life. Although it only took a few minutes per person, Robert felt that he really knew the team, after just one brief meeting.

Teams can be emotionally intelligent, or unintelligent, and the effect that EI has on a team are fairly striking. High EI teams tend to bond more quickly and achieve higher levels of performance, over shorter periods of time, than do lower EI teams [9]. Perhaps one reason for this is that high EI teams are also more likely to create meaningful and powerful vision statements. Such teams also have stronger social networks and links [10]. Similarly, Robert's team worked well together. The rest of the meeting was spent productively, addressing conflicts and concerns with efficiency. It was remarkable to be part of such a well-functioning group, Robert marveled.

Robert was still reflecting on his new job, congratulating himself on his good fortune, when his peaceful reverie was disturbed by angry voices in one of the windowed offices just down the hall from his cubicle. Robert was trying not to eavesdrop on the conversation, but the voices were so loud that it was hard not to hear every word spoken by the two angry people. Robert glanced over at his next-door cubicle neighbor, who returned his look, and got up to walk toward Robert. "They always do that," she stated without any introduction. "They don't usually get into shouting matches, but they are not known for being wallflowers." Robert told his colleague that such behavior was also common in his previous work environment, but he was surprised to find people being so blatant about it in this company. "It's not that common here. Just a few people," she informed Robert. "But these are two of the best we've got around here. They get really passionate about their ideas and about their work. They hash it out, all of it, until they resolve whatever it was that created the problem to start with."

Sure enough, the loud voices turned from anger and frustration to merriment a few minutes later. Two people emerged from the office—Marsha and Matthew—still engaged in intense conversation. At the end of the hallway, they each turned to go in opposite directions, and much to Robert's surprise, they warmly wished each other well. "I thought for sure there would be fists flying," Robert murmured to himself. His colleague smiled as she heard that observation, and told Robert "they respect each other a lot. They recognize when they are almost going too far, and are really superb at taking the other person's perspective. They can walk in the other guy's shoes and understand their point of view, whether they agree with it or not. It's something their team learned last year. It's called . . ." Robert put his had up to interrupt his colleague, and he finished the sentence with "emotional intelligence?" "Yes, exactly," she responded, "that was part of their training last year."

Such constructive resolution of conflict is an outcome, in part, of emotional intelligence. The quality of our social interactions is determined, to some extent, by our level of EI (see [11]). This makes sense: emotions serve as signals, especially signals about interpersonal events (see [12]). Emotions signal impending behaviors and acts—for example threat, dominance and aggression—that play a key role in generating and resolving interpersonal conflicts.

By now, Robert was intrigued by this term and concept "emotional intelligence" and did a quick online search and discovered that the term itself came to popular attention in 1995 when a book by that name first appeared. Robert, ever the data-driven type, dug a bit deeper and discovered that the topic was quite controversial, with many researchers deriding the concept claiming that it did not exist, that there was no science behind the term, and that EI was merely a myth. Yet Robert had seen the concept in action, had heard it described in some detail and intuitively, it made sense to him. Robert was perplexed, and Marsha, who was just happening to walk by Robert's cubicle, noticed that something seemed to be consuming his attention. She stopped and asked if anything was wrong. "No, nothing," he replied. But something in the way Marsha asked the question made Robert feel that he could answer candidly. "Well, maybe something. I've been hearing about this emotional intelligence stuff today, and was really interested in the subject, so I did a quick search. The stuff I read really panned the concept. It seems that it must be one of those pop psych fads, without much behind it. So, I'm kind of surprised and, maybe, a little disappointed."

"If you have a few minutes," Marsha said, "Let me tell you about this thing called emotional intelligence." And this is the story Marsha related. "Our company was approached 18 months ago by a consultant that our President knew. The consultant proposed an organization-wide initiative on emotional intelligence. The HR folks looked into it and concluded that the proposal was just warmed-over interpersonal skill training. Nothing new or different, except the new and fancy term, emotional intelligence. Or, as the consultant called it, 'EQ.' One of our senior HR generalists dug deeper into the field and quickly discovered that emotional intelligence meant different things. There was the faddish, pop psych approach, that you just uncovered, and that the consultant tried to foist on us."

"And then there was the scientific approach. There was indeed something real behind the hype. Trouble was, it was found only in the realm of academic circles for about 15 years. The HR generalist located some of the people conducting the academic work on EI and found that there were a few practical, workplace applications available. That's the approach we took. And it has worked quite well. What I learned was that EI, as opposed to EQ, sees emotions as data, rather than as something to be tightly regulated. EI is not 'twice as important as IQ,' far from it, and EI is really a form of general intelligence, it is actually related to IQ, not something completely different. EQ consisted of stuff like assertiveness and optimism, things our company already measured and trained. EI was a lot different, both in how it was defined and how it was measured and developed. I found out that the statement that anyone can learn EQ was not supported by any good science. In fact, EQ has been called a myth. EI seemed to have some decent research behind it. A lot of us managers were given a chance to learn more about EI, to get assessed, and to develop some of the underlying skills. There may be a chance for you to get some training, if you're interested."

The story made a lot of sense to Robert. It explained some of the information he had quickly scanned online. Although it might be unusual to find a company that possesses this strong an EI ability culture, aspects of such an approach are available to most organizations. Research findings indicate that ability-based EI offers potential positive impacts in the activities, relationships and behaviors that are the "nuts and bolts" of organization members' interactions each and every day. EI is not the silver bullet of organizational effectiveness. Despite claims to the contrary, there is no evidence demonstrating that EI is the single most important predictor of success. However, EI—defined as a set of abilities—exists, can be objectively assessed and relates to many important organizational and individual outcomes.

We hope that you found this story to be of interest and value. Our aim was to both engage and to inform you through combining creative narrative with substantiated findings and literature citations. We conclude this chapter with a review of the extant literature on the ability model of emotional intelligence and its application to the workplace.

## ☐ The Ability Model of EI at Work

What should EI predict? Which workplace outcomes should be related to EI and which should not? We, and others, have speculated as to the nature of EI-workplace outcomes, but unlike the claims associated with the popularized notion of "EQ," we do not expect EI to be related to all aspects of work performance.

The areas where EI should matter are those involving frequent interpersonal contact and where such contacts form the basis for effectiveness. For example, EI should not play much of a role in a classic assembly-line operation where individual workers are separated from one another. However, EI might be important in the self-directed teams of the modern factory floor. EI should matter in team contexts because it has consistently been found to be related to the quality of interpersonal relationships, satisfaction measures, empathy, pro-social behaviors and affiliation (for a review, see [13]).

## EI and Individual Work Performance

Although it makes sense that EI facilitates customer relationships, data are only recently becoming available to test this hypothesis. In one of the few experiments examining this application of the ability-based model of EI, Daus, Rubin, Smith, and Cage [14] simulated a customer service interaction with an angry customer. They found that one's ability to successfully manage the difficult customer was related to aspects of managing emotions (as assessed by the precursor to the MSCEIT, the MEIS). They also found that EI was related to job satisfaction and emotional labor. These results have been replicated in a field study using mystery shopper ratings (where researchers disguised as shoppers evaluate the performance of sales people) and sales performance [15].

Another study concluded that EI enhanced the performance of workers engaged in direct customer contact. In this study, ability EI predicted supervisor ratings, above and beyond a measure of "g" (general intelligence [16]). EI (as measured by the MSCEIT) also correlated with performance on a decision-making task.

One of the more impressive data sets comes from a study of 44 financial analysts working for a large health care insurance organization. Lopes and his colleagues found that those scoring higher on the MSCEIT received greater merit increases, held higher company rank, and received better peer and supervisor ratings of interpersonal facilitation, stress tolerance and leadership potential [17]. Of great interest was that these findings were still significant after the researchers controlled for the effects of cognitive ability and personality variables.

Daus and her colleagues [14] have been examining the performance of police officers using qualitative interview data as well as quantitative performance metrics. They found that certain aspects of emotional intelligence are predictive of job performance and the police officers' responses to workplace stress.

Emotional stress may be related to the type and frequency of emotional labor that employees engage in. A recent study found that ability EI predicted the use of surface acting (expressing an emotion that one does not feel). This relationship held after controlling for measures of emotional labor and emotional expressivity.

## EI and Teams

Emotional intelligence is also important in work groups or teams. Rice studied 26 teams of claims adjusters working in the financial services center of a large insurance company [18]. She found that teams with higher average EI received higher performance ratings from managers, particularly for customer service. (Other results were negative.)

Lopes et al. examined the emotional intelligence of 91 students working on a 10-week project in small teams [17]. Individuals who were better able to manage emotions were more satisfied with other group members and with team communication, and also reported receiving more social support.

A long-term study of teams low and high on EI concluded that low EI teams ultimately end up at the same level of performance as high EI teams [9]. Of greatest interest in this study, however, was the fact that high EI teams started off their projects with a higher level of effectiveness and that it took some weeks for low EI teams to catch up.

## EI and Leadership

Over the past several years there has been a good deal of speculation regarding the relationship of EI and certain aspects of leadership, such as transformational leadership (see [5], [19–20]), but these speculative inferences were not based upon empirical research. Today we have additional data that are helping us to better understand the complex relationship between EI and leadership. Empirical support for a link between EI and leadership has been demonstrated in these areas: emerging and transformational leadership, ratings of leadership potential, subordinate and managerial rankings of leadership, organizational commitment, and leader self-awareness. Several of the studies contributing to these findings are summarized in the following paragraph.

In a semester-long study of college students, leader emergence and transformational leadership appear to be related to aspects of EI [21]. Similar results for managers in South Africa have been found. Coetzee and Schaap's study of 100 managers demonstrated that transformational leadership is related to overall EI, and that "laissez-faire" leadership was negatively related to one of the EI abilities (using emotions) [22]. A small-scale study by Lopes and colleagues examined supervisor-related leadership potential, and found significant relationships with EI [17]. Most importantly, these relationships remained significant after controlling for Big Five personality traits and verbal ability. A study of executives found that those executives scoring higher on EI achieved better business outcomes and were rated as more effective leaders by their subordinates and direct manager than were their lower EI peers [23]. In addition, this study found that the identifying emotion ability predicted effective leadership over and above traditional personality and cognitive measures. This is a critical finding, because if EI is to remain within our sphere of interest it must predict important outcomes, and add to our understanding of a phenomenon based upon pre-existing constructs (such as conscientiousness or analytical intelligence). Leadership self-awareness is sometimes assessed via discrepancy scores on 360° assessments, and this aspect of performance appears to be correlated with ability EI. People lower in EI overrated their own leadership capabilities (as assessed by direct reports), while those with higher levels underrated their own leadership [24].

Casting a more skeptical eye towards the importance of EI in positions of leadership, a small study utilizing the MSCEIT found that MSCEIT scores decreased for those higher up on the corporate ladder [24]. However, it was assumed that this low EI effect was in career tracks where EI skills are not critical or necessary for effective performance. Also, in the previously cited claims adjustor teams study by Rice [18], some team outcomes were negatively related to leader EI. This appeared to be the case for teams engaged in production-type tasks rather than relationship-intensive aspects of the job. This finding is consistent with our contention that EI is not equally critical across all types of tasks, job, or roles.

## ☐ Conclusions

We are pleased that a chapter on EI in the workplace is able to include empirical data from a range of studies. Such was not the case a few short years ago. The studies we have briefly reviewed in this chapter are the first installment in what we hope is a long line of publications on this topic. If this field is to advance, there needs to be much greater sophistication in the way research is conducted.

### Four Prescriptions

For researchers interested in contributing to this field of study we would offer four prescriptions.

## Specify Roles

Where is EI predictive? EI does not guarantee health, wealth or happiness. It is not critical or even necessary for performance in a number of roles. Researchers should specify the roles for which they believe EI plays an important part, and they need to indicate why this is so. For example, if investigating the importance of accurately identifying emotions for sales people, researchers should differentiate between relational sales and transactional sales jobs, such as cold calling. (We would not hypothesize that EI ability is critical to success in the latter type of sales role.)

To borrow an illustration from our story, Marsha's team leadership role, for example, depends to some extent upon the quality of her interpersonal network and the nature of her social interactions with team members. Conflict must be handled constructively and competing needs met. This is the type of role where we hypothesize that ability EI is important. Robert, on the other hand, might not be in an EI-critical role if he serves mainly as an independent contributor.

## Specify Outcomes

How will EI manifest itself? Researchers need to translate the ability of EI into observable behaviors and outcomes. The critical question is, how can we observe EI at work? For example, we don't necessarily "see" accurate emotional identification in play; the results of applying this skill are usually not recognized as an event or an outcome separate from the interaction in which this occurs. Researchers must carefully consider the outcomes of EI, how to observe them, how to capture them, and how to measure them. While we previously cited a study that found performance based merit increases to be associated with EI, we are not sure that such metrics are the best indicators of EI.

Taking a page from EI research conducted on non-work outcomes, perhaps researchers should focus on qualitative aspects of interpersonal encounters, satisfaction measures, organizational climate and related factors. For example, Robert and his colleagues would likely rate Marsha fairly high on leadership satisfaction measures. Matthew's actions in bringing Robert on board on day one could be captured via worker diary studies, real-time emotion ratings and climate surveys.

## Examine Training Effectiveness

Can EI be taught? The popular notion of EI would have you implicitly believe that EI is learned, whereas IQ is fixed at a young age. Research to date seems to suggest that EI, *per se*, cannot be increased. The two EI intervention studies of which we are aware both failed to demonstrate that EI could be improved [25–26]. However, we hypothesize that EI-related knowledge and skills can be developed. This is a subtle distinction for some, but one we feel compelled to make. We simply do not know if EI itself, as measured by the MSCEIT for example, is malleable, or to what extent it is so. However, our assumption is that specific emotional abilities can be developed. Our friends Marsha and Matthew's experience would likely lead them to conclude that, unlike IQ, EI can be increased, and they can point to their own training as proof of this belief. But this small workplace intervention had no outcome measures and lacked any control group. In addition, a pre-test was not followed up with an EI post-test, and there were no attempts at examining changes in other outcomes. The field is still in its infancy when it comes to training efficacy studies and intervention, and this research gap must be filled before we can claim that EI itself can be increased.

## Determine Incremental Validity

Does EI predict outcomes above and beyond intelligence and personality? Robert was hired as the result of his interviews and reference checks. His organization has also screened certain candidates using omnibus personality measures and, for some positions, a measure of intellectual ability. Should they add an ability measure of EI to their selection process? Maybe.

On-going research on EI must examine what it adds, if anything, to our understanding of important outcomes. If EI predicts outcomes, but does not add to the prediction based upon existing constructs, then it might be an interesting area of study but of less practical utility than originally thought. Researchers don't need to include dozens of constructs in their work, but should consider measures of "g" (general intelligence), and core personality traits such as the Big Five. The current evidence on the incremental value of EI is encouraging as research has shown that EI predicts important outcome variance even after controlling for traditional measures of IQ and personality [8], [10], [17].

## Next Application Steps

Practical applications of EI abound. Our concern regarding the explosion of training programs has to do with their lack of rigor and theoretical underpinnings. We have seen many programs labeled as EI programs whose content bears no resemblance at all to either emotions or to intelligence. Unfortunately, the term has become a convenient marketing tool more than a body of professional practice. Our experiences in EI training and review of adult cognition and learning lead us to propose four ways in which practitioners can enhance their ability-based EI training.

## Provide an Underlying Model

Trainers should not assume, or allow, an "anything goes" approach to EI training. Training must be based upon a clear definition of EI. While we strongly advocate an ability-based approach to EI, training must be based on a clearly stated model of EI, and training needs to flow from that EI model.

Learner's expectations are an important part of learning effectiveness. Given that most learners are familiar with non-ability approaches to EI, providing an explicit model of EI, and comparing it to the pre-existing notions of learners, can result in enhanced training programs. For example, we provide an overview of the ability model of EI in all training programs. The four-step blueprint becomes a model for the entire training experience.

## Experience with Substance

Once a model of EI is established, and learner models addressed, training must incorporate experiential components in order to be maximally effective. There is a danger to such training, of course, and that is exposing people to emotions that they do not wish to feel. There is also a considerable ethical issue facing trainers: to allow participants to easily opt out, to protect personal disclosures as confidential information and to provide emotional support after the end of the session.

Experiential training needs to meet a stated objective: it is not enough to feel good about the experience, it has to tie into a basic training objective.

## Practice the Skills

Once an experiential component has been completed, many trainers move on to the next module. But if we desire to obtain transfer of training to the daily life of participants then we need to provide them with ample time to practice the skills we are teaching. Role plays with corrective feedback, with scenarios developed by participants or drawn from their stock of experiences, can provide greater transfer of training.

Our approach has been to provide a case study role play early in our training to provide a baseline for participants. The role plays follow the ability-based model of EI, and get people using the four-step emotional blueprint right away. Skill practice is built throughout the other modules, and includes more complex cases and role plays as the training progresses. Participants also develop their own emotional blueprints based upon a current, important interpersonal situation they are facing.

### Offer Follow-Up Support

Effective training requires us to be available to participants after the formal session has ended. It also requires trainers to provide the means for participants to continue their learning after the session has ended. Whether this is achieved through follow-on training, individual development plans, or written or online training resources, providing people with an opportunity to continue their learning is another critical component of good and effective training.

Our story of Marsha, Robert and Matthew illustrates how an organization can have a training program that is based on sound theory. On-going access to training professionals means that this organization continues to learn, to transform itself, and to leverage the skills of EI in meaningful ways. Trainers constantly face time constraints and budgetary limitations, and so we recognize that training is not conducted under ideal circumstances. But if we start with a simple set of principles for EI training, we can begin to develop greater professionalism and rigor in such programs.

Emotional intelligence has come to mean different things to people, and there seems to be a split between academic researchers' use of the term and practitioners' use of the term. We believe that this does not have to be the state of this field. It was our intent in this chapter to present you with a structured, focused model of EI that can be used as a platform for research as well as for practice.

## ☐ References

1. Paulhus, D. L., Lysy, D. C., & Yik, M. S. M. (1998). Self-report measures of intelligence: Are they useful as proxy IQ tests? *Journal of Personality Psychology, 66*, 525–554.
2. Atkins, P. W. B., & Wood, R. E. (2002). Self- versus others' ratings as predictors of assessment center ratings: Validation evidence for 360-degree feedback programs. *Personnel Psychology, 55*, 871–904.
3. Damasio, A. R. (1994). *Descartes' error*. New York: G. P. Putnam's Sons.
4. Salovey, P., & Mayer, J. D. (1990). Emotional intelligence. *Imagination, Cognition, and Personality, 9*, 185–211.
5. Caruso, D. R., Mayer, J. D., & Salovey, P. (2002). Emotional intelligence and emotional leadership. In R. E. Riggio, S. E. Murphy, & F. J. Pirozzolo (Eds.), *Multiple intelligences and leadership* (pp. 55–74). Mahwah, NJ: Lawrence Erlbaum Associates, Inc.
6. Caruso, D. R., & Salovey, P. (2004). *The emotionally intelligent manager*. San Francisco: Jossey-Bass.

7. Mayer, J. D., Salovey, P., & Caruso, D. R. (2002). *Mayer-Salovey-Caruso Emotional Intelligence Test (MSCEIT) user's manual.* Toronto, Canada: Multi-Health Systems.
8. Brackett, M., & Mayer, J. D. (2003). Convergent, discriminant, and incremental validity of competing measures of emotional intelligence. *Personality and Social Psychology Bulletin, 29,* 1147–1158.
9. Jordan, P. J., Ashkanasy, N. M., & Hartel, C. E. J. (2002). Workgroup emotional intelligence: Scale development and relationship to team process effectiveness and goal focus. *Human Resource Management Review, 12*(2), 195–214.
10. Lopes, P. N., Salovey, P., & Straus, R. (2003). Emotional intelligence, personality, and the perceived quality of social relationships. *Personality and Individual Differences, 35,* 641–658.
11. Brackett, M., Mayer, J. D., & Warner, R. M. (2004). Emotional intelligence and the prediction of behavior. *Personality and Individual Differences, 36,* 1387–1402.
12. Plutchik, R. (1980). *Emotion: A psychoevolutionary synthesis.* New York: Harper & Row.
13. Mayer, J. D., Salovey, P., & Caruso, D. R. (2004). Emotional intelligence: Theory, findings, and implications. *Psychological Inquiry, 15,* 197–215.
14. Daus, C. S., Rubin, R. S., Smith, R. K., & Cage, T. (2005). *Police performance: Do emotional skills matter?* Paper presented at the 19th annual meeting of the Society for Industrial and Organizational Psychologists, as part of the symposium, "Book 'em Danno!: New developments in law enforcement performance prediction."
15. Cage, T., Daus, C. S., & Saul, K. (2005). *An examination of emotional skill, job satisfaction, and retail performance.* Paper presented at the 19th annual meeting of the Society for Industrial/Organizational Psychology, as part of a symposium.
16. Janovics, J., & Christiansen, N. D. (2002). *Emotional intelligence in the workplace.* Paper presented at the 16th annual conference of the Society of Industrial and Organizational Psychology, San Diego, CA.
17. Lopes, P. N., Salovey, P., Côté, S., & Beers, M. (2005). Emotion regulation abilities and the quality of social interaction. *Emotion, 5,* 113–118.
18. Rice, C. L. (1999). *A quantitative study of emotional intelligence and its impact on team performance.* Unpublished master's thesis, Pepperdine University, Malibu, CA.
19. Ashkanasy, N. M., & Tse, B. (1998). *Transformational leadership as management of emotion: A conceptual review.* Paper presented at the first conference on Emotions and Organizational Life, San Diego, CA.
20. George J. M. (2000). Emotions and leadership: The role of emotional intelligence. *Human Relations, 53,* 1027–1055.
21. Daus, C. S., & Harris, A. (2003). *Emotional intelligence and transformational leadership in groups.* Paper presented at the 18th annual meeting of the Society for Industrial and Organizational Psychologists, Orlando, FL.
22. Coetzee, C., & Schaap, P. (2003). *The relationship between leadership styles and emotional intelligence.* Paper presented at the sixth annual conference of the Society for Industrial and Organisational Psychology, South Africa.
23. Rosete, D., & Ciarrochi, J. (2005). Emotional intelligence and its relationship to workplace performance outcomes of leadership effectiveness. *Leadership and Organization Development Journal, 26,* 388–399.
24. Collins, V. L. (2001). *Emotional intelligence and leadership success.* Unpublished doctoral dissertation, University of Nebraska, Lincoln, NE.
25. Forrey, J. S. (2000). *The effect of biblically based peer counselor training on emotional intelligence.* Unpublished dissertation, Trinity Evangelical Divinity School, Deerfield, IL.
26. Stephenson, S. F. (2003). *Teaching emotional intelligence in elementary school: The effectiveness of a specialized curriculum.* Chico, CA: Whitman College.

# 10 CHAPTER

Joseph Ciarrochi
John T. Blackledge

# Mindfulness-Based Emotional Intelligence Training: A New Approach to Reducing Human Suffering and Promoting Effectiveness

There has been substantial confusion in the field of emotional intelligence (EI). People seem to disagree on what EI is, what it predicts, and whether EI is distinctive from traditional measures. Despite all these disputes, EI continues to attract substantial interest from both the public and from scientists. What is so appealing about EI? Perhaps people recognize a fundamental paradox: science has helped us to gain amazing control over our external world, yet we have made little progress it getting control of our internal, emotional worlds. For example, we can travel around the world in less than a day, but we don't seem to have made much progress in reducing road rage, racism, murder, and suicide. If we look honestly at the human condition, we must admit that emotional *un*intelligence is everywhere. People may be turning to EI, perhaps hoping that it will help them get control of their lives.

The purpose of the present chapter is to provide a theory about why people often act so ineffectively in the context of emotions. We then use the theory to hopefully accomplish two goals, namely, (1) to provide an organizing framework for the vast number of EI-relevant measures currently in the field, and (2) to connect these measures to a coherent intervention.

# ☐  Definining a Few Terms

We work within a functional contextualist framework [1]. This means that our primary focus is on *influencing* behavior, rather than merely predicting it. Specifically, the goal of our EI work is to identify the conditions that promote effectiveness and reduce suffering. We define effectiveness as the achievement of goals that are determined by each individual client. "Reduction of suffering" is a bit more difficult to define, but can be operationally defined by high scores on negative indices of well-being (e.g., depression and anxiety), and/or an increase of scores on positive indices of well-being (e.g., life satisfaction).

Our discussion focuses on processes that are presumed to promote emotionally intelligent behavior and indirectly reduce suffering. It is critical to distinguish between emotional intelligence and emotionally intelligent behavior. Emotional intelligence refers to people's ability to process emotions and deal effectively with them (see Chapter 1 in this volume). EI refers to people's *potential*. In contrast, "emotionally intelligent behavior" refers to how effectively people actually behave in the presence of emotions and emotionally charged thoughts.

Simply put, emotionally unintelligent behavior occurs when emotions impede effective action, and emotionally intelligent behavior occurs when emotions do not impede effective action, or when emotions facilitate effective action. Emotional intelligence (as an ability) is one set of processes hypothesized to promote emotionally intelligent behavior. There are other potential processes, many of which will be discussed in this chapter.

Perhaps a few examples of emotionally intelligent behavior will clarify our definition. If you are anxious, does that feeling stop you from going to get a health checkup (we assume this would be inconsistent with your goal of maintaining health)? If you are very angry at your friend, do you hit him (assuming your goal is to maintain friendly relations)? If you feel sad, does this stop you from caring for a loved one (assuming you value such "care")? These are three examples of emotionally unintelligent behavior. The processes that we specify in this chapter are hypothesized to help people act more intelligently and more effectively pursue their personal values and goals when they feel anxious, angry, or sad. Emotionally intelligent people would, according to our definition, feel anxious *and* get a health checkup, feel angry *and* treat people with respect, and feel sad *and* still support loved ones.

In our model, emotionally intelligent behavior (EIB) is presumed to reduce unnecessary suffering. Thus, reduced suffering is essentially an after-effect of people moving towards what they value (or engaging in EIB). For example, if people feel sad and continue to do the things they value, they may be less likely to experience depression because their abilities to consistently engage in personally meaningful and vital activities would be expected to minimize depression over the long term. Similarly, if someone experiences anxiety about an upcoming test, and focuses on studying for it, rather than procrastinating, then they may be less likely to experience excess anxiety and regret. In contrast, if they try to avoid studying and avoid thinking about the test, then they may ironically experience more anxiety about the test in the long run (see section on emotional orientation, below).

Our review focuses on processes that are both presumed to promote emotionally intelligent behavior, and that can be modified by an intervention. By talking about these processes, we do not make any assumptions about whether the processes refer to either a "potential," or a "tendency." The ultimate purpose of everything done within a our EI approach is about intervening to help people lead better, more vital lives. Thus, we are not interested in EI-relevant measures in themselves, but rather how these measures facilitate effective interventions.

## Why People Seem to be so Emotionally Unintelligent—Language-Based Processes

Relational Frame Theory (RFT), a modern behavioral theory of language and cognition that has undergone rigorous empirical testing (see [2] for an initial summary of this work), suggests that psychological suffering is virtually ubiquitous in human beings primarily because of the way language works. Very briefly, RFT posits that the way we think about our experiences dramatically changes those experiences by transforming direct contingency stimulus functions—or, in other words, by pervasively altering our impressions of what is actually going on in ways that lead us to act as if the illusory world created through abstract thoughts is real.

RFT endorses the notion that, although we can only ever be completely certain that thoughts referring to phenomena we can directly perceive with our five senses are effectively "real," we are often erroneously convinced that thoughts referring to abstract, non-sensible phenomena are just as true and accurate. For example, I can be certain that I feel anxious in the sense that I can physically sense bodily components of anxiety (rapid heart beat, tense shoulders, sweaty skin, etc.). But the evaluative thoughts that anxiety is a *bad* thing and that *there is something wrong with me* for feeling anxious, and the prescriptive thought that *I must avoid* anxiety or bad things will happen, do not refer to formal stimulus properties that can be directly sensed. Although the thoughts that there is something wrong with me, and anxiety is bad and must be avoided, are not immutable truths, I may act as if they are, and correspondingly go to great and often counterproductive lengths to avoid anxiety.

Evaluative and prescriptive language surrounding experiences like anxiety are only the tip of the iceberg. RFT predicts that virtually any emotion or other aspect of human experience can be arbitrarily evaluated and involved in unnecessary behavioral limitations and prescriptions. In blunt language, there are virtually unlimited ways in which we can be weighed, measured, and found wanting. The hope lies in the fact that these measurements are not real.

The hallmark of an RFT-informed perspective on what makes a person emotionally intelligent thus involves an awareness of the illusory qualities of language that allow emotions and other aspects of our experience to be negatively evaluated and to participate in *apparent* causal relations with subsequent behavior. The emotionally intelligent person, from our perspective, is able to recognize unpleasant emotions for what they are: constellations of physiological sensations, thoughts, and behavioral predispositions that are not intrinsically harmful, can be fully and willingly experienced, and need not determine what is done next. The emotionally unintelligent person views the negative evaluations and prescriptive thoughts surrounding emotions as fundamentally true and behaviorally binding (e.g., if I feel angry, I must act aggressively and get revenge).

The FEAR acronym (fusion, evaluation, avoidance, reason giving), drawn from RFT-based Acceptance and Commitment Therapy (ACT [3]) describes in more detail how this kind of emotional unintelligence develops.

## Fusion

In a basic sense, cognitive fusion occurs when we "take our thoughts too seriously" and assume that what we believe corresponds to immutable truths. In a more technical sense, cognitive fusion is a process that enables language's ability to transform direct stimulus functions (to literally change the characteristics and implications of our experience).

When negative evaluations and inaccurate or dysfunctional verbal rules (referred to as "reasons" or "reason giving" in the FEAR acronym) are cognitively fused with, problems arise. When one fuses with negatively valanced evaluations of one's experience, the stimulus functions of that experience are transformed and become correspondingly more negative or aversive than they actually "are" from the perspective of a nonverbal organism. (Or, more precisely, than they actually would be from a direct contingency perspective.) While such negative evaluations can confer an advantage (e.g., when framing one's experience negatively

leads oneself to successfully change unsatisfactory or unnecessarily pro-
hibitive circumstances), they often create more aversive stimulation and
harmful experiential avoidance than necessary. For example, a man who
becomes depressed following a run of bad luck, and subsequently fuses
with thoughts that he is hopelessly inadequate to life's challenges, is then
likely to feel even worse about himself and to avoid potentially constructive challenges likely to test his worthiness.

Similarly, fusion with problematic verbal rules or "reasons" can lock
one in to actions prescribed by those rules and prohibit actions discordant
with them. For example, a woman who fuses with a verbal rule stating
that anger must never be expressed may be ineffective at solving interpersonal conflicts because following this rule would often prohibit an
open discussion of her perspective and her grievances. Thus, while fusion
with evaluations and verbal rules/reasons can often confer a psychological
and behavioral advantage, such fusion can often enhance psychological
suffering and contribute to more maladaptive behavior as well.

## Evaluation

Language allows us to create labels (such as "anxiety" and "sadness") for
our internal states. Once labeled, such states can be readily evaluated, and
these evaluations are very often negative [3]. When these negative evaluations are fused with, we may then try to avoid the internal states just as
we avoid genuinely threatening external events. We may even verbally
generate more global and abstract labels such as "our life." As
it can with any other stimulus, our minds can then verbally evaluate "our
life" as "worthless" and "unbearable," thereby providing the impetus for a
variety of problematic behaviors designed to avoid the sizable psychological pain associated with such thoughts—substance abuse, social isolation,
even suicide. Finally, language allows us to create ideals about ourselves,
other people, and the world around us. Our minds can then compare the
ideal to present reality, and find the present to be unacceptable.

Consistent with this view, evidence suggests that social comparison and
negative self-evaluation are pervasive and linked to suffering [4–5], and
that negative self- and global evaluations play critical roles in a great
number of psychological disorders, including post-traumatic stress disorder [6] and depression [7].

## Avoidance

It is often adaptive to avoid threats in the outside world. Humans create
an internal, private world of symbols, and learn to avoid aspects of it.
Such avoidance can be attempted by directly suppressing unpleasant

experiences or by seeking to modify such experiences. Experiential avoidance may work in the short run, but often not in the long run. Indeed, it can have a paradoxical rebound effect. The more one tries to avoid the experience, the more it can dominate one's life [3], [8].

The downsides to experiential avoidance are now well documented. Research has shown that when subjects are asked to suppress a thought, they later show an increase in this suppressed thought as compared with those not given suppression instructions [9]. Indeed, the suppression strategy may actually stimulate the suppressed mood in a kind of self-amplifying loop [10].

### Reason Giving/Rule Creation

People learn to put forth reasons as valid and sensible causes of behavior [3]. Unfortunately, people begin to believe their own reasons and stories [3], even when they do not correspond well to actual, direct contingencies and are harmful or unproductive if followed. People tell themselves, "I am worthless" and behave accordingly. They might tell themselves "I must have other people's approval," and waste a great deal of energy trying to get approval from every significant other. Or they might think, "I can't take a risk, because I am too anxious." They act as if they really can't take a risk, although experience can show them that they can take risks *and* be anxious [11].

## ☐ EI-Relevant Processes Derived from the Theory

We now turn our attention to the different dimensions that we believe undermine the harmful influence of FEAR-based action and that promote emotionally intelligent behavior. For a book-length treatment of how to undermine FEAR, please see Hayes et al. [3] and other work under the heading of Acceptance and Commitment Therapy (ACT). We view Mindfulness-based Emotional Intelligence Training (MBEIT) as an ACT intervention applied to organizations.

After describing each dimension, we will review a number of individual difference measures that appear to tap into the dimensions, and discuss their relationship to well-being. The purpose of discussing the measures is not to rename old measures as "EI." We use the original names. These measures index processes that are presumed to promote emotionally intelligent behavior. Our purpose is to put a wide range of measures into a coherent theoretical framework that is tied to specific interventions.

From a functionalist perspective, the main reason to talk about these measures is because they may help to make a difference in people's lives.

Such measures may help people to evaluate which aspect of an intervention is or is not working. It may also help to identify client's strengths and weaknesses and thereby create an intervention that is tailored to each individual's needs.

# ☐ Effective Emotional Orientation

## Defining Effective Emotional Orientation

Effective emotional orientation (EEO) involves willingness to have private experiences (e.g., anxiety), when doing so fosters effective action (Table 10.1). It also involves accepting the inevitability of unpleasant affect and negative self-evaluation, and recognizing that these private experiences do not have to stop us from pursuing a valued direction [3].

People quite reasonably avoid things in the world that are aversive. Cognitive fusion with negative evaluations exponentially increases the amount of stimuli in one's world experienced as aversive. People naturally evaluate their aversive thoughts as bad and seek to avoid them. As discussed above, avoidance often does not work and indeed can make matters worse. A rule of thumb regarding private experience is, "If you're not willing to have it, you have it" [3]. This is completely different from the rule of public experience. If you not willing to have something unpleasant in the public world (say, an ugly sofa), you can usually get rid of it.

## The Link between Well-Being and Individual Differences in EEO

EEO is more of a family of constructs, rather than a single construct. The "family" members are interrelated, yet sometimes statistically separable. In general, all of the measures of EI-relevant processes described in this chapter have this family property. This chapter will focus on measures that have found empirical support from multiple, independent laboratories.

The first individual difference we discuss—problem orientation—reflects the tendency to see emotional problems as a challenge rather than a threat, and the tendency to face problems, rather than avoid them. There is considerable evidence supporting the link between problem orientation and negative indices of well-being. It has been associated with low depression, anxiety, hopelessness, suicidal ideation, health complaints, and neuroticism [12–15]. It has been shown to be associated with low psychological distress and positive coping strategies, even when controlling for optimism,

**TABLE 10.1. Processes that are hypothesized to promote emotionally intelligent behavior**

| EI-relevant process | Description |
|---|---|
| Effective emotional orientation | • Letting go of unhelpful emotion control strategies<br>• Willingness to have emotionally charged private experiences (thoughts, images, emotions), when doing so fosters effective action<br>• Accepting the inevitability of a certain amount of unpleasant affect and negative self-evaluation<br>• Understanding that private experiences do not have to stop one from pursuing a valued direction (and therefore one doesn't have to get rid of them) |
| Using emotion as information | • Identifying emotions<br>• Understanding the appraisals that activate different emotions<br>• Understanding the consequences of emotions on cognition, health, etc.<br>• Understanding how emotions progress over time<br>• Distinguishing between helpful and unhelpful emotions and emotionally charged thoughts |
| Defusing from unhelpful thoughts and emotions (i.e., Undermining the power of unhelpful thoughts and emotions to act as barriers to effective action) | • Seeing that emotionally charged thoughts about life are not equivalent to life<br>• Looking *at* emotionally charged ways of framing (thinking about) experiences, rather than *through* them<br>• Being able to be mindful and accepting of moment to moment experience (either internal or external) |
| Defusing from unhelpful self-concepts (i.e., undermining the power of unhelpful self-concepts to act as barriers to effective action) | • Recognizing that self-evaluations are not descriptions of our essence<br>• Escaping the perceived need to defend self-esteem<br>• Looking at, rather than through, self-evaluations<br>• Recognizing that emotionally charged evaluations of the self do not have to stop us from pursuing our goals<br>• Making contact with the "observer self;" finding the safe place from which to accept all negative emotions, self-doubts, and other unpleasant inner experiences |
| Effective action orientation | • Clear awareness of values and their relative importance<br>• Ability to take action that is consistent with goals and values, even in the context of:<br>   ◦ impulses, fears, lack of confidence<br>   ◦ uncertainty, doubt<br>   ◦ feelings of exhaustion or fatigue<br>   ◦ physical pain<br>   ◦ intense emotion<br>• Ability to sustain committed action in the face of inconsistent feedback, frustration, and failure |

pessimism, positive affectivity, negative affectivity, and stressful life events [15–16]. Other research provides some evidence that problem orientation is causally related to well-being. Davey and his colleagues have shown that experimentally induced reductions in effective orientation lead to increases in subsequent catastrophic worrying [17].

The White Bear Suppression Inventory measures poor orientation, in that people who score high on it seek to avoid or suppress their private experiences. It has been found to correlate with measures of obsessional thinking and depressive and anxious affect [18].

The Acceptance and Action Questionnaire (AAQ) measures the willingness to experience thoughts, feelings, and physiological sensations without having to control them, or let them determine one's actions [19–20]. It has been associated with a range of negative emotional states [19]. A longitudinal study found that the AAQ predicts mental health and an objective measure of performance, over and above job control, negative affectivity, and locus of control [20]. In another study utilizing the AAQ, participants high in emotional avoidance showed more anxiety in response to $CO_2$ (biological challenge), particularly when instructed to suppress their emotions [10].

# ☐ Using Emotion as Information

The second dimension of our model involves the ability to use emotions as information (UEI) to inform effective action (see Table 10.1). Emotions are messengers. They usually tell us something about the world and about our own desires. For example, anxiety results from the appraisal that something undesirable might happen. Anger results from the appraisal that someone has acted unfairly and this has resulted in something undesirable [21].

The FEAR framework suggests that we tend to evaluate our unpleasant or otherwise unwanted private experiences as bad and subsequently try to avoid them. Unfortunately, avoiding the messenger (the emotion) does not change the message. Importantly, if we do not know what the message is, we will find it difficult to act effectively. If we do not know that we are anxious, then we may mistakenly think our anxious sensations are due to a physical sickness [22]. Or we may mistakenly blame our anxiety on some irrelevant event (our colleague's behavior), and seek to change this irrelevant event, rather than focusing effectively on the real problem. Essentially, we need to be able to utilize emotions as information if we are to effectively solve our emotional problems.

# The Link Between Well-Being and Individual Differences in Using Emotional Information

The measures discussed here focus on people's ability to identify their emotions, which is essential to being able to use emotional information.

Alexithymia refers to people who have trouble identifying and describing emotions and who tend to minimize emotional experience and focus attention externally. This construct appears to be a mix of using emotional information and effective emotional orientation. The Toronto Alexithymia Scale (TAS-20) is one of the most commonly used measures of alexithymia. It has been shown to be highly related to Bar-On's self-report EI measure [23], and to a number of important life outcomes. For example, people high in alexithymia are more prone to drug addiction, eating disorders, and to report medically unexplained symptoms [24]. The alexithymia subscales—difficulty identifying and describing emotions—are related to a variety of negative indices of well-being (e.g., depression), even after controlling for other measures of emotional intelligence [15]. A longitudinal study found that alexithymia predicts persistent somatization at 2-year follow-up [25].

The emotional clarity subscale of the Trait Meta-Mood Scale (TMMS) also appears to measure an aspect of using emotion as information [26]. This scale predicts how much people seem to dwell unproductively on sad thoughts [26]. In general, just about every measure of emotional intelligence appears to have a subscale that assesses skill at emotional identification. Such measures include the Mayer-Salovey-Caruso Emotional Intelligence Test [27] and the Schutte et al. emotional intelligence inventory [28].

In contrast to the above scales, the Levels of Emotional Awareness Scale (LEAS) is based on performance rather than self-report [29]. People low in emotional awareness tend not to use specific emotion terms (sadness, anger) to describe their emotional experience. Instead, they focus on cognitions ("I'd feel confused"), bodily sensations ("I'd feel tired") and undifferentiated emotional states ("I'd feel bad"). Research has shown people high in emotional awareness are less likely to allow moods to bias their judgments in mood congruent directions [30]. Other research suggests that people high in emotional awareness have higher levels of social well-being. Ciarrochi et al. found that emotionally aware adults have a higher number of social supports [30]. More recently, Bajgar found that emotionally aware boys are less likely to be involved in anger outbursts and fights and emotionally aware girls are more likely to be popular with their peers [31].

We acknowledge that their are rather substantial differences between self-report and ability-based measures of emotion perception. However, discussion of these differences is beyond the scope of this chapter—please see other chapters in this volume.

## ☐ Defusing from Unhelpful Emotions and Thoughts

The third dimension of our model involves the ability to undermine fusion with unhelpful emotions and thoughts. Table 10.1 lists the key components of this skill (see also the above subsection on fusion).

When language processes dominate, "humans fuse with the psychological contents of verbal events. The distinction between thinking and the referent of thought is diminished. As a result, emotionally charged thoughts or feelings (particularly those with provocative or pejorative meanings) become connected to powerful and predictable behavior patterns" [3, p. 149].

In other words, language has the power to bring forth its own reality. The word "milk" psychologically brings forth the taste of milk, images of frothy whiteness, and even the near sensation of coldness. It is as if simply speaking or thinking of the word has made the milk present. Language is so powerful that people come to see their verbal constructions of life as equivalent to life itself [3]. People fail to distinguish between the verbal constructions and the actual experience. We sometimes see life through "horrible" colored glasses [3], [32], and when these colored sights are taken at face value, life itself can become horrible.

One key to undermining fusion is to learn to look *at* our emotionally charged thoughts, rather than *through* them. Normally, we do not even notice the process of thinking that occurs through virtually all our waking hours. Thoughts occur but are not recognized as thoughts *per se*. Rather, they are implicitly assumed to be accurate descriptions of our experiences. A first step in viewing thinking simply as behavior we engage in (rather than immutable reflections of reality) is to notice that we are indeed "creating" strings of words and to notice how these words might be coloring our perceptions of our direct experiences. This involves realizing first hand that words are simply maps of the terrain, not the terrain itself—and that these maps are often grossly inadequate.

Defusion involves a fundamental shift in context. It involves looking at the feelings, thoughts, sensations, and memories that show up from moment to moment and watching them as they go by. It involves a context shift from the "here and now" ("I am depressed") to the "there and then" (I have had the evaluation that "I am depressed"). Such shifts help us see our actual, direct experiences for what they are—streams of words and changing physical sensations and urges—rather than what our minds say our direct experiences are [3], [33]. Very often, vast differences exist between basic experiences created by direct, non-verbal contingencies, and the confabulated versions of these same experiences created by verbal processes.

The antidote to the FEAR-based behaviors just described involve the highly interrelated processes of cognitive *defusion* and acceptance. Procedures instilling the shift in context described above instantiate this defusion and disrupt problematic transformations of stimulus function created through language. Once defusion has "de-thorned" the bushes one metaphorically stands in, it becomes easier to accept one's position and orient toward behavior more instrumental in achieving personally held values. Some defusion and acceptance-based techniques, for example, involve those elsewhere referred to as "mindfulness." Mindfulness can be broken down into a number of components, including "what" skills (i.e., observing things as they come and go, describing them, and participating fully in life), and "how" skills (i.e., taking a non-judgmental stance, mindfully focus on what you are doing, doing what works [34]). Essentially, mindfulness helps people to look at their private experience, rather than through it, and to see their moment-to-moment experience as it is (not as it seems to be when seen through language or intense emotion).

Mindlessly seeing life through unhelpful thoughts is expected to be a major source of suffering [32]. Ellis has proposed four major classes of unhelpful thoughts [32]. These include demandingness ("Things *must* be a certain way"), low distress tolerance ("I can't stand it"), awfulizing ("My life is awful"), and global evaluations ("I am completely good or bad; work is completely bad"). The key goal in mindfulness training is not to get rid of the thoughts, as they are not harmful in and of themselves. Rather, the key is to accept whatever thoughts show up during the course of pursuing goals (effective orientation) and to learn to look at thoughts, rather than through them. One must be willing to have unpleasant thoughts, and not believe them.

The last two decades have found substantial support for interventions that are designed to facilitate the strategic use of defusion and acceptance. Acceptance and Commitment Therapy (ACT) is an acceptance- and defusion-based approach that addresses processes designated by the FEAR framework. There are now nearly two decades of work specifically supporting the efficacy of ACT, as well as over 60 empirical RFT studies supporting aspects of the ACT model. Published randomized control trials provide evidence that ACT may do as well or better than traditional cognitive behavioral therapy in reducing depression and anxiety, and that it is effective in the treatment of substance abuse, pain, and psychosis [35–36]. ACT has also been shown to be effective at reducing stress and sick leave utilization in "normal" populations [37–38].

There is also substantial support for other acceptance or mindfulness-based interventions, including Dialectic Behavior Therapy [34], Mindfulness-based Cognitive Therapy for Depression [39], mindfulness-based meditation [40], and Mindfulness-based Stress Reduction [33]. Many other approaches have benefited by adding mindfulness and acceptance components to their inventions (for a review see [3]).

## Individual Differences in Mindfulness and Fusion with Particular Types of Unhelpful Thoughts

There are several scales related to this dimension. The Mindfulness Attention Awareness Scale (MAAS) measures people's tendency to be mindful of moment to moment experience. This scale has been shown to relate to various aspects of well-being and to how effectively people deal with stressful life events [41].

The Dysfunctional Attitudes Scale (DAS [42]) is commonly used in clinical practice and measures the extent people believe, or fuse with, certain unhelpful thoughts. It can be divided into two dimensions [43–44]. The first dimension is about the "dire need" for power and success, and includes beliefs that relate to perfectionism (being perfectly achieving), performance evaluation, not seeming weak, and a need for admiration and control. The second dimension relates to acceptance, and includes feeling a "dire need" for social acceptance, love, and approval. The DAS (and similar scales) have been shown to relate to well-being, discriminate between clinical and non-clinical groups, and predict changes in well-being in a longitudinal design [43–44]. In addition, there is evidence that reduction in dysfunctional beliefs due to clinical interventions are associated with reductions in disturbing emotional states [42], [45–46].

Another group of measures reflect unhelpful beliefs about uncertainty (e.g., "that uncertainty is awful or intolerable"). These include measures of intolerance of uncertainty [47], rigidity [48], and intolerance of ambiguity [49]. These measures have been shown to relate to depression and anxiety in both clinical and normal populations [47], [50].

Finally, individual differences in rumination seem to reflect high fusion. Rumination can be measures using self-reports measures such as the Emotion Control Questionnaire [51]. Ruminators seem to be stuck in their thoughts, engaging in repetitive and passive thinking about a problem [52]. Rumination involves mindlessly bouncing from one negative thought to another, perhaps in an attempt to escape unpleasant affect by controlling the uncontrollable (e.g., uncertainty [47]). It has been associated with a range of emotional difficulties, including anger and depression [53–54]. Longitudinal studies have established that people who engage in more rumination have higher levels of depressive symptoms over time and perceive themselves to be receiving less social support, even when controlling for their baseline levels of depressive symptoms [54–56]. High rumination has also been associated with delayed recovery from stress, as indicated by delayed heart rate and physiological (cortisol) recovery [57–58].

Rumination might also be seen as an ineffective emotional orientation, since it appears to involve attempts to use reasoning to escape from unpleasant private experiences [59]. However, we include it here because it seems to involve a mindless absorption in the content of thought (fusion), rather than looking at thought, and a focus on the future or the past, whilst the present goes unnoticed.

The measures may seem quite different from each other in this section, and to some extent they are. However, there is also some evidence that they interrelate. For example, Brown and Ryan found across several studies that higher mindfulness scores were modestly associated with higher self-reported emotional intelligence and lower rumination [41]. Dugas and his colleagues found that intolerance of uncertainty is related to ruminative activity [59]. More recently, Godsell and Ciarrochi found that the measures discussed in this section and other sections all tend to correlate, sometimes substantially [60].

It is also worth noting that these measures tend to correlate with neuroticism, or the tendency to experience negative affect [59], [61–62]. This overlap with personality is sometimes seen as a problem in EI research, as it suggests that the measure may not predict variance over and above personality. We should emphasize again that our goal is not primarily incremental prediction or the creation of new EI measures. Thus, for our purposes, it is not a problem if these measures correlate with neuroticism or other personality measures. In fact, we expect that all the measures reviewed in this paper reflect processes that *lead* to neuroticism. Thus, it would be absurd to posit that they are independent of this variable.

Again, our goal is pragmatic. We seek to reduce suffering. To some extent, the two personality traits, positive and negative affectivity, are just two imperfect indices of suffering. They don't necessarily provide clues as to what one does about suffering.

# ☐ Defusing Self-Concepts

The last aspect of our model involves the ability to free oneself, at least briefly, from fusion with unhelpful self-concepts (see Table 10.1). Humans develop a concept of self. The mind then proceeds to evaluate it. We readily evaluate this "self" as "good," "bad," "kind," "flawed," "incomplete," "special," and/or "unethical." Cognitive fusion means we tend to treat these evaluations as literal properties of our self. For example, we can evaluate a cup as "bad," but this badness is not a formal or direct property of the cup—a property that can be directly perceived by one of the five senses. "Roundness" or "hardness" can be said to be a formal property of the cup, but abstract notions like "badness" or "goodness," with no directly perceivable physical referent, cannot be considered a formal property of the cup. Similarly, abstract verbalizations like "bad" or "good" cannot be said to be an innate property of the "self." While logical or pseudo-logical arguments might conclude that one is "bad," such an abstraction relies on arbitrary (but conventionalized) criteria and thus is not as uniformly verifiable as one's physical properties and attributes.

This apparently philosophical distinction between formal (physical sensible) and abstract stimulus properties actually has some vital and pertinent implications for human suffering. If abstractions inherent to negative evaluations and problematic verbal rules literally do not have concrete physical referents like those that formally descriptive words have, then these abstractions are not formally binding. The universe does not know or care if one is "bad" or "good" because the concepts of badness and goodness are simply verbal constructions. They are not immutable truths, but rather are verbal illusions that need not have a binding domination over one's life. Yet humans tend to confuse the nebulous quality of evaluations ("I'm bad") with the solidity of formal descriptions ("I'm made up of about 70% water"). If you believe badness was a primary property of your self, then it would be very difficult, if not impossible, to change [3], [32].

Problems arise when people come to identify with unhelpful self-concepts. Whatever verbal concept of "me" I have becomes, for all practical purposes, the equal of the actual "me." People are then drawn into protecting the concept of self as if it is part of the self [3]. They seek to feed it, or defend it against attack. People begin to talk about "building self-esteem" or repairing "damage" done to it. They become "hurt" when someone "attacks" their self-esteem.

Low self-esteem seems to involve at least two parts: negative evaluations of the entire self ("I am worthless") and fusion with these evaluations. In other words, one could have a negative self-evaluation yet not believe (fuse with) it. Undermining fusion with self-concepts is very different from "building self-esteem." The goal in undermining fusion is not to get rid of the negative evaluations and replace them with positive evaluations. Rather, it is to accept the negative self-evaluations as words that may inevitably show up, and to look *at* them, rather than through them.

## Individual Differences in Fusing with Unhelpful Self-Concepts and Well-Being

It appears to be reasonably well established that low self-esteem is associated with higher levels of negative affect [4]. Self esteem is often measured using a self-report scale by Rosenberg [63]. It also appears to be measured by the Bar-On emotional quotient inventory [64].

What is somewhat more surprising is that some aspects of high self-esteem have been associated with poor well-being, at least in some circumstances [65–66]. For example, the Narcissist Personality Inventory (NPI) assesses a person's sense grandiosity, self-importance, and specialness [67]. Narcissists scan the social context for evidence that supports their elevated sense of self and tend to construct high self-esteem in the absence of objective evidence. Their self-esteem is fragile, and they are prone to respond to threatening feedback with shame, humiliation, anger, and interpersonal aggression [68].

A related line of research has examined individual differences in the stability of self-esteem. Stability can be measured by administering a standard self-esteem inventory at multiple times, and then using the variance between different measurements to predict outcomes [65]. People who have unstable high self-esteem have been shown to experience more anger and hostility, perhaps because they feel the "need" to defend their self-worth [65]. Other research shows that unstable self-esteem is associated with goal-related affect characterized by greater tenseness and less interest [69].

## ☐ Effective Action Orientation

Effective action orientation (EAO) involves the ability to take value-congruent action in the context of strong emotions and self-doubts. It also involves the ability to sustain this action even in the face of inconsistent feedback, frustration, and failure (see Table 10.1).

### Measuring Effective Action Orientation

There are a number of well-researched measures of people's self-control, or the ability of people to manage their lives, hold their tempers, keep their diets, fulfill their promises, stop after a couple of drinks, save money, persevere at work, and keep secrets [70].

The *action-state orientation scale* measures people's ability to move from a desired goal state to some future goal state (action orientation) versus their tendency to engage in persistent, ruminative thoughts, which reduces the resources available for goal striving [71]. Strong action orientation is associated with lower levels of anxiety, depression, and rigidity, higher levels of positive attitudes, positive job-related positive behavior, and better performance in cognitive and athletic tasks [71–73].

The *self-control scale* is another measure of action orientation. Self-control purportedly involves the ability to "override or change one's inner responses, as well as to interrupt undesired behavioral tendencies and refrain from acting on them" [70, p. 274]. This conceptualization of self-control runs contrary to MBEIT, which suggests that one does not have to change one's inner responses to act effectively [3]. However, an examination of the self-control scale reveals that every single item focuses on behavior, rather than inner responses (e.g., "I do certain things that are bad for me, even if they are fun"). Thus, whilst this conceptualization is inconsistent with ACT, the scale is in fact consistent. Research has demonstrated the validity of this scale and shown that high self-control is related to higher grade point average, lower levels of anxiety and depression, less alcohol abuse, and better relationships [70].

Self-control can be measured using behavioral tasks, as well as the self-report measures described above. Specifically, a substantial amount of developmental research has looked at children's ability to delay gratification in particular situations [74–76]. For example, one study offered adolescents $7 immediate payment or $10 one week later [76]. Compared to students who delayed gratification, those who chose the immediate fee showed more self-regulatory failures, such as greater use of drugs and greater academic underperformance. In another study, pre-school children where offered the choice of one marshmallow immediately versus two at a later time. This task predicted performance 10 years later. Specifically, it was found that the children who delayed gratification were more academically and socially competent and more able to deal well with frustration and stress [74].

# ☐ MBEIT and Other EI Frameworks

The MBEIT model seeks to specify the causes or "normal" human suffering that are expected to be relevant to every language able human being (see above paragraphs on FEAR). Much of the theory and evidence for MBEIT comes from the clinical domain. Its distinctive emphasis is on intervening to improve emotional functioning. It does not seek to specify how emotional information is processed, unless such a specification is of direct relevance to an intervention.

In contrast, Mayer's Ability model of EI (see Chapter 1 in this volume) developed out of basic research in emotion and in intelligence. Their theory seeks to specify how emotional information processing occurs and can be located within a mechanistic philosophical framework. One key premise of this framework is that if the information processing and emotions systems can be understood, then it will help researchers to plan interventions.

Finally, there are a number of empirically driven models of emotional intelligence, most notably that of Bar-On [64] and Goleman [77]. These approaches have used research and past experience to identify emotionally relevant characteristics that appear to be useful for people at work, in relationships, and other domains. For example, Goleman's model [77] includes such characteristics as impulse control, hope, enthusiasm, social adroitness, and character. Bar-On's model [64] includes empathy, social responsibility, flexibility, problem solving, and happiness.

At the conceptual level, there is remarkably little overlap between the major approaches. For example, value-laden dimensions such as "character" and "social responsibility" are found in the empirically driven models, but not in MBEIT or ability-based models. The approaches also differ in their emphasis on measuring ability versus measuring typical performance (MBEIT and empirical approaches). One may in principle have a high potential to act effectively, but often fail to do so (e.g., when one is not motivated to do so).

We believe that the different approaches may have the ability to inform each other. MBEIT may suggest dimensions of optimal performance that are not currently measured by the Mayer's ability-based measure of EI (the MSCEIT). For example, the future MSCEIT may measure the ability to act effectively even when experiencing strong emotion and impulses (termed "effective action orientation" in our approach). Similarly, the ability-based approach may suggest useful directions for interventions that are not currently captured in the MBEIT model. For example, one might examine how to improve the "emotional facilitation" dimension of Mayer's ability model. There is certainly much integrative research that still needs to be done.

# ☐  Conclusions

We have presented a framework, which captures the core processes (FEAR) that are proposed to underlie emotionally unintelligent behavior and suffering. This framework helps to organize a substantial amount of individual difference research, and structure it in such a way that it can be linked to a coherent theory. Previously, many of the measures reviewed here were treated in isolation. Research involving one measure rarely made reference to other, seemingly related measures. Researchers thus risked "rediscovering" what had already been found with the other measures. This review will hopefully prompt researchers to look across research areas and to gain a better understanding of how their research fits in with the other research.

Importantly, this framework allows one to connect each of the individual difference measures to a coherent intervention strategy [3]. The measures may be useful in guiding the intervention strategies (e.g., in specifying what processes most need to be targeted). They may also be useful in measuring progress in the intervention. Future research is needed to evaluate these possibilities.

# ☐ References

1. Laudan, L. (1981). A confutation of convergent realism. *Philosophy of Science, 48*, 19–49.
2. Hayes, S. C., Barnes-Holmes, D., & Roche, B. (Eds.). (2001). *Relational frame theory: A post-Skinnerian account of human language and cognition.* New York: Kluwer Academic/Plenum Publishers.
3. Hayes, S. C., Strosahl, K. D., & Wilson, K. G. (1999). *Acceptance and commitment therapy: An experiential approach to behavior change.* New York: Guilford Press.
4. Blascovich, J., & Tomaka, J. (1991). Measures of self-esteem. In J. P. Robinson, P. R. Shaver, & L. S. Wrightsman (Eds.), *Measures of personality and social psychological attitudes* (Vol. 1, pp. 115–160). New York: Academic Press.
5. Lyubomirsky, S. (2001). Why are some people happier than others? The role of cognitive and motivational processes in well-being. *American Psychologist, 56*(3), 239–249.
6. Blackledge, J. T. (2004). A functional-contextual account of post-traumatic stress. *International Journal of Psychology and Psychological Therapy, 4*(3), 443–467.
7. Beck, J. S. (1995). *Cognitive therapy: Basics and beyond.* New York: Guilford Press.
8. Wegner, D. M. (1994). Ironic processes of mental control. *Psychological Review, 101*(1), 34–52.
9. Wenzlaff, R. M., & Wegner, D. M. (2000). Thought suppression. *Annual Review of Psychology, 51*, 59–91.
10. Feldner, M., Zvolensky, M., Eifert, G., & Spira, A. (2003). Emotional avoidance: An experimental test of individual differences and response suppression using biological challenge. *Behaviour Research and Therapy, 41*(4), 403–411.
11. Bourne, E. J. (2000). *The anxiety and phobia workbook* (3rd ed.). Oakland, CA: New Harbinger Publications, Inc.
12. Elliott, T. R., Herrick, S. M., MacNair, R. R., & Harkins, S. W. (1994). Personality correlates of self-appraised problem solving ability: Problem orientation and trait affectivity. *Journal of Personality Assessment, 63*(3), 489–505.
13. Elliott, T. R., & Marmarosh, C. L. (1994). Problem-solving appraisal, health complaints, and health-related expectancies. *Journal of Counseling and Development, 72*(5), 531–537.
14. D'Zurilla, T. J., Chang, E. C., Nottingham, E. J., & Faccini, L. (1998). Social problem-solving deficits and hopelessness, depression, and suicidal risk in college students and psychiatric inpatients. *Journal of Clinical Psychology, 54*(8), 1091–1107.
15. Ciarrochi, J., Scott, G., Deane, F. P., & Heaven, P. C. L. (2003). Relations between social and emotional competence and mental health: A construct validation study. *Personality and Individual Differences, 35*, 1947–1963.

16. Chang, E. C., & D'Zurilla, T. J. (1996). Relations between problem orientation and optimism, pessimism, and trait affectivity: A construct validation study. *Behaviour Research and Therapy, 34*(2), 185–194.

17. Davey, G. C., Jubb, M., & Cameron, C. (1996). Catastrophic worrying as a function of changes in problem-solving confidence. *Cognitive Therapy and Research, 20*(4), 333–344.

18. Wegner, D. M., & Zanakos, S. (1994). Chronic thought suppression. *Journal of Personality, 62*(4), 615–640.

19. Hayes, S. C., Strosahl, K. D., Wilson, K. G., Bissett, R. T., Pistorello, J., Toarmino, D., et al. (2003). Measuring experiential avoidance: A preliminary test of a working model. *The Psychological Record, 54*, 553–578.

20. Bond, F. W., & Bunce, D. (2003). The role of acceptance and job control in mental health, job satisfaction, and work performance. *Journal of Applied Psychology, 88*(6), 1057–1067.

21. Ortony, A., Clore, G., & Collins, A. (1988). *The cognitive structure of emotion.* New York: Cambridge University Press.

22. Taylor, G. J. (2000). Recent developments in alexithymia theory and research. *Canadian Journal of Psychiatry, 45*(2), 134–142.

23. Taylor, G. J., Bagby, R., & Luminet, O. (2000). Assessment of alexithymia: Self-report and observer-rated measures. In R. Bar-On & J. D. A. Parker (Eds.), *The handbook of emotional intelligence: Theory, development, assessment, and application at home, school, and in the workplace* (pp. 301–319). San Francisco: Jossey-Bass.

24. Taylor, G. J. (2001). Low emotional intelligence and mental illness. In J. Ciarrochi & J. P. Forgas (Eds.), *Emotional intelligence in everyday life: A scientific inquiry* (pp. 67–81). Philadelphia: Psychology Press.

25. Bach, M., & Bach, D. (1995). Predictive value of alexithymia: A prospective study in somatizing patients. *Psychotherapy and Psychosomatics, 64*, 43–48.

26. Salovey, P., Mayer, J. D., Goldman, S. L., Turvey, C., & Palfai, T. P. (1995). Emotional attention, clarity, and repair: Exploring emotional intelligence using the Trait Meta-Mood Scale. In J. W. Pennebaker (Ed.), *Emotion, disclosure, and health* (pp. 125–154). Washington, DC: American Psychological Association.

27. Mayer, J. D., Salovey, P., & Caruso, D. (2002). *Mayer-Salovey-Caruso Emotional Intelligence Test (MSCEIT): User's manual.* North Tonawanda, New York: Multi-Health Systems.

28. Schutte, N. S., Malouff, J. M., Hall, L. E., Haggerty, D. J., Cooper, J. T., Golden, C. J., et al. (1998). Development and validation of a measure of emotional intelligence. *Personality and Individual Differences, 25*(2), 167–177.

29. Lane, R. D., Kivley, L. S., Du Bois, M. A., Shamasundara, P., et al. (1995). Levels of emotional awareness and the degree of right hemispheric dominance in the perception of facial emotion. *Neuropsychologia, 33*(5), 525–538.

30. Ciarrochi, J., Caputi, P., & Mayer, J. D. (2003). The distinctiveness and utility of a measure of trait emotional awareness. *Personality and Individual Differences, 34*(8), 1477–1490.

31. Bajgar, J., & Deane, F. P. (2004). *Does emotional awareness help in the popularity stakes?* Unpublished manuscript, University of Wollongong.

32. Ellis, A. (2001). *Overcoming destructive beliefs, feelings, and behaviors: New directions for Rational Emotive Behavior Therapy.* Amherst, NY: Prometheus Books.

33. Kabat-Zinn, J. (1990). *Full catastrophe living: Using the wisdom of your body and mind to face stress, pain, and illness.* New York: Dell Publishing.

34. Linehan, M. M. (1993). *Cognitive-behavioral treatment of borderline personality disorder.* New York: Guilford Press.

35. Hayes, S. C., Strosahl, K. D., & Wilson, K. G. (2002). Acceptance and commitment therapy: An experimental approach to behavior change. *Child and Family Behavior Therapy, 24*(4), 51–57.

36. Zettle, R. D. (2003). Acceptance and commitment therapy (ACT) vs. systematic desensitization in treatment of mathematics anxiety. *Psychological Record, 53*(2), 197–215.

37. Bond, F. W., & Bunce, D. (2000). Mediators of change in emotion-focused and problem-focused worksite stress management interventions. *Journal of Occupational Health Psychology, 5*(1), 156–163.

38. Dahl, J., Wilson, K. G., & Nilsson, A. (2004). Acceptance and commitment therapy and the treatment of persons at risk of long-term disability resulting from stress and pain symptoms: A preliminary randomized clinical trial. *Behavior Therapy, 35*(4), 785–801.

39. Segal, Z. V., Williams, J. M. G., & Teasdale, J. D. (2002). *Mindfulness-based cognitive therapy for depression: A new approach to preventing relapse.* New York: Guilford Press.

40. Cormier, L. S., & Cormier, W. H. (1998). *Interviewing strategies for helpers: Fundamental skills and cognitive behavioral interventions.* Pacific Grove, CA: Brooks/Cole.

41. Brown, K. W., & Ryan, R. M. (2003). The benefits of being present: Mindfulness and its role in psychological well-being. *Journal of Personality and Social Psychology, 84*(4), 822–848.

42. Weissman, A. (2000). Dysfunctional Attitude Scale (DAS). In K. Corcoran & J. Fischer (Eds.), *Measures for clinical practice: A sourcebook* (Vol. 2, pp. 187–190). New York: Free Press.

43. Blatt, S. J., Quinlan, D. M., Pilkonis, P. A., & Shea, M. (1995). Impact of perfectionism and need for approval on the brief treatment of depression: The National Institute of Mental Health Treatment of Depression Collaborative Research Program revisited. *Journal of Consulting and Clinical Psychology, 63*(1), 125–132.

44. Brown, G. P., Hammen, C. L., Craske, M. G., & Wickens, T. D. (1995). Dimensions of dysfunctional attitudes as vulnerabilities to depressive symptoms. *Journal of Abnormal Psychology, 104*(3), 431–435.

45. Hajzler, D. J., & Bernard, M. E. (1991). A review of rational-emotive education outcome studies. *School Psychology Quarterly, 6*(1), 27–49.

46. Engels, G. I., Garnefski, N., & Diekstra, R. F. W. (1993). Efficacy of rational-emotive therapy: A quantitative analysis. *Journal of Consulting and Clinical Psychology, 61*(6), 1083–1090.

47. Dugas, M. J., Gagnon, F., Ladouceur, R., & Freeston, M. H. (1998). Generalized anxiety disorder: A preliminary test of a conceptual model. *Behaviour Research and Therapy, 36*(2), 215–226.

48. Neuberg, S. L., & Newson, J. T. (1993). Personal need for structure: Individual differences in the desire for simpler structure. *Journal of Personality and Social Psychology, 65*(1), 113–131.

49. Frenkel-Brunswik, E. (1949). Intolerance of ambiguity as an emotional and perceptual personality variable. *Journal of Personality, 18,* 108–143.

50. Freeston, M. H., Rheaume, J., Letarte, H., Dugas, M. J., et al. (1994). Why do people worry? *Personality and Individual Differences, 17*(6), 791–802.

51. Roger, D., & Najarian, B. (1989). The construction and validation of a new scale for measuring emotion control. *Personality and Individual Differences, 10*(8), 845–853.

52. Nolen-Hoeksema, S. (1987). Sex differences in unipolar depression: Evidence and theory. *Psychological Bulletin, 101*(2), 259–282.

53. Rusting, C. L., & Nolen-Hoeksema, S. (1998). Regulating responses to anger: Effects of rumination and distraction on angry mood. *Journal of Personality and Social Psychology, 74*(3), 790–803.

54. Nolen-Hoeksema, S., Larson, J., & Grayson, C. (1999). Explaining the gender difference in depressive symptoms. *Journal of Personality and Social Psychology, 77*(5), 1061–1072.

55. Nolen-Hoeksema, S., Parker, L. E., & Larson, J. (1994). Ruminative coping with depressed mood following loss. *Journal of Personality and Social Psychology, 67*(1), 92–104.

56. Nolen-Hoeksema, S., & Davis, C. G. (1999). "Thanks for sharing that": Ruminators and their social support networks. *Journal of Personality and Social Psychology, 77*(4), 801–814.

57. Roger, D., & Jamieson, J. (1988). Individual differences in delayed heart-rate recovery following stress: The role of extraversion, neuroticism and emotional control. *Personality and Individual Differences, 9*(4), 721–726.

58. Roger, D., & Najarian, B. (1998). The relationship between emotional rumination and cortisol secretion under stress. *Personality and Individual Differences, 24*(4), 531–538.

59. Dugas, M. J., Freeston, M. H., & Ladouceur, R. (1997). Intolerance of uncertainty and problem orientation in worry. *Cognitive Therapy and Research, 21*(6), 593–606.

60. Godsell, C., & Ciarrochi, J. (2004). *A factor analysis of emotional competence measures.* Unpublished manuscript, University of Wollongong.

61. Ciarrochi, J., Forgas, J. P., & Mayer, J. D. (Eds.). (2001). *Emotional intelligence in everyday life: A scientific inquiry.* Philadelphia: Psychology Press.

62. Ciarrochi, J. (2004). Relationships between dysfunctional beliefs and positive and negative indices of well-being: A critical evaluation of the Common Beliefs Survey III. *Journal of Rational-Emotive and Cognitive Behavior Therapy, 22*(3), 171–188.

63. Rosenberg, M. (1965). *Society and the adolescent self-image.* Princeton, NJ: Princeton University Press.

64. Bar-On, R. (1997). *Bar-On Emotional Quotient Inventory (EQ-i): Technical manual.* Toronto, Canada, Multi-Health Systems.

65. Kernis, M. H., Grannemann, B. D., & Barclay, L. C. (1989). Stability and level of self-esteem as predictors of anger arousal and hostility. *Journal of Personality and Social Psychology, 56*(6), 1013–1022.

66. Rhodewalt, F. (2001). The social mind of the narcissist: Cognitive and motivational aspects of interpersonal self-construction. In J. P. Forgas & K. D. Williams (Eds.), *The social mind: Cognitive and motivational aspects of interpersonal behavior* (pp. 117–198). Cambridge, UK: Cambridge University Press.

67. Raskin, R., & Terry, H. (1988). A principal-components analysis of the Narcissistic Personality Inventory and further evidence of its construct validity. *Journal of Personality and Social Psychology, 54*(5), 890–902.

68. Rhodewalt, F., & Eddings, S. K. (2002). Narcissus reflects: Memory distortion in response to ego-relevant feedback among high- and low-narcissistic men. *Journal of Research in Personality, 36*(2), 97–116.

69. Kernis, M. H., Paradise, A. W., Whitaker, D. J., Wheatman, S. R., & Goldman, B. N. (2000). Master of one's psychological domain? Not likely if one's self-esteem is unstable. *Personality and Social Psychology Bulletin, 26*(10), 1297–1305.

70. Tangney, J. P., Baumeister, R. F., & Boone, A. L. (2004). High self-control predicts good adjustment, less pathology, better grades, and interpersonal success. *Journal of Personality, 72*(2), 271–322.

71. Diefendorff, J. M., Hall, R. J., Lord, R. G., & Strean, M. L. (2000). Action-state orientation: Construct validity of a revised measure and its relationship to work-related variables. *Journal of Applied Psychology, 85*(2), 250–263.

72. Heckhausen, H., & Strang, H. (1988). Efficiency under record performance demands: Exertion control—an individual difference variable? *Journal of Personality and Social Psychology, 55*(3), 489–498.

73. Kuhl, J., & Beckmann, J. (1994). *Volition and personality: Action versus state orientation.* Gottingen, Germany: Hogrefe & Huber Publishers.

74. Mischel, W., Shoda, Y., & Peake, P. K. (1988). The nature of adolescent competencies predicted by preschool delay of gratification. *Journal of Personality and Social Psychology, 54*(4), 687–696.

75. Shoda, Y., Mischel, W., & Peake, P. K. (1990). Predicting adolescent cognitive and self-regulatory competencies from preschool delay of gratification: Identifying diagnostic conditions. *Developmental Psychology, 26*(6), 978–986.
76. Wulfert, E., Block, J. A., Ana, E. S., Rodriguez, M. L., & Colsman, M. (2002). Delay of gratification: Impulsive choices and problem behaviors in early and late adolescence. *Journal of Personality, 70*(4), 533–552.
77. Goleman, D. (1995). *Emotional intelligence*: New York: Bantam Books, Inc.

CHAPTER

Peter Salovey

# Applied Emotional Intelligence: Regulating Emotions to Become Healthy, Wealthy, and Wise

This chapter is going to be a little different from many of the others in this book. Rather than talk about emotional intelligence *per se*, I am going to discuss two particular applications of what we have learned about emotional intelligence. The focus will be on staying physically well and on making good financial decisions—health and wealth. I am going to argue that the appropriate regulation of emotions is an important predictor of good health and a key to investing money wisely.

The view of emotional intelligence that forms the backdrop for this chapter is that of Mayer and Salovey [1–4]. This theory describes emotional intelligence as a set of interrelated abilities organized along four dimensions: (a) identifying and expressing emotions, (b) using emotions, (c) understanding emotions, and (d) managing or regulating emotions. Although all four of these sets of skills may be important in staying healthy and accumulating wealth, in this chapter I focus only on the last of these four, managing one's feelings.

## ☐ The Salubrious Consequences of Emotional Regulation

You are driving on the interstate and a car cuts in front of you at 70 miles per hour. Then the driver jams on the brakes. You do the same and feel

**229**

yourself becoming enraged: "Where did this guy get his driver's license . . . Sears?" Emotional challenges like this one present themselves every day: should I express my anger—perhaps rolling down the window, yelling, or gesturing obscenely? Or should I "sit on" my emotions, suppressing them until, it would seem, they go away? The challenge of expressing versus suppressing is a fundamental dimension of emotional self-management. And I am going to argue in this section of the chapter that emotional expression and emotional suppression represent a double-edged sword: both strategies can lead to health problems.

## Emotional Expression and Health Outcomes

How would you answer the following questions? True or false? "Some of my family members have habits that bother and annoy me very much." True or false? "I tend to be on my guard with people who are somewhat friendlier than I had expected." True or false? "It makes me feel like a failure when I hear of the success of someone I know well." People who answer "true" to questions like these tend to be prone to hostile, angry outbursts [5], and the tendency to respond to social situations with hostility seems to be associated with coronary heart disease [6–7].

What is interesting in this line of research is that it is not just any kind of hostility and anger that bodes poorly for the health of one's heart, but rather, a particular kind: cynical hostility. Cynical hostility is a special example of the failure of emotional self-management. It is characterized by suspiciousness, resentment, florid displays of anger, antagonism, and distrust. These folks are not hard to find in a crowd. More often than not, they are men [8]. They tend to be verbally aggressive and behaviorally antagonistic. Not surprisingly, they have difficulty making friends or maintaining relationships [9–10].

All of this cynical hostility takes it toll on the heart. First of all, it creates excessive cardiovascular reactivity. The heart and vascular system tend to over-react to minor stressors [11], and this is especially true in situations involving other people [12]. The blood vessels feeding the heart muscle tend to constrict, while the heart itself beats faster. This puts a real strain on the coronary system. The emotional arousal often experienced by cynically hostile people is associated with lipids being shunted to the bloodstream (perhaps to provide "fuel" for the ensuing fight that the body is expecting). This increase in blood cholesterol and triglycerides creates a risk for the buildup of plaques, which can block arteries feeding heart muscle and result in a heart attack [13]. Worse in some ways, when people are experiencing a lot of anger and hostility, they may cope with it by smoking cigarettes, drinking alcohol, or eating fatty foods, which can lead to longer term health damage too.

## Emotional Suppression and Health Outcomes

So, is the answer simply to "stuff it"—to suppress hostile feelings, maintain a calm exterior, and minimize the expression of negative emotions? That strategy does not appear to be very healthy either [14]. For one, suppressed anger seems to raise one's blood pressure just as much as expressed anger [15]. It is also possible—though the evidence is quite weak at this point—that suppressing negative emotions may increase susceptibility to and progression of cancer [16–18]. In fact, the course of the illness among cancer patients who are openly angry and combative may actually be better than for those who suppress their anger [19–20]. Denial and repression, on the other hand, may be related to cancer progression [21].

In one set of studies, recent stressors and coping abilities were measured in over 1500 women sent to a specialist because of a lump or tenderness in a breast. Those women who were experiencing the most stress, but at the same time denied its existence, were especially likely to be diagnosed with breast cancer. However, women who indicated that they were comfortable expressing anger were less likely to receive this diagnosis [22–24]. So, acting like the stressors in one's life are not bothersome may be dangerous to one's health. And, at least in the breast cancer context, expressing anger might protect a person from cancer. Again, it looks like anger is a double-edged sword. Too much results in one kind of health problem; too little, another.

Luckily, we can learn to express the right amount of anger. David Spiegel and his colleagues at Stanford University enrolled women with metastatic breast cancer into a support group that met weekly and, in part, helped women to learn to express their feelings about having cancer, extract meaning from the experience, and develop a social support system [25–26]. A control group received only standard medical care. Those women who participated in the support group lived an average of 37 months from the start of the study; those women who received only standard medical care died, on average, after only 19 months. Unfortunately, recent work on expressive group therapies for cancer patients has produced a more mixed set of findings (e.g., [27–28]).

## Confiding: Might This be the Answer?

If expression of cynical hostility is related to heart disease but suppressing emotions may be associated with cancer progression, what is a person to do with such feelings? Perhaps the Greeks were correct in urging moderation in all things. We may need to express negative feelings, but in a way that is neither mean-spirited nor stifled. It is likely that this is what he had in mind when Jamie Pennebaker at the University of Texas proposed that confiding our traumas may have beneficial effects on physical and mental health. Pennebaker has studied the effects of emotional disclosure extensively and finds that the simple act of disclosing emotional experiences in writing, even anonymously, improves individuals' subsequent physical and mental health (see [29] for a review). For instance, students assigned to write about a traumatic emotional experience subsequently made fewer health center visits and received higher grades than students assigned to write about a trivial topic (e.g., [30–31]). The benefits of emotional disclosure also include broadly enhanced immunological functioning (e.g., [32]), and decreases in self-reported physical symptoms, distress, and depression (e.g., [33–34]). These impressive findings have proved robust across dozens of studies conducted by several investigators and among such disparate populations as college students, maximum security prisoners, and recently unemployed professionals (see [35] for a meta-analysis).

## Learning to Regulate Our Emotions for Better Health

Perhaps the expression of emotions has only a positive impact on physical health when we are confident about our abilities to regulate them. In one study, we investigated the hypothesis that adapting successfully to a stressful experience depends, in part, on beliefs that one has the capacity to regulate feelings. Goldman, Kraemer, and Salovey conducted a prospective study examining whether beliefs about one's moods, in particular, the belief that one can repair negative moods, are related to physical health complaints [36]. The reasoning behind this study was that individuals who cannot repair or regulate their feelings may look to others for help in doing so. As a result, they may be more likely to seek the attention of a physician when they are feeling stressed because they do not know how to regulate these feelings themselves. Such individuals may simply be using the health care system as a mood regulation strategy. Of course, it is also possible that these individuals are actually more likely to become physically ill when stressed.

Goldman et al. assessed 134 student volunteers at three different times during the semester: at the start of the year, during midterm examinations, and during final examinations [36]. At these times, Goldman et al. administered the Trait Meta-Mood Scale (TMMS), which includes an index of one's beliefs about being able to regulate feelings, as well as measures of stress, physical symptoms, and health center visits [36]. When the researchers divided the sample into three groups of people (those with a high degree of skill in repairing negative moods, those with average skills in this area, and those with low skills), they found some intriguing results. When stress was low, the three groups differed very little. But, as stress increased, those individuals who said that they could not easily regulate their feelings were more likely to visit the health center, and those individuals who were good at repairing negative moods actually visited the health center less often.

## Summing Up

Affective self-regulation appears to be the aspect of emotional intelligence most relevant to physical health [37]. As we have seen, individuals unable to control their anger and hostility are prone to heart disease. The data connecting hostility to cardiovascular problems are quite strong. At the same time, individuals who suppress their anger and hostility—and negative feelings more generally—may be engaging in an emotional style that exacerbates certain kinds of cancer. However, the data linking suppressed negative emotions, like hostility, to cancer are, at present, not nearly as convincing as that linking hostility and heart disease. In general, the inability to regulate negative emotions, indeed, even the belief that one does not have strong skills in this domain, seems to make one vulnerable to stress. When the going gets tough, the tough get going; but when the going gets tough for individuals who lack confidence in their emotional regulatory skills, they are more likely to end up going to the doctor's office.

## ☐ The Emotionally Intelligent Investor: Avoiding the Pathologies of Loss Aversion

It's January. You've paid off your holiday bills. For the first time in years, you have some extra cash—$4000 to be exact. Usually you would just add this to your savings account, but you've noticed of late the paltry 2% interest rate the bank is paying. Maybe there is a better place to invest your money. What about the stock market? You read a book last year suggesting that even non-experts like yourself can make money in stocks, just invest in what you know. Well, you know about General Motors; you have a 1993 Chevrolet parked in the garage and a 1997 Pontiac in the driveway. And your daughter works as a hostess in that new restaurant in town, the celebrity-endorsed Planet Hollywood. It always seems pretty crowded there when you drop by to see how she is doing.

So you set up an account with one of those web-based brokerages on your home computer and buy $2000 worth of General Motors (50 shares at $40 each) and $2000 in Planet Hollywood (100 shares at $20 each).

For a while, nothing much happens one way or the other. You check your stocks every day; they go up, they go down. But over a few months time, you notice a trend. General Motors seems to be creeping up just a bit, but the overall inclination of Planet Hollywood seems downward. After 6 months, General Motors is now worth $50 a share and Planet Hollywood $16.

"Time to make some decisions?" you wonder. You think about the situation with General Motors. In just a few months, you've made $500 on a $2000 investment. "Pretty good," you think to yourself. "Let's lock in that gain and sell it." You log on to your broker, type in a sell order, and find that you have $2500 in cold hard cash, minus a few dollars commission. "This is pretty easy," you think to yourself. "But what to do about Planet Hollywood?" Your $2000 investment there is now worth only $1600. You mull over your options and decide, "why turn a $400 loss on paper into a real loss by selling? Might as well just hold on. Planet Hollywood will turn around. If it doesn't make a big run, I'll hang on at least until it drifts back to $20 a share. When I'm even, I'll sell it. Besides, I think Planet Hollywood is a pretty good restaurant. I am sure others will see how wonderful it is before too long. Maybe I should think about buying some more shares using some of the money in our household emergency account. Probably best just to sit tight."

Do these investment ruminations ring a bell with you? Most experts in behavioral finance and investor psychology would suggest that they've led to precisely the wrong choices (e.g., [38]). That selling winners quickly and hanging on to losers for a long time waiting for them to turn around are defeatist strategies. That taking risks in order to get out of a hole no matter how compelling is not an emotionally intelligent decision. That overvaluing what we already own is commonplace but irrational. And that making no decision at all—maintaining the status quo—often feels like the easiest decision to make, the path of least resistance. This section of the chapter explores some of the reasons why investors make these kinds of decisions and argues that by intelligently managing our emotions—our pride and, in particular, by not being quite so afraid of feeling regret, we may be able to make more profitable choices.

## Prospect Theory

Obviously people feel better when their investments rise in value than when they fall. But why is it that, say, a 20% gain only makes us feel pretty good while a 20% loss leads to wretched misery? Winning some amount certainly brings pleasure. But take that same amount and lose it: now we feel truly horrible. Before we can understand the investor pathologies described in this chapter, we need to appreciate this emotional imbalance.

How are we to comprehend this asymmetry between how winning and losing makes investors feel? We need to consider one of the most influential theories in both behavioral economics and psychology. It is called *prospect theory*, and it was articulated by Stanford University's Amos Tversky and Princeton's Daniel Kahneman. Although this theory has profound and complex implications, its essence can be captured in a single graph that looks like an "S." This graph, depicted in Figure 11.1, relates outcomes in the world—such as gaining or losing money—to how they make us feel, their subjective value [39–40].

There are a few things to notice about this graph. First of all, if humans were completely rational creatures—mechanical androids like Commander Data on Star Trek—the figure would not be an S-shaped curve at all but rather a straight line. Every dollar gained makes us one unit happier; every dollar lost makes us one unit sadder. In terms of its influence on

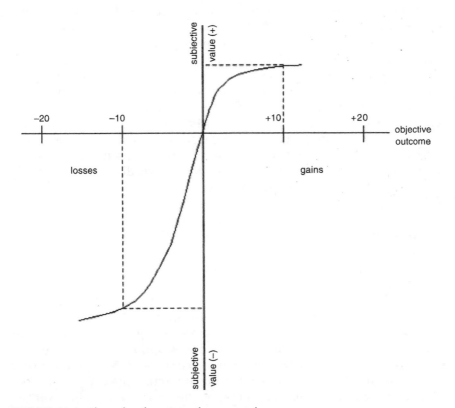

**FIGURE 11.1.** The value function of prospect theory.

our emotions, each dollar is like every other dollar. But this is not the case. As we "win" dollars, each new dollar adds less to our enjoyment than the previously won dollar. The first few dollars gained make us feel the best. No reason to take any risks in order to gain more dollars, once we've won a few, we already feel pretty good, right?

Now take a look at the left side of the graph. Here, with each dollar lost we feel worse and worse, but the losses that pack the strongest negative punch are those first few dollars lost. We already feel pretty badly when we lose, so if we lose more, we only feel a bit worse. If we are losing, perhaps we might as well take some risks; we are already feeling pretty badly, so who cares if we lose more?

There is something else that is interesting about this graph. Notice how the "S" curve is not as steep for winning as it is for losing. Start at the middle of the graph—called the "reference point"—and notice what happens to one's feelings as you move the same distance right (gain) or left (loss). The negative emotional reaction to losing is always bigger than the positive emotional reaction is to gaining the same amount. A $5 win is okay, but a $5 loss is sad. A $10 win is nice, but a $10 loss is miserable. A $1000 win is terrific, but a $1000 loss is total tragedy. As psychologists like to say, losses loom larger than comparable gains.

So why am I taking so much time telling you about this graph? Well, this simple S-shaped curve helps us to understand several classic and interrelated investor mistakes and the emotions that drive them: (a) refusing to sell losing investments but selling winners prematurely, (b) taking bigger and bigger risks when losing in order to "get even," (c) overvaluing an investment simply because we own it, and (d) staying with the investments we already have, that is, preserving a bias toward the status quo. In the remainder of this chapter, we discuss each of these emotionally rooted investor pathologies.

## Refusing to Sell at a Loss

Some years ago, a manufacturer of sports apparel moved to New Haven, Connecticut, the city where I live. This company provides uniforms for many professional sports teams and also sells t-shirts and sweat clothes to the general public. With great fanfare, this company "went public," selling stock in an initial public offering for about $24 a share. Wanting to support a local employer and get in on this action, I began to follow the stock price of this company. When it dropped to about $12 a share a year later, I bought 500 shares. At half the initial offering price, it seemed like a bargain. The price of this stock, however, never saw $12 again. Over the next several years, in the face of labor problems in professional sports leading to strikes and shortened hockey and basketball seasons, it dropped to $6 then to $3 then to $2 and finally bottomed out near $1. A $6000 initial investment was now worth a bit over $500.

As this situation unfolded, it would have been adaptive to have asked, "Is there a better place for my money?" If yes—and these were years when the market as a whole was rising dramatically, so nearly any investment alternative may have been better than this one—the rational thing to do was sell the stock, despite the loss, and put the money to work somewhere else. In fact, some money managers have a "stop-loss rule," that says if their initial investment drops in value more than some predetermined amount, often 10%, sometimes a bit more, they sell it. Period. No questions asked. But I would not be telling you about this particular investment if that's what I did. Instead, refusing to admit I was wrong about this company (even though I read their annual reports indicating negative earnings year after year), I hung on. "Why turn a paper loss into a real one?" I would tell my wife. "Some day, when all these strikes in professional sports end, I'll get even. Then I'll sell."

Well, this story has an interesting ending, which I will describe later when I talk about the pathology of risk taking in the face of losses. But for now, let me discuss the emotional turmoil that plagued and paralyzed me. Investment guru Leroy Gross in *The Art of Selling Intangibles: How to Make Your Million $ Investing Other People's Money* [41] captures it very well:

> Many clients will not sell anything at a loss. They don't want to give up the hope of making money on a particular investment, or perhaps they want to get even before they get out. The "getevenitis" disease has probably wrought more destruction on investment portfolios than anything else. . . . Investors are reluctant to accept and realize losses because the very act of doing so proves that their first judgment was wrong.

This is called *loss aversion*, the reluctance to accept a loss [40], [42]. And it can manifest itself in two ways: the tendency to hold on to an investment that has declined in value for much too long, and the tendency to sell an investment that has appreciated prematurely. In other words, rather than stopping losses but letting profits run (as is usually advised), we are emotionally wired up instead to refuse to cut our losses with a bad investment and fail to take full advantage of a good one. Behavioral economists Hersh Shefrin and Meir Statman note, we "sell winners too early and ride losers too long" [43].

Refusing to sell losers and invest our money elsewhere is especially interesting, given that the IRS rewards us with a nice tax deduction if we could bring ourselves to admit we were wrong and sell that losing stock. But no, we hang on. Pride goeth before a fall: why admit we made a mistake by turning a paper loss into a real one? And hope springs eternal: if we hold on just a little longer, we know that the investment will turn around.

The best way to understand this investor pathology is to consider, once again, the S-shaped curve. Notice how as one contemplates a gain—the right side of the figure—the curve from the reference point (the center) is concave, but that as one contemplates a loss—the left side of the figure—the curve from the reference point is convex. They way in which the curve flattens out for both gains and losses reflects the fact that once feeling good about a gain, it is hard to feel much better with additional gains, and once feeling pretty bad about a loss it is unlikely one will feel even worse with additional losses. Hence, why not sell gainers and "lock in" these good feelings now, without risking that they could go away. And why not hang on to losers, after all, how much worse could I feel? Sounds like a good emotional self-regulation strategy, no?

An emotionally intelligent investor might look at the tendency to hang on to losers but to sell winners in yet another way: as a battle between pride and regret [43–44]. The potential pride in selling an investment at a profit ("I was right") is offset by the even stronger emotion of regret when one contemplates selling an investment at a loss ("I was wrong"). We are delighted to experience pride whenever we can, and hence sell our winners when, perhaps, we should hold on to them. But we will work very hard to avoid experiencing the more powerful emotion of regret. As a result, we postpone selling losers. Richard Thaler suggests that "the regret at having erred may be exacerbated by having to admit the mistake to others, such as one's spouse or the IRS" [44], an admission that never has to be made if one refuses to sell! Not surprisingly, then, an analysis of the accounts of 10,000 individual investors with a particular brokerage firm revealed that these investors were 50% more likely to sell a stock that had gone up as compared with one that had gone down [45]. In this analysis, if each investor had sold a loser rather than a winner, on average they would have made 4.4% more profit in the subsequent year. But, "forgone gains are less painful than perceived losses" [46].

Emotionally intelligent investors can benefit from the advice of legendary Wall Street executive Alan C. (Ace) Greenberg, the chairman of the investment firm Bear Stearns. Considering his father's approach to selling clothing retail through a chain of stores in the Midwest, Greenberg says:

> If you've got something bad, sell it today because tomorrow it's going to be worse. . . . People don't hesitate for a minute to take a small profit, but they don't want to take losses. Which is, of course, just the opposite of what you should do. If you're wrong, you're wrong. Sell, and buy something else. (quoted in [47])

An emotionally intelligent way to get over the concern about feeling regret when a losing stock position is sold is to reframe what one is trying to do. Rather than thinking in terms of selling a loser and buying something else with the proceeds, reframe this decision as the transferring of money from one investment to another. Don't even use the word "sell," in describing what you are doing. You are simply reallocating investments, not "buying" and "selling."

## Risk Taking When Confronted by Losses

In one of their early papers on prospect theory, Kahneman and Tversky observed that "a person who has not made peace with his losses is likely to accept gambles that would be unacceptable to him otherwise" [39, p. 287]. Because losses are so painful, investors are motivated to take risks as a way to avoid them. Think about casino gambling for a moment. It is very hard to walk away from the table a loser, isn't it? But suppose that luck wasn't much of a lady for you last night, and today is the final day of your vacation in Atlantic City. What are you most likely to do? Frequently, people will head back to the casino and try one last time to get even. Now, because time is of the essence and they are already so far in the hole, they take much bigger risks—betting at the $20 blackjack table rather than the $5 table. Investors often engage in similar behavior—buying more and more of a loser as it drops in price hoping that if there is a price turnaround, they'll break even. Perhaps also, they are attempting to demonstrate to themselves (and anyone who is watching) that they did not make a mistake, that they have no regrets. Peter Lynch calls this, "watering weeds" [48].

Now, if you really believe in the fundamental value of your investment—it's an excellent company, in a leading industry, with quality management—but that it is just going through a temporary difficult period, by all means buy more of it. What was a good deal at $20 per share is an even better one at $10, right? Alas, often decisions to buy more do not represent taking advantage of temporary discounts—a New York Stock Exchange Fire Sale—but rather throwing good money after bad.

Recall my investment in the New Haven sports apparel company that I purchased at $12 and that sank like a stone for the next several years thereafter. How should I have handled that mistake? No doubt, when the stock dropped some predetermined amount—say to $9 or $10—and there was no reason to believe that the fundamental value of the company in terms of sales or profits was going to improve quickly—I should have cut my losses and sold. True, $6000 would have turned into $5000, or even less, but the loss could be used to offset gains at tax time. More importantly, the question to ask is "if I had $5000 to invest, would I buy shares of this company or put the money somewhere else?" No doubt, other options would have appeared to be better investment opportunities.

But is this what happened? Alas, no. Desperate and not being able to admit my folly by "booking" the loss, I bought more of the stock—at $6, then at $4, and then again at $2. With no hope on the horizon for this company, the value slipped to $1 per share, and now an approximately $15,000 original investment was starting to look pretty worthless. With an overwhelming case of "getevenitis," I bought a final 2000 shares at $1.25 each. Over the next several months, the stock price bounced around between $1.00 and $1.75. The likelihood that this company would ever make a profit was in great doubt. Maybe it wouldn't even survive. What was bad, only got worse.

This gamble paid off, but only because of a small miracle. Scanning the stock quotes on my office computer one afternoon (while I should have been working), I noticed unusual activity in the stock of this company: massive amounts of buying and selling. Volume was hundreds of times greater than normal. And the price was going up—$2, then $3, then, $4—all in a matter of 15 minutes. At just under $5, I sold everything I had, a small profit, actually. For five more minutes, the stock rose, to 6, 7, and 8 or so, but then, just as quickly it sank back to $4. One day later, it was trading at $2, and within a week it was back around $1.50. The company has since gone into bankruptcy and was "delisted" by the stock exchange.

What caused this unusual activity? It is not really clear—the company made no announcements during this period, and it was not covered in the financial media. Perhaps day traders were churning the stock and then lost interest. No one is quite sure. For me, the end of the story is a relatively happy one: I got out alive—after several years of stress—although my money during this time could have done much better invested elsewhere. But for every minor miracle of this kind are dozens of stocks that continue to sink and never rise to the level at which they were purchased. Should you sit around waiting for such lightning to strike in order to sell them? I don't think so. Get out. Put your money somewhere else. Pretend you had the cash in hand that you would if you sold the investment; would you now invest that cash in this company? If the answer is "no," and it probably is, "book" the loss.

The tendency to take big risks when losing, hoping against hope that one can get out from under the loss, results in investors throwing good money after bad. They are engaging in what is called a *sunk-cost* strategy [44], [49]. The more money we have thrown at some idea—consider how I continued to throw money at the losing sports apparel stock—the more we ignore associated risks and justify throwing even more money at it. As every owner of an old car knows, the reason for not selling your jalopy is that you just put $500 into a new exhaust system for it (despite knowing that the transmission is likely to go next, and that will be even more expensive to fix). The emotional power of sunk costs is illustrated at the theater when we do not leave at intermission even though we are not enjoying the play, at restaurants when we overeat simply because the meal was expensive, and at the department store when we value something more after paying full price than when we purchase the same item on sale.

## The Endowment Effect: If It's Mine It's Worth More

Losers are the hardest investments for us to get ourselves to sell. But, in fact, we have emotional difficulties selling anything. The subjective value of what we own (that is, its value to us) is always higher than its actual, objective value (its price in the marketplace). This is called the endowment effect: investors overvalue what they own and devalue what others own. More formally, people demand much more to give something up than they would be willing to pay to buy it [44].

If humans were the rational automatons on which traditional economic theory is based, the value of something would not change depending on whether one owned it or not. I should be as willing to sell my laptop computer for $1500 as I would be willing to buy the exact same one from my neighbor at the same price. But this is not what happens. I want $1800 for mine, and I wouldn't touch my neighbor's for more than $1200. Similarly, people fall in love with their investments, especially stocks and mutual funds, and have great difficulty parting with them.

The endowment effect is another implication of that S-shaped function of prospect theory, described earlier in the chapter. It is a kind of loss aversion. Because of the extra emotional impact associated with losing something as compared to winning it, we have strong motivations not to lose things—not to let go of anything we have. This behavior is often seen among homeowners who sell their houses without help from real estate brokers. These FSBO—For Sale By Owner—homes are often priced above the market because their owners so desperately want to avoid the regret associated with accepting too low a price, and there is no broker to encourage them to set a more realistic figure. How many of you know someone who refused to sell their house, despite a reasonable offer, hoping to get full price (even with a broker encouraging them to accept) only to find that a better offer never materialized?

The endowment effect is easily demonstrated in the laboratory. For example, suppose I recruit individuals to participate in one of my experiments and compensate half of them with $1.00 and the other half with a state lottery ticket. At the end of the experiment, I give the folks who received the dollar the option of exchanging it for a lottery ticket and the folks who received the lottery ticket the option of exchanging it for a dollar. It turns out that most individuals, regardless of whether they first received a dollar or a lottery ticket, are reluctant to give it up in exchange for the alternative option. Because they own it, it is now worth more to them (after [50]). Similar results have been obtained for individuals given coffee mugs or ball-point pens: for mugs, the average "owner" was unwilling to sell for less than $5.25, but the average "buyer" was unwilling to pay more than about $2.75; the ratio of selling to buying prices for pens was also about 2 to 1 [51].

Perhaps in the most dramatic demonstration of *instant endowment*, George Loewenstein and Daniel Kahneman gave half of the students in a class a nice ball-point pen and the other half a token redeemable for a mystery gift. Everyone was then asked to rate the attractiveness of various possible gifts and then to choose between a pen and two chocolate candy bars. Fifty-six per cent of the individuals who already had a pen preferred it as the gift of choice, but only 24% of the others chose the pen. However, when everyone rated the attractiveness of the gift options, the people given a pen did not rate it as more attractive than those who did not get one. It appears that the endowment effect is driven more strongly by the emotion of regret at having to give something up than an enhanced pride of ownership [52].

The potential impact of regret is so strong that people often make very strange financial decisions merely to avoid regret. For instance, suppose you can choose Retirement Plan A or Retirement Plan B. Last year, Retirement Plan A featured two mutual funds, a very risky small-cap stock fund that returned a whopping 50% and a more conservative blue-chip stock fund with a 20% return. If you select Retirement Plan A, your employer will only let you invest in the conservative blue-chip fund option. Alternatively you can pick Retirement Plan B, which has only one fund, a different conservative blue-chip fund that last year returned 15%. Surprisingly, many people will choose Retirement Plan B, even though its blue-chip fund wasn't as successful as a comparable fund with Retirement Plan A. Why? Well, to choose Retirement Plan A means to experience the regret of not being allowed to invest in its very successful small cap fund. With Plan B, this non-option is not salient—you don't see its fantastic return in the quarterly fund report—and regret is less likely to be experienced. In an actual experiment, Richard Thaler found that people would rather win $100 than $150, if winning $150 also meant that someone else won $1000. They'd take less money to avoid feeling the regret at not having been the "big" winner [44]. In this study, regret avoidance was purchased for $50.

The endowment effect creates a bias that plagues investors, making it difficult to "pull the trigger" on a transaction. Is it any wonder that manufacturers risk very little when they offer money-back guarantees on their products? Once possessed, these products are worth more than their purchase price to the consumer. The same status quo bias holds, of course, for all kinds of financial products, and so we turn to this issue next.

## The Status Quo Bias: Paralyzed in the Present

It all starts to add up: if investors fear selling stocks that have gone down, value what they have more than what they don't have, and are willing to pay a premium not to experience regret, the overwhelming psychological bias must be to do nothing at all. After all, if all of one's ducks appear to be swans, why sell them? And if no one else has anything that is worth what they want me to pay for it, why buy? Besides, if we just hang on, it will all work out, we convince ourselves. Even in the end, Pandora's box contained one last item: hope. As prospect theory's S-shaped function suggests, the disadvantages of change always loom larger than the advantages of remaining in the status quo [46].

The status quo bias may be the dominant emotion management strategy among investors. All things being equal, options that have the appearance of being the status quo—of requiring no change to maintain them—are favored. For example, in one experiment, individuals were told that they would receive a substantial inheritance. Some of these individuals were told that they were to decide on an investment portfolio for these funds (high risk stock, moderate risk stock, treasury bills, or municipal bonds); others were given these options but told that the money was already invested predominantly in one of them. Anticipated returns for each of these options were provided. Both groups were told to allocate the inheritance in any way that they wanted and that they should ignore any tax consequences or possible commissions. The participants who were given a pre-existing portfolio allocation showed a strong bias toward the status quo—they generally left things invested in the way that they already were. For example, 32% of the individuals chose the municipal bond option when no prior investments were mentioned. The number of individuals choosing municipal bonds rose to 47% when they were told that the money they were to receive was already invested that way—when it was the status quo option. The status quo option was especially attractive when the number of investment choices was increased. The more alternatives for investment people were given, the more they simply wanted to leave things alone [53].

Once one decides on an investment strategy, it is important to stick with it. "Stay the course" is a mantra, for example, of the Vanguard family of mutual funds. However, often an investment strategy is selected precisely because it is the course that things were already on, without an active decision that this is the most appropriate one. So avoiding excessive buying and selling is certainly a good investment principle, but only once a strategy has been developed, a strategy that is decided upon actively not merely inherited.

## Summing Up

So let's return to our investor from the beginning of the chapter—the person who purchased $2000 worth of General Motors (at $40 per share), only to sell it a few months later when it went to $50 and was worth $2500. What if this investor, who also bought $2000 worth of Planet Hollywood (at $20 per share) and decided to hold on to it, even after a 20% drop in its value, rode her winner, General Motors, but sold the loser, Planet Hollywood, instead?

In today's newspaper, as I write this chapter, is a story about General Motors opening a new luxury car plant in Lansing, Michigan and revealing plans for a new Saturn small sport-utility vehicle to be available in 2002. There is also a column about Planet Hollywood. Under the headline, "Planet Hollywood Spinning Out of Orbit," is a discussion of the restaurant chain's $238 million loss in 1998, reflecting an 18% drop in sales. Accounting firm PricewaterhouseCoopers is quoted as saying they are concerned about Planet Hollywood's ability to continue as a going concern. In May 1999, to pick a date at random, General Motors was selling for $95 per share and Planet Hollywood for 81 cents. We can only hope our hypothetical investor repurchased General Motors but sold Planet Hollywood while it still had some market value.

The trouble, though, is that our psychological instincts and consequent emotional reactions are more likely to lead us to make the same mistakes as this investor. Because realizing losses packs such an emotional punch and forces us to confront the fact, semi-publicly, that we were wrong, it is easier to hang on to stocks like Planet Hollywood, hoping they will turn around and we will get even. Not only that, we tend to fall in love with what we own, and so we are overly optimistic about the prospects of Planet Hollywood despite objective data to the contrary—we might even be tempted to take a risk and buy more in the face of mounting losses and sinking stock prices. Does Planet Hollywood really look like it will be selling around $20 a share in the near future? Finally, because we feel pretty good about having made some money on General Motors, we get out early, locking in those warm feelings along with a small profit. Regret is no longer risked. Alas, we miss out on even larger gains.

If there is one overarching lesson as we contemplate the pathology of loss aversion and its close cousins, instant endowment and status quo biases, it is that the past tends to be too much with us. We get emotionally hung up on the history of our investments, from whence they came. Ask yourself, "if all my investments were liquidated now, and I had the cash in hand and the freedom to put it anywhere, what would my investment portfolio look like? Where is the best place to put my money for the future?" To the extent that your current portfolio deviates from this ideal one, transferring investment dollars may be desirable—and you should think of it as just that, a transfer or shift of funds. Our emotions are likely to be more cooperative with our investment goals if we think in terms of reallocating our money rather than buying and selling.

# ☐ Conclusion

This chapter has discussed some of the pathologies and advantages of intelligent emotional self-management. In the health arena, appropriate levels of emotional expression may help us to avoid the negative consequences of, for example, anger expression, or of emotional suppression. As for investing, learning to manage regret and anxiety seems like the key to avoiding the pathologies of loss aversion. Emotional intelligence, then, appears to be central to maintaining good health and making the most of the money we earn in life. It is a twist on the old saying, but being emotionally wise may help a person become healthy and wealthy.

# ☐ Note

Preparation of this manuscript was facilitated by the following grants: American Cancer Society (RPG-93-028-05-PBP), National Cancer Institute (R01-CA68427), and National Institute of Mental Health (P01-MH/DA56826). We also acknowledge funding from the Ethel F. Donaghue Foundation Women's Health Investigator Program at Yale University.

# ☐ References

1. Mayer, J. D., & Salovey, P. (1997). What is emotional intelligence? In P. Salovey & D. J. Sluyter (Eds.), *Emotional development and emotional intelligence* (pp. 3–31). New York: Basic Books.

2. Salovey, P., & Mayer, J. D. (1990). Emotional intelligence. *Imagination, Cognition, and Personality, 9*, 185–211.

3. Salovey, P., Mayer, J. D., & Caruso, D. (2002). The positive psychology of emotional intelligence. In C. R. Snyder & S. J. Lopez (Eds.), *The handbook of positive psychology* (pp. 159–171). New York: Oxford University Press.

4. Salovey, P., Woolery, A., & Mayer, J. D. (2000). Emotional intelligence: Conceptualization and measurement. In G. Fletcher & M. Clark (Ed.), *The Blackwell handbook of social psychology: Interpersonal processes* (pp. 279–307). London: Blackwell.

5. Cook, W. W., & Medley, D. M. (1954). Proposed hostility and pharisaic-virtue scales for the MMPI. *Journal of Applied Psychology, 38*, 414–418

6. Miller, T. Q., Smith, T. W., Turner, C. W., Guijarro, M. L., & Hallet, A. J. (1996). A meta-analytic review of research on hostility and physical health. *Psychological Bulletin, 119*, 322–348.

7. Smith, T. W. (1992). Hostility and health: Current status of a psychosomatic hypothesis. *Health Psychology, 11, 139–150.*

8. Matthews, K. A., Owens, J. F., Allen, M. T., & Stoney, C. M. (1992). Do cardiovascular responses to laboratory stress relate to ambulatory blood pressure levels? Yes, in some of the people, some of the time. *Psychosomatic Medicine, 54*, 686–697.

9. Benotsch, E. G., Christensen, A. J., & McKelvey, L. (1997). Hostility, social support, and ambulatory cardiovascular activity. *Journal of Behavioral Medicine, 20*, 163–182.

10. Lepore, S. J. (1995). Cynicism, social support, and cardiovascular reactivity. *Health Psychology, 14*, 210–216.

11. Siegman, A. W., & Snow, S. C. (1997). The outward expression of anger, the inward expression of anger, and CVR: The role of vocal expression. *Journal of Behavioral Medicine, 20*, 29–46.

12. Suls, J., & Wan, C. K. (1993). The relationship between trait hostility and cardiovascular reactivity: A quantitative review and analysis. *Psychophysiology, 30*, 1–12.

13. Dujovne, V. F., & Houston, B. K. (1991). Hostility-related variables and plasma lipid levels. *Journal of Behavioral Medicine, 14*, 55–56.

14. Gross, J. J., & Levenson, R. W. (1997). Hiding feelings: The acute effects of inhibiting positive and negative emotions. *Journal of Abnormal Psychology, 106*, 95–103.

15. Brownley, K. A., Light, K. C., & Anderson, N. B. (1996). Social support and hostility interact to influence clinic, work, and home blood pressure in black and white men and women. *Psychophysiology, 33*, 434–445.

16. Bahnson, C. B. (1981). Stress and cancer: The state of the art. *Psychosomatics, 22*, 207–220.

17. Gross, J. J. (1989). Emotional expression in cancer onset and progression. *Social Science in Medicine, 28*, 1239–1248.

18. Temoshok, L. (1987). Personality, coping style, emotion, and cancer: Towards an integrative model. *Cancer Surveys, 6*, 545–567.

19. Derogatis, L. R., Abeloff, M., & Melasaratos, N. (1979). Psychological coping mechanisms and survival time in metastatic breast cancer. *Journal of the American Medical Association, 242*, 1504–1508.

20. Levy, S. M., Herberman, R. B., Maluish, A. M., Schlien, B., & Lippman, M. (1985). Prognostic risk assessment in primary breast cancer by behavioral and immunological parameters. *Health Psychology, 4*, 99–113.

21. McKenna, M. C., Zevon, M. A., Corn, B., & Rounds, J. (1999). Psychosocial factors and the development of breast cancer: A meta-analysis. *Health Psychology, 18*, 520–531.

22. Cooper, C. L., & Faragher, E. B. (1992). Coping strategies and breast disorders/cancer. *Psychological Medicine, 22*, 447–455.

23. Cooper, C. L., & Faragher, E. B. (1993). Psychosocial stress and breast cancer: The interrelationship between stress events, coping strategies, and personality. *Psychological Medicine, 23*, 653–662.

24. Faragher, E. B., & Cooper, C. L. (1990). Type A stress prone behavior and breast cancer. *Psychological Medicine, 20*, 663–670.

25. Spiegel, D. (2001). Mind matters: Group therapy and survival in breast cancer. *New England Journal of Medicine, 345*, 1767–1768.

26. Spiegel, D., Kraemer, H. C., Bloom, J. R., & Gottheil, E. (1989, October 14). Effect of psychosocial treatment on survival of patients with metastatic breast cancer. *The Lancet,* pp. 888–891.

27. Classen, C., Butler, L. D., Koopman, C., Miller, E., DiMiceli, S., Giese-Davis, J., et al. (2001). Supportive-expressive group therapy and distress in patients with metastatic breast cancer: A randomized clinical intervention trial. *Archives of General Psychology, 58*, 494–501.

28. Goodwin, P. J., Leszcz, M., Ennis, M., Koopmans, J., Vincent, L., Guther, H., et al. (2001). The effect of group psychosocial support on survival in metastatic breast cancer. *New England Journal of Medicine, 345*, 1719–1726.

29. Pennebaker, J. W. (1997). Writing about emotional experiences as a therapeutic process. *Psychological Science, 8*, 162–166.

30. Cameron, L. D., & Nicholls, G. (1998). Expression of stressful experiences through writing: Effects of a selfregulation manipulation for pessimists and optimists. *Health Psychology, 17*, 84–92.

31. Pennebaker, J. W., Colder, M., & Sharp, L. K. (1990). Accelerating the coping process. *Journal of Personality and Social Psychology, 58*, 528–537.

32. Pennebaker, J. W., Kiecolt-Glaser, J. K., & Glaser, R. (1988). Disclosure of traumas and immune function: Health implications for psychotherapy. *Journal of Consulting and Clinical Psychology, 56*, 239–245.

33. Greenberg, M. A., & Stone, A. A. (1992). Emotional disclosure about traumas and its relation to health: Effects of previous disclosure and trauma severity. *Journal of Personality and Social Psychology, 63*, 75–84.

34. Petrie, K. J., Booth, R. J., Pennebaker, J. W., Davison, K. P., & Thomas, M.G. (1995). Disclosure of trauma and immune response to a hepatitis B vaccination program. *Journal of Consulting and Clinical Psychology, 63*, 787–792.

35. Smyth, J. M. (1998). Written emotional expression: Effect sizes, outcome types, and moderating variables. *Journal of Consulting and Clinical Psychology, 66*, 174–184.

36. Goldman, S. L., Kraemer, D. T., & Salovey, P. (1996). Beliefs about mood moderate the relationship of stress to illness and symptom reporting. *Journal of Psychosomatic Research, 41*, 115–128.

37. Salovey, P., Rothman, A. J., Detweiler, J. B ., & Steward, W. T. (2000). Emotional states and physical health. *American Psychologist, 55*, 110–121.

38. Hilton, D. J. (2001). The psychology of financial decision-making: Applications to trading, dealing, and investment analysis. *Journal of Psychology and Financial Markets, 2*, 37–53.

39. Kahneman, D., & Tversky, A. (1979). Prospect theory: An analysis of decision under risk. *Econometrica, 47*, 263–291.

40. Kahneman, D., & Tversky, A. (1984). Choices, value, and frames. *American Psychologist, 39*, 341–350.

41. Gross, L. (1988). *The art of selling intangibles: How to make your million $ investing other people's money.* New York: Prentice Hall.

42. Kahneman, D., & Tversky, A. (1991). Loss aversion and riskless choice: A reference dependent model. *Quarterly Journal of Economics, 106*, 1039–1061.

43. Shefrin, H., & Statman, M. (1985). The disposition to sell winners too early and ride losers too long: Theory and evidence. *Journal of Finance, 40*, 777–790.

44. Thaler, R. H. (1980). Toward a positive theory of consumer choice. *Journal of Economic Behavior and Organization, 1*, 39–60.

45. Odean, T. (1998). Are investors reluctant to realize their losses? *Journal of Finance, 53*, 1775–1798.

46. Kahneman, D., Knetsch, J. L., & Thaler, R. H. (1991). The endowment effect, loss aversion, and the status quo bias. *Journal of Economic Perspectives, 5,* 193–206.

47. Singer, M. (1999, April 26, May 3). The optimist: Is Ace Greenberg the sanest man on Wall Street? *The New Yorker,* pp. 140–149.

48. Lynch, P. (2000). *One up on Wall Street: How to use what you already know to make money in the market* (Fireside ed.). New York: Simon & Schuster.

49. Arkes, H. R., & Blumer, C. (1985). The psychology of sunk cost. *Organizational Behavior and Human Decision Processes, 35,* 124–140.

50. Knetsch, J. L., & Sinden, J. A. (1984). Willingness to pay and compensation demanded: Experimental evidence of an unexpected disparity in measures of value. *Quarterly Journal of Economics, 99,* 507–521.

51. Kahneman, D., Knetsch, J. L., & Thaler, R. H. (1990). Experimental tests of the endowment effect and the Coase Theorem, *Journal of Political Economy, 98,* 1325–1348.

52. Loewenstein, G., & Kahneman, D. (1991). *Explaining the endowment effect.* Unpublished manuscript.

53. Samuelson, W. F., & Zeckhauser, R. (1988). Status quo bias in decision making. Journal of *Risk and Uncertainty, 1,* 7–59.

# INTEGRATION
# AND
# CONCLUSIONS

CHAPTER

Joseph Ciarrochi

# The Current State of Emotional Intelligence Research: Answers to Some Old Questions and the Discovery of Some New Ones

The main objective of this book is to contribute to a more helpful and comprehensive definition of what emotional intelligence is, and how it can be applied to deal with the many problems we all face in everyday life. We hope we have achieved this objective. Nevertheless, as a careful reading of the chapters in this volume will suggest, we are not quite there yet. Indeed, our book cannot but reflect the continuing existence of some degree of confusion in the literature about how one might define emotional intelligence (EI). Some of the chapters seem to adopt a slightly different approach and define EI in a somewhat different way. Despite these apparent differences, however, there are also some important similarities. As can be seen in Table 12.1, all the chapters focus on skills or processes that promote effective action in emotionally charged situations. The skills are also intended to improve emotional well-being. Interestingly, there is also reasonable overlap with the content of the theories. For example, emotional awareness is described as important in all of these chapters. Similarly, effective emotion management (or coping) appears as a component of EI in almost all of these chapters.

Despite these similarities, there are also important differences in the theories. For example, some of the approaches focus on ability-based measures (e.g., Chapter 9) and others focus on self-report measures (e.g.,

**TABLE 12.1. Outline of EI-relevant processes and behaviors, and their proposed benefits to everyday life**

| Chapter | Skills | Benefit of the skills |
|---|---|---|
| 3 | Skills related to regulation/coping, expressive behavior, and social/emotional awareness | Help children and adolescents to develop positive relationships |
| 4 | Awareness of mood<br>Understanding the causes and consequences of mood | Prevent mood from having unwanted influences on judgment and behavior |
| 5 | Skill at coping with emotions and stressful events<br>What is considered "skilful" depends on the situation | Deal effectively with situational and emotional demands |
| 6 | Perceiving own and others' emotions accurately in marriages. Ability to utilize, understand, and manage emotions | More loving, supportive Marriage |
| 7 | Empathic accuracy: knowing what people are feeling during an interaction<br>Effective management of empathic accuracy | Building friendships<br>Managing relationship threat<br>Developing intimacy |
| 8 | Self-awareness, social awareness, responsible decision making, self-management, relationship management | Help children and adolescents to deal with bullying, peer pressure, and school work<br>Help kids to build quality relationships with peers, teachers, family, and the community |
| 9 | Ability to identify, effectively express, use, understand, and manage emotions | Managerial effectiveness<br>Dealing well with workplace conflict<br>Motivating colleagues<br>Effective teamwork<br>Workplace performance |
| 10 | Effective emotional orientation<br>Emotional awareness and identification<br>Skills related to defusing (disbelieving) unhelpful thoughts and emotions<br>Skill at taking value-congruent action in the context of difficult emotions and impulses | Improved mental health (less suffering)<br>More intimate, supportive relationships<br>Managerial and workplace effectiveness<br>Dealing effectively with difficult social situations |
| 11 | Ability to identify, express, use, understand, and manage emotions | Improved physical health<br>Better financial decisions |

Chapter 10). Self-report and ability-based measures correlate only weakly, suggesting that they tap into different processes (see Chapter 2). Other chapters focus on situational influences (e.g., Chapters 4 and 5), rather than stable individual differences (i.e., as measured via ability or self-report measures). How can these differences be understood? I propose two distinctions that I hope will lend some clarity.

## ☐ Emotional Intelligence Versus Emotionally Intelligent Behavior

I propose that emotional intelligence be used to refer to a latent ability (i.e., what people are capable of at their best). In contrast, "emotionally intelligent behavior" (EIB) refers to how effectively people actually perform in the context of emotions and emotionally charged thoughts. If people allow emotions to act as barriers to effective action, then we would say they are engaging in emotionally *unintelligent* behavior. If, in contrast, emotions do not interfere with effective action, or facilitate effective action, we would say they are engaging in emotionally intelligent behavior (see Chapter 10 for a more complete discussion).

People high in EI should be more likely to engage in emotionally intelligent behavior. However, people may often fail to live up to their EI potential. There are factors that influence EIB other than EI. For example, Chapters 4 and 5 focus on situtional factors that influence EIB. Other chapters focus on processes that are likely to lead to EIB (e.g., Chapter 5 and "flexible use of coping strategies"; Chapter 10 and effective emotional orientation). Still other chapters discuss variables that might be considered EIB, rather than a process that leads to EIB. For example, Chapter 8 discusses "relationship management," which focuses on actual behavior such as working co-operatively and effective conflict management.

## ☐ Ability versus typical performance

The theories differ in terms of whether they focus on people's peak ability (as measured by ability tests) or typical functioning (often measured with self-reports). The ability approach is exemplified by the work of Jack Mayer (Chapter 1) and David Caruso (Chapter 9). The typical functioning approach is emphasized in the Ciarrochi and Blackledge chapter (Chapter 10), and appears to some extent in many of the other chapters. "Typical" approaches focus on how people perform in their everyday life, rather than what they are capable of doing (as in the ability approach). Thus, someone might be quite *capable* of being aware of their partners emotions, but may typically not achieve awareness, perhaps because of lack of motivation or because of some other barrier [1] (see Chapters 6 and 7).

The ability-based measures and the self-report based measures tend to correlate only weakly, suggesting that they reflect different underlying processes. In constrast, the different self-report measures tend to correlate moderately with each other, suggesting they are more similar to each other than they are to the ability measures. Thus, although the different models of EI in Table 12.1 are similar sounding and similar in function, they are actually quite different.

At present, there are at least two distinguishing features of the ability verus typical EI approaches. First, ability assessment of EI is based on performance tests with right or wrong answers, whereas "typical" assessment tends to be based on self-reports. Second, the stimuli in ability-based measures are not sampled directly from people's lives. For example, ability tests ask people to identify emotions in stimuli that they have never seen before (i.e., unfamiliar faces and figures). In contrast, self-report measures are likely to draw people's attention to what they do in their lives from day to day. For example, when people are asked, "do you have trouble identifying your feelings," they are likely to look to what they do in their lives to answer this question. To use another example, people with an ineffective emotional orientation (see Chapter 10) tend to endorse items such as "When I feel uneasy, I do whatever I can to get rid of those feelings." These people typically do not accept their feelings. However, this does not mean they do not have the *ability* to accept their feelings. Indeed, once an intervention puts people into contact with the advantage of accepting feelings in some circumstances, people do demonstrate the ability to accept them, and such increased acceptance leads to improvements in well-being [2–3].

Though typical EI tends to be assessed with self-report measures (or so I hypothesize), there is no reason why it can not also be assessed using performance measures. For example, in the Flury and Ickes (Chapter 7) empathic accuracy task, couples assess how their partner was feeling and thinking at various points in an interaction. The extent that the partner correctly identifies what the partner felt is the extent they are said to be "empathically accurate." This is a performance measure because people's accuracy is observed during a performance task, rather than being self-reported. It also seems to reflect some level of "typical" rather that ability because situational manipulations can lead people to perform better (see Chapter 7).

To summarize, the term "emotional intelligence" is useful for organizing a body of research that focuses on effectiveness in the context of emotions and emotionally charged thoughts. However, the approaches to EI differ markedly. It would seem advisable for future researchers to distinguish between different approaches to emotional intelligence, in terms of whether the approach focuses on ability (EI proper), or emotionally intelligent behavior, and whether the approach measures typical versus optimal responding.

## ☐ How Does One Evaluate the Usefulness of an EI Measure?

### Predictive Power

As discussed in Chapter 2, the value of an EI measure depends upon its purpose. One important purpose in psychology is prediction. Does an EI test predict who will be the best manager? Does it predict who will form the best peer relationships, and have the most successful marriages? It is important for a new measure to be able to predict variance over and above that predicted by traditional measures of personality and IQ. Otherwise, why would you create the new measure?

Ability measures have thus far showed good incremental and predictive value (Chapter 2). The story is more mixed for self-report measures. For example, the Bar-On EQ-I [4] appears to correlate substantially with measures of personalty and thus contribute relatively little cumulative value to our understanding of EI. Furthermore, the wording of the actual items on this scale also seem to be substantially similar to items on personality measures such as self-esteem (e.g., "I lack self-confidence") and neuroticism (e.g., "I get anxious"). Thus, one can not empirically justify using the EQ-I over traditional personality measures in trying to predict behavior. Other self-report EI measures show somewhat more promise, though research is still needed to fully evaluate them (see Chapter 2).

### Usefulness in Guiding and Evaluating Intervention Research

Even though self-reports may not show much predictive power over and above traditional personality measures, they may still be useful as a guide for intervention research. For example, in Chapter 10 we discussed an EI dimension labelled "effective emotional orientation." People low on this dimension tend to chronically avoid negative affect, which ironically increases the frequency that they experience negative affect (see Chapter 10 [3], [5]). Thus, ineffective emotional orientation (IEO) and negative affect (NA) are moderately correlated, presumably because IEO leads to negative affect.

Consider a model in which IEO leads to negative affectivity and negative affectivity in turn leads to higher likelihood of experiencing burnout at a job (Figure 12.1). In this model, IEO will not predict variance over and above negative affect, because the effect of IEO occurs indirectly through negative affect. (In fact there is evidence that IEO predicts variance over and above negative affect, but for the purposes of this section we will assume the model in Figure 12.1; see [5].)

The IEO construct and similar ones presented in Figure 12.1 might be helpful in guiding intervention research, even if they don't predict unique variance. For example, based on the model in Figure 12.1, we know that if we can reduce negative affect, we can reduce job burnout. How does one reduce negative affect? Chapter 10 provides evidence that direct attempts to reduce negative affect often don't work, and indeed can make things worse. Instead, we propose that one can target IEO, and improvements in IEO are expected to *indirectly* reduce negative affect and burnout. Many EI-relevant measures are linked to negative affect in a similar fashion as IEO. For example, negative affectivity has been linked to self-reported emotional clarity [6], emotion identification [7], and in some contexts, to certain coping styles (Chapter 5). One can seek to alter all of these EI-relevant variables in an attempt to indirectly influence negative affectivity.

In conclusion, if one's goal is prediction, and not influence, then the best predictor of future behavior is usually past behavior [8]. Thus past negative affectivity is probably the best predictor of future negativity. However, if the goal is prediction *and* influence, then the EI-relevant variables can be used to understand *why* negativity occurs, in order to understand how you might reduce negativity.

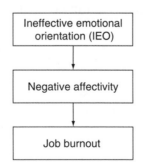

**FIGURE 12.1.** A causal model in which an emotional competency (IEO) does not predict unique variance in an outcome (burnout), but nevertheless helps one to understand and potentially influence the outcome.

# ☐ The Big EI Questions that Still Need to be Answered

In Chapter 1, Mayer asked a series of questions by way of organizing the field. Let me conclude by posing my own questions.

### Question 1: What Aspects of EI Are Not yet Measured Adequately, and How Might they be Measured?

For example, Chapter 10 reviewed evidence which suggests that people differ in their effective action orientation, or skill at moving in a value congruent direction when emotions are inconsistent with that direction (e.g., ability to give a speech even when speech anxious). Currently, there is no comprehensive, well-valided ability measure of effective action orientation, though there are some interesting behavioral measures of this construct in the developmental literature (e.g., see [9]). Future research is needed to evaluate whether ability-based measures can be developed to measure effective action orientation and other EI dimensions discussed in the chapters (see Table 12.1).

### Question 2: To What Extent Can Ability Verus Self-Report EI Measures Predict Important Outcomes, Over and Above Personality and IQ?

Much progress has been made on this question already, but still more work to be done. Can self-report measures, such as the Bar-On, be improved to show incremental value over personality? Will the next decade of research continue to support the distinctiveness and utility of ability-based measures?

### Question 3: To What Extent Are Different Measures Reflecting What People Typically Do Versus What they Are Capable of Doing (i.e., Ability)?

I have hypothesized that self-report measures of EI-relevant processes tend to reflect typical performance rather than ability, but future research needs to evaluate this possibility directly.

The distinction between typical performance and ability is quite important, in that it suggests quite different approaches to EI intervention. For example, if someone is capable of managing their aggressive behavior, but does not do so, then an intervention might target the barriers to effective management (e.g., lack of motivation, failure to realize that the management strategies help them to achieve their goals, etc.). In contrast, if people do not know how to manage their aggressive behavior, then the intervention might provide them with the skills of effective management (e.g., "stop, take a breath, count to ten, etc.").

Some research has begun to address the issue of typical performance versus ability. These studies have examined whether motivational manipulations can increase people's performance. If a measure reflects people's ability, then motivation should have little effect (e.g., because either you know the answer or you don't).

There is evidence that motivational manipulations improve performance on an empathic accuracy task (Chapter 7). In a related research, Ciarrochi et al. [1] showed that a motivational intervention significantly increased both male and female participants' Level of Emotional Awareness (LEA), although women generally demonstrated greater emotional awareness than men [1]. Furthermore, the LEA of motivated men equalled those of women in the control condition, but the motivated men had to work significantly longer on the task to achieve this equality. Sex differences held even after controlling for self-report and behavioral measures of motivation. This study provides evidence that differences in emotional awareness can be due to differences in both motivation and ability. Future research is need to evaluate the extent that the skills listed in Table 12.1 are influenced by motivational instruction.

## Question 4: Can EI be Improved?

The answer to this question may depend on whether we are talking about ability or typical performance. Little research to date has looked at improving ability EI. However, given that ability EI is considered to be similar to IQ (normal intelligence) in many ways, we might look at IQ interventions to see if they offer any suggestions for EI interventions. The evidence suggests that interventions often improve IQ in the short run, but that IQ gains diminish in the long run [10]. The loss of IQ may be due in part to a lack of support after the intervention, as children are sent back to an impoverished environment. Indeed, research suggests that if children receive early intervention (e.g., starting as early as 3 weeks old) and this intervention is then supported with a school-aged intervention, then the children do show increased IQ that is sustained over time [11–12]. The

IQ research suggests that if ability EI is to be improved, then interventions need to start at a very young age, and be maintained in some form throughout the school years (see also Chapters 3 and 8).

In contrast to ability, typical performance may be far more influenced by interventions. For example, research has shown that many of the EI dimensions described in Chapter 10 can be modified. Similarly, Chapters 3 and 8 suggest that many aspects of typical performance can be successfully improved in school-based interventions. Even with these encouraging results, much more research is needed to evaluate the efficacy of EI interventions. Can an EI intervention improve marital interactions (Chapter 6), the quality of friendships (Chapter 7), and the ability to cope with difficult situations (Chapter 5)? Can it improve our physical health and our ability to make financial decisions (Chapter 11)? Research is also needed to assess why EI interventions work, i.e., what is the process by which EI interventions work?

## ☐ Conclusions

Understanding how affect influences our everyday thoughts and actions remains one of the last frontiers for psychology. Writers, philosophers and scientists have been wondering about the nature of human affectivity for millennia, yet empirical research into this critically important domain is a relatively recent development. Social life and interpersonal behavior are arguably more complex and demanding in the twenty-first century than ever before. The disappearance of traditional, small-scale societies since the eighteenth century and the emergence of complex, impersonal industrialized mass societies has presented humans with unparalleled challenges. Our cognitive and emotional capacities evolved as an adaptation for living in small-scale, face-to-face groups where life-long kinship and acquaintanceship were the norm. Yet we now find ourselves living in a society of strangers, surrounded by people we know only fleetingly or not at all. It is not surprising that our affective reactions are sometimes inappropriate and dysfunctional. Understanding our emotional nature is thus of greater urgency today than ever before.

In some ways it is not surprising that the EI concept arose just at this time. The EI field shows no signs of slowing in the near future. If we look at the proposed benefits of EI (Table 12.1), we can see why there is such interest. EI measurement and intervention has the potential to be relevant to every aspect of people's lives, including parenting skill, marital satisfaction, investment decisions, managerial effectiveness, and physical health. We hope that researchers continue to stay the course and conduct rigorous EI research in the coming years. We also hope non-academics remain open to the possibility of EI interventions in their schools and businesses. If so, then EI researchers and practitioners will have a chance to make a lasting difference in people's lives.

# ☐ References

1. Ciarrochi, J., Hynes, K., & Crittenden, N. (2005). Can men do better if they try harder: Sex and motivational effects on emotional awareness. *Cognition and Emotion, 19*(1), 133–141.
2. Hayes, S., Masuda, A., Bissett, R., Luoma, J., & Guerrero, L. F. (2004). DBT, FAP, and ACT: How empirically oriented are the new behavior therapy technologies? *Behavior Therapy, 35*, 35–54.
3. Hayes, S. C., Strosahl, K. D., & Wilson, K. G. (1999). *Acceptance and commitment therapy: An experiential approach to behavior change*: New York: Guilford Press.
4. Bar-On, R. (1997). *Bar-On Emotional Quotient Inventory (EQ-i): Technical manual.* Toronto, Canada: Multi-Health Systems.
5. Bond, F., & Bunce, D. (2003). The role of acceptance and job control in mental health, job satisfaction, and work performance. *Journal of Applied Psychology, 88*(6), 1057–1067.
6. Mayer, J. D., & Gaschke, Y. N. (1988). The experience and meta-experience of mood. *Journal of Personality and Social Psychology, 55*(1), 102–111.
7. Bagby, R. M., Parker, J. D. A., & Taylor, G. J. (1994). The twenty-item Toronto Alexithymia Scale: I. Item selection and cross-validation of the factor structure. *Journal of Psychosomatic Research, 38*(1), 23–32.
8. Anastasi, A. (1982). *Psychological testing* (5th ed.). New York: Macmillan.
9. Shoda, Y., Mischel, W., & Peake, P. K. (1990). Predicting adolescent cognitive and self-regulatory competencies from preschool delay of gratification: Identifying diagnostic conditions. *Developmental Psychology, 26*(6), 978–986.
10. Lazar, I., & Darlington, R. B. (1982). Lasting effects of early education: A report from the Consortium for Longitudinal Studies. *Monographs of the Society for Research in Child Development, 47*(2–3), 1–151.
11. Campbell, F. A., & Ramey, C. T. (1994). Effects of early intervention on intellectual and academic achievement: A follow-up study of children from low-income families. *Child Development, 65*(2), 684–698.
12. Reynolds, A. J., & Temple, J. A. (1998). Extended early childhood intervention and school achievement: Age thirteen findings from the Chicago Longitudinal Study. *Child Development, 69*(1), 231–246.

**13**
CHAPTER

John D. Mayer
Joseph Ciarrochi

# Clarifying Concepts Related to Emotional Intelligence: A Proposed Glossary

The use of clear terminology promotes better communication and understanding within a discipline. An individual who reads even a few articles on emotional intelligence is likely to be struck by shifts, from one article to the next, in how specific terms are employed, as well as by shifts in how those terms are defined. Some terms arguably represent creative new usage in the field, but other terms represent somewhat out-of-date concepts, and still others seem, for little reason, to fly in the face of standard scientific terminology. For that reason we offer the following brief discussion of some terminology, and a proposed glossary of terms in and related to the field. In it, we have tried to identify representative usages that are consistent with psychological usage more generally.

## ☐ Matters of Emotion, Intelligence, and their Intersection

### Emotion and Intelligence

Many things might be described by the term emotional intelligence. For the term to be taken seriously, it must reflect its constituent terms—emotion, and intelligence—and their combination. The matter might be easier if there were one definition of emotion, and one of intelligence. As it is, researchers often employ different definitions within each area—and yet some areas of agreement can be found [1–2]. Our first definition of emotion was developed based on Nicole Frijda's wide-ranging discussion of what emotion is:

> **Emotion**—a progressive activity of the organism, in response to a perceived predicament, that involves a (usually) integrated combination of psycho-physiological reactions, subjective feelings, and related cognitive activities. (Based on a discussion by [1, p. 63].)

Here is a second general definition from a contemporary psychology textbook:

> **Emotion**—a state of arousal involving facial and bodily changes, brain activation, cognitive appraisals, subjective feelings, and tendencies toward action, all shaped by cultural rules. [3, p. 386]

Such definitions are typically followed by a list of examples of emotions: happiness, sadness, fear, anger, and the like.

Turning now to intelligence, here again is a summary definition of intelligence drawing on work by two eminent researchers [2]:

> **Intelligence**—the capacity to learn accurately and to reason abstractly so as to adapt to one's environment.

This is similar to the definition proposed a number of years before by David Wechsler:

> **Intelligence**—[the individual's] global capacity to act purposefully, to think rationally, and to deal effectively with his environment. [4]

And here are two textbook definitions:

> **Intelligence**—an inferred characteristic of an individual, usually defined as the ability to profit from experience, acquire knowledge, think abstractly, act purposefully, or adapt to changes in the environment. [3, p. 321]

> **Intelligence**—an attribute used to describe a person that is based on the assumptions that (1) a person has a range of different abilities and (2) intelligence can be equated with how a person measures up on a particular ability scale, as valued by a culture. [5, p. 257]

## Emotional Intelligence itself

A definition of emotional intelligence must sensibly describe the intersection of emotion and intelligence. Here is a recent example from our laboratory:

> **Emotional intelligence**—the capacity to reason about emotions, and of emotions to enhance thinking. It includes the abilities to accurately perceive

emotions, to access and generate emotions so as to assist thought, to understand emotions and emotional knowledge, and to reflectively regulate emotions so as to promote emotional and intellectual growth. [6, p. 197]

We employed a different phraseology in a 1999 definition:

**Emotional intelligence**—refers to an ability to recognize the meanings of emotion and their relationships, and to reason and problem-solve on the basis of them. Emotional intelligence is involved in the capacity to perceive emotions, assimilate emotion-related feelings, understand the information of those emotions, and manage them. [7, p. 267]

Other researchers working in the area have generally followed our definition, often changing its phrasing just slightly:

**Emotional intelligence**—refers to the competence to identify and express emotions, understand emotions, assimilate emotions in thought, and regulate both positive and negative emotions in oneself and others. [8, p. xv]

## ☐ Qualities Distinct from, though Related to, Emotional Intelligence

### Non-Standard Uses of the Term Emotional Intelligence

There are other markedly different uses of the term emotional intelligence, of course. Many of these come from popularizations of the topic. Although these definitions are used fairly widely among some who study emotional intelligence, they are non-standard in the sense that they are discrepant with broader psychological and scientific usage.

For example, Goleman generally equated emotional intelligence with a long list of traits (e.g., motivation, persistence, sociability, and self-awareness), and also with character more generally [9]. These definitions appear to inflate the meaning of emotional intelligence so that includes a number of unrelated, albeit important, personality parts and processes. Although the personality parts and processes are important, they are unrelated to emotion, or to intelligence, as commonly understood. A particularly striking example of this is when Goleman refers to emotional intelligence as equivalent to character [9, p. 285]. Good character is typically defined as far more than emotion, intelligence or their combination.

For instance, emotional intelligence defined in the standard way, above, could certainly co-exist with selfish motives, a lack of self-control (in all areas except emotional self-control), poor cognitive judgment, and a short time horizon, among many other qualities. A person high in emotional intelligence, in other words, could be motivated by greed, lack sufficient self-control to work hard, fail to distinguish irrational arguments from rational ones, and employ a live-for-the-moment philosophy. Most people would judge such an individual as possessing a questionable character, at best.

It is worth identifying some further terminology that might be useful in sorting out some aspects of personality distinct from emotional intelligence. These further concepts/terms can then be used alongside emotional intelligence itself.

## Considering the Term, "Trait"

Petrides and Furman seriously struggled with the terminology of self-reported traits that often go under the name of emotional intelligence [10]. They made two suggestions for substitute terms. The first was "trait-emotional intelligence." As they themselves point out, however, the term requires a non-standard definition of the term "trait," because traits are typically defined to include abilities such as intelligence. For example, here are two textbook definitions of traits:

> **Trait**—a characteristic of an individual, describing a habitual way of behaving, thinking, or feeling. [3, p. 454]

> **Personality trait**—a relatively consistent characteristic exhibited in different situations. [11, p. 438]

A "trait emotional intelligence" that includes, say, motivation and excludes intelligence makes sense (according to Petrides and Furnham [10]) only if one adheres to a very specific conceptual scheme of trait classification and terminology employed by Hans Eysenck. Petrides and Furnham made (what seems to us) a better suggestion: that is, to employ the term emotional self-efficacy for personality characteristics related to some aspects of emotional functioning. Applying this term (as opposed to trait EI) to their idea of emotional intelligence, one arrives at:

> **Emotional self-efficacy**—a person's belief that he or she possesses empathy and assertiveness . . . as well as elements of social intelligence . . . personal intelligence . . . and ability EI. [10, p. 427]

Elsewhere, the suggestion has been made that, where psychologists employ emotional intelligence in an unqualified manner, their usage could be referred to as involving a "mixed model" approach:

> **Mixed models of emotional intelligence**—these models describe a conception of emotional intelligence that includes not only mental abilities related to intelligence and emotion, but also other personality dispositions and traits such as motives, sociability and warmth. [7, p. 399]

Another possibility is to define a style of thinking that involved the appearance of emotional effectiveness, rather than emotional intelligence itself. A parallel distinction is sometimes drawn in intelligence research where intelligence refers to the mental ability but intellect refers to the personality style—the appearance of intelligence. The term is based on a suggestion by Hofstee.

> **Stylistic emotional intellect**—a personality style that reflects the appearance of emotional competence, including, perhaps, such attributes as sociability, warmth, and appropriate assertiveness. [12, p. 49]

A combination of emotional intellect, social effectiveness, and, perhaps, emotional intelligence itself might be represented by the term socio-emotional effectiveness.

> **Socio-emotional effectiveness**—an individual's capacity to navigate the social world in an effective manner, accomplishing his or her goals as needed.

Note that socio-emotional effectiveness need not rely heavily on intelligence. It might involve, for example, being attractive and assertive, or coping effectively with a disability, or even using money and wealth to buy oneself out of difficulties, independent of more sophisticated problem solving with emotions.

Another distinction within the field is that between cognitive and non-cognitive capacities. As one author saw it: *"Emotional intelligence is defined by the author as an array of noncognitive capabilities, competencies, and skills that influences one's ability to succeed in coping with environmental demands and pressures"* [13, p. 14, italics in original]. "Non-cognitive" is undefined in the foregoing. But we can turn to Wechsler's original idea of non-intellective traits, from which the above was drawn [14, p. 103], and integrate the ideas in this way:

> **Non-cognitive capacities**—motivational and emotional qualities or traits that contribute to effective behavior.

## Psychological Processes Versus Psychological Expression and Behavior

One of the fundamental distinctions in psychology is between the internal psychological processes, on the one hand, and external expressions of those processes in the individual's life space.

> **Life space** (or life sphere)—the individual's surrounding life area, his or her physical self, possessions, interactions and behaviors, and group memberships. [15]

**Socio-emotionally effective behavior**—the observable acts of the individual that lead to emotional and social effectiveness in interactions with others. (See also Chapter 10.)

**Emotionally-intelligent behavior**—the subset of socio-emotionally effective behavior that is specifically associated with emotional intelligence. (See also Chapter 10.)

# ☐ Types of Measurement Approach/Types of Data

Many EI researchers speak of self-report data and paper-and-pencil tests. Yet those terms are imprecise and carry several different meaning. Does self-report, for example, refer to anything an individual says, or only to judgments about the self? There is nothing wrong with a term having multiple definitions, of course, except that as a scientific matter, it leads to confusion. For example, some psychologists have criticized self-report data as involving "deliberate faking, lack of insight, and unconscious defensive reactions" [16, p. 236]. Surely, however, self-reports such as "I am 20 years old," or "I am female" are trustworthy in many contexts.

Based on comments such as these, and a similar critique by Funder [17], we suggest the following terminology for data and measures of data in the emotional intelligence field:

**Self-judgment**—self-judgment refers to data or test items in which a person endorses a statement involving a judgment about him or herself (e.g., I like parties; I clearly know my emotions most the time). [17–18]

**Process report** (e.g., process-report data, process-report tests)—process reports refer to data in which the person reports on ongoing mental states at the time they occur (e.g., I know how I'm feeling right now). [18]

**Observer report or peer report** (e.g., observer-report data, observer-report test)—observer report refers to data or responses in which a first person (the observer or peer) reports or judges the characteristics of a second, target individual. [17–18]

**Criterion-report data; ability data** (e.g., ability data, ability tests, criterion-report tests)—tests and data for which a person answers questions so as to meet a criterion of correctness. [18]

# ☐ Conclusions

The list could go on and on of course, we haven't touched on social intelligence, practical intelligence, or emotional creativity. We believe that the choices we began with here, however, are among those most central to the field. We hope the brief discussion of these terms can promote clearer thinking about, and clearer discussions of, emotional intelligence in the scientific literature and beyond.

# ☐ References

1.  Frijda, N. H. (2000). Handbook of emotions. In M. Lewis & J. M. Haviland-Jones (Eds.), *Handbook of emotions* (2nd ed., pp. 59–74). New York: Guilford Press.
2.  Sternberg, R. J., & Detterman, D. R. (1986). *What is intelligence?* Norwood, NJ: Ablex.
3.  Wade, C., & Tavris, C. (2006). *Psychology* (8th ed.). Upper Saddle River, NJ: Pearson Prentice Hall.
4.  Wechsler, D. (1958). *The measurement and appraisal of adult intelligence.* Baltimore: Williams & Wilkins.
5.  Gazzaniga, M. S., & Heatherton, T. F. (2003). *Psychological science: Mind, brain, and behavior.* New York: W. W. Norton.
6.  Mayer, J. D., Salovey, P., & Caruso, D. R. (2004). Emotional intelligence: Theory, findings, and implications. *Psychological Inquiry, 60,* 197–215.
7.  Mayer, J. D., Caruso, D. R., & Salovey, P. (1999). Emotional intelligence meets traditional standards for an intelligence. *Intelligence, 27,* 267–298.
8.  Matthews, G., Zeidner, M., & Roberts, R. D. (2002). *Emotional intelligence: Science and myth.* Cambridge, MA: MIT Press.
9.  Goleman, D. (1995). *Emotional intelligence.* New York: Bantam.
10. Petrides, K. V., & Furnham, A. (2001). Trait emotional intelligence: Psychometric investigation with reference to established trait taxonomies. *European Journal of Personality, 15,* 425–448.
11. Kosslyn, S. M., & Rosenberg, R. S. (2004). *Psychology: The brain, the person, the world* (2nd ed.). Boston: Pearson Allyn & Bacon.
12. Hofstee, W. K. B. (2001). Intelligence and personality: Do they mix? In J. M. Collins & S. Messick (Eds.), *Intelligence and personality: Bridging the gap in theory and measurement* (pp. 43–60). Mahwah, NJ: Lawrence Erlbaum Associates, Inc.
13. Bar-On, R. (1997). *Bar-On Emotional Quotient Inventory: Technical manual.* Toronto, Canada: Multi-Health Systems.
14. Wechsler, D. (1943). Non-intellective factors in general intelligence. *Journal of Abnormal and Social Psychology, 38,* 101–103.
15. Mayer, J. D., Carlsmith, K. M., & Chabot, H. F. (1998). Describing the person's external environment: Conceptualizing and measuring the life space. *Journal of Research in Personality, 32,* 253–296.
16. Mischel, W. (1968). *Personality and assessment.* New York: John Wiley & Sons.
17. Funder, D. C. (2001). *The personality puzzle.* New York: W. W. Norton.
18. Mayer, J. D. (2004). A classification system for the data of personality psychology and 15.

# AUTHOR INDEX

# SUBJECT INDEX